S0-BRE-267

BALLOTS AND
FENCE RAILS

*Reconstruction
on the Lower Cape Fear*

BALLOTS AND FENCE RAILS

*Reconstruction
on the Lower Cape Fear*

by W. McKee Evans

The Norton Library
W·W·NORTON & COMPANY·INC·
NEW YORK

COPYRIGHT 1966, 1967 BY THE UNIVERSITY OF NORTH CAROLINA PRESS

First published in the Norton Library 1974
by arrangement with The University of North Carolina Press

Books That Live
The Norton imprint on a book means that in the publisher's estimation it is a book
not for a single season but for the years.
W. W. Norton & Company, Inc.

Library of Congress Cataloging in Publication Data
Evans, William McKee.
    Ballots and fence rails.
    (The Norton library)
    Reprint of the ed. published by University of North
Carolina Press, Chapel Hill.
    Bibliography: p.
    1. Cape Fear River Valley—History. 2. Reconstruc-
tion—North Carolina. I. Title.
F262.C2E9   1974   975.6′04   73-20293
ISBN 0-393-00711-1

Printed in the United States of America
1 2 3 4 5 6 7 8 9 0

To LEVI COFFIN
(1789-1877)

❦ Preface

IN DISTANT AGES PAST THE WATERS RECEDED FROM EASTERN North Carolina. Yet the sea has left its mark on this land that the ages have not erased. The flat, sandy coastal plain recalls the floor to the ocean, while the Sand Hills to the west evoke the wind-blown dunes of an ancient shore. To man, this coastal plain has been, in general, rather grudging. But with at least one resource it rewarded the European settlers from their earliest migrations. The sterile, white soil, that would grow practically nothing else, grew the noble long leaf pine, a tree that puts to shame all of its brother pines and inspires the lumberman as well as the poet. When the botanist, François André Michaux, reached America in 1801, he found these trees, rising a magnificient sixty and even ninety feet, forming a straw-carpeted forest, extending in a vast arc along the coastal plain from Norfolk, Virginia, to the Mississippi, and beyond. This was the great Piney Woods.

A river rises in the hills of Piedmont North Carolina, spills over the fall line to the plain, and wanders slowly through the Piney Woods to find the ocean by Cape Fear, from which it derives its name. Eight southeastern North Carolina counties lying along the lower reaches of this river will be the focus of our attention. But for the sake of certain comparisons, we shall have occasion to glance elsewhere, to Piedmont North Carolina, to the southern Appalachians, and even to the Gulf Coast.

The co-ordinate of time, like the one of space, will be small. We shall be preoccupied chiefly with the years of political Reconstruction, 1865-77. But here too, from this central core of time, we shall make certain departures. For example, the economic developments and the evolutions of ideas, both of which tend to unfold more slowly than, say, military or political events, will be extended down to the end of the nineteenth century. Furthermore there will be points where, in order to gain perspective, we shall find it illuminating to look even further, backward into the colonial period, or forward into the twentieth century.

But even when these liberties have been taken, the focus of this book remains a narrow one. If one is ever to write definitively about any phase of history, it will surely be by working within such close limitations as these. However, should the reader close this book with the feeling that this has not been done, that there is more to be said about Reconstruction on the lower Cape Fear, then at least one object of the present effort has been realized. Because indeed there is much more to be said, particularly since the events of the mid-twentieth century make us always see Reconstruction with new eyes.

The purpose of this work is neither to deal exhaustively with institutions, nor to explore any conventional list of topics that one customarily finds in a local history. For example, attention is focused in chapter one for a moment on the human conflict that gave rise to the African Methodist Episcopal Church, but this is not followed by a history of that institution on the lower Cape Fear. The smallness of scope rather is intended to serve a different end: that the stage might be peopled with men and women instead of with abstractions, men and women caught in a moment of crisis that tore their world apart more completely than any that has occurred before or since, a crisis in which their built-in responses provided them with few answers, in which they had to shape the future without reliable blueprints from the past. If to deal defini-

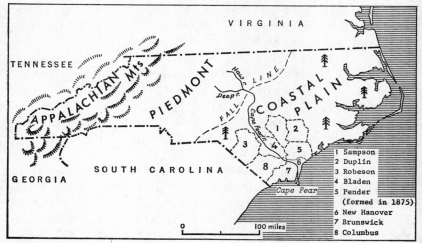

North Carolina: Physical Features

tively with such subject matter is beyond our grasp, perhaps one can strive to illuminate certain themes in southern history which are still vital.

Of the many people to whom I am indebted in writing this book, originally offered as a doctoral dissertation for the Department of History at The University of North Carolina at Chapel Hill, none has been more helpful than Dr. George Tindall. His searching criticism has called me back from more than one barren departure. Other historians at the University at Chapel Hill have been unstinting in sharing their experience with me. Dr. Hugh T. Lefler has been especially helpful in guiding me to more fruitful sources, while Dr. Frank Klingberg and Dr. Joseph Carlyle Sitterson have read portions of the manuscript and offered their encouragement.

In carrying out a project such as this, one comes to appreciate the high concept that library personnel have of their profession.

Thus the work that I have done at The University of North Carolina at Chapel Hill, Duke, Fisk, the Wilmington Public Library, the North Carolina Archives, the Library of Congress and the National Archives has not only been productive but pleasurable as well. At the Wilson Library, The University of North Carolina, Mr. J. Douglas Helms of the Southern Historical Collection and Mr. William Powell of the North Carolina Room; and, at the National Archives, Mrs. Sarah Jackson, have been exceptionally magnanimous in the way they have interpreted their responsibilities toward a visiting scholar.

A number of people in Wilmington have helped me more than they suspect. Mr. Roger Hewlett was kind enough to allow me to examine some private records of his family, while Mrs. L. V. Porter helped me piece together some family relationships that were not apparent from the printed sources. Mr. Charles H. Foard obtained for me some charts of the Cape Fear estuary and made some valuable suggestions concerning the harbor and the economic development of the lower Cape Fear. On the basis of highly fragmentary information Mr. Charles Bryant helped me identify many nineteenth-century figures. Furthermore anyone working in the history of the lower Cape Fear has both the benefit and the challenge of a well-developed heritage of local history-writing. In this project, for example, the work of people such as Louis Toomer Moore and Ida Brooks Kellam is more significant than an occasional footnote might suggest.

I find that I have an important debt to three generations of my family. Especially helpful have been my parents, Alfreda and J. Browne Evans; my wife, Ruth V. Evans; her brother, Jerome Van Camp; and our son, Owen Thomas Evans; all of whom have offered valuable criticism and insights. In addition to sharing their ideas, the latter three persons have helped in more practical ways, preparing maps and assembling data.

A book like the present one is often called a "monograph." It deals with a single subect and is usually presumed to be the work of a single hand. How spurious this concept is when one thinks of the many hands that have helped along the way!

Contents

⟨ Maps

BALLOTS AND FENCE RAILS

Reconstruction
on the Lower Cape Fear

I ⟞ *"Blow Gabriel, blow,*
for God's sake, blow"

IT WAS IN THE DARKNESS BEFORE DAWN, IN THE LATE SUMMER OF 1863, that the "Mary Celeste" arrived before the New Inlet bar. Before her the horizon glowed red from the eternal fires of the Confederate salt works. On her portside lay Cape Fear, a dark mound of sand that pointed like a warning finger to Frying Pan Shoals, a treacherous span of water stretching twenty miles out to sea.

But for blockade-runners, like the "Mary Celeste," it was the very treachery of these waters in which lay the greatest hope for escaping the Federal warships. Because on board each blockade-runner was a Cape Fear pilot, trained from boyhood in these tortuous, shifting channels. No Union navy chart could match their skill. A Cape Fear pilot would be able to tell you that if today you were to return to a certain spot, where only a few months ago you had seen deeply-laden ships riding at anchor, you would find at that place neither ships nor even water, but rather a broad, glistening strand, a beach that would remain for a season only to be reclaimed by the Atlantic with the onset of the autumn storms.

For a lifetime the pilots had studied the ceaseless action of the winds and the currents in the unending work of building new islands and shoals and returning old ones to the sea. On the fleeing blockade-runner, the unblinking eyes of the pilot seemed to see through the dark waters to the spot where the speeding keel fairly skimmed the deadly shoal heads, while the Federal picket-ships trailed far behind gingerly feeling their way with the sounding line.

But the "Mary Celeste" was in trouble. Her Cape Fear pilot, John William Anderson of Smithville, later Southport, had taken yellow fever while the ship lay in port at Nassau. So swiftly had the disease borne down upon him that it appeared that death might overtake Anderson before his shipmates could raise the Carolina coast. But faster still they had sailed the "Mary Celeste," riding the Gulf Stream northward, then through the region of the mists, where the warm waters of the Gulf Stream mingled with the cool coastal current, until at last, peering through the darkness, they had seen the horizon blaze red, and they knew that once again they stood before the cape of fear, where their way was barred by the muzzles and spars of the Federal fleet.

With the pilot stricken in his bunk below, and the moments of darkness ebbing fast, the skipper decided to attempt a blind dash for the bar. Death blazed in the Federal broadsides, and surged in the black shoal waters, as the "Mary Celeste" fled "like a scared greyhound," the exploding shells tearing her rigging, and sending jets of water skyward. Anderson heard the firing and asked his shipmates to carry him to the wheel house, where he stood supported by "two strong sailors. His face was as yellow as gold, and his eyes shone like stars. He fixed his unearthly gaze upon the long line of breakers ahead, then upon the dim line of pines that stood higher than the surrounding forest, then at the compass for a moment, and then said calmly, 'Hard starboard!' " The "Mary Celeste" cleared the bar, and swept under the protective guns of Fort Fisher, then over the still dark waters of Smithville Bay. Pilot Anderson died soon after the "Mary Celeste" dropped anchor opposite Deep Water Point near town. Not far away his mother stood waiting "at the open door, ready to receive him."[1]

1. This account is taken chiefly from Alfred Moore Waddell, *Some Memories of My Life* (Raleigh: Edwards and Broughton, 1908), pp. 85-88, hereinafter cited as Waddell, *Memories*, with certain details drawn from Walter Gilman Curtis, *Reminiscences, 1848-1900* (Southport, N.C.: Herald Job Office, n.d.), p. 30, hereinafter

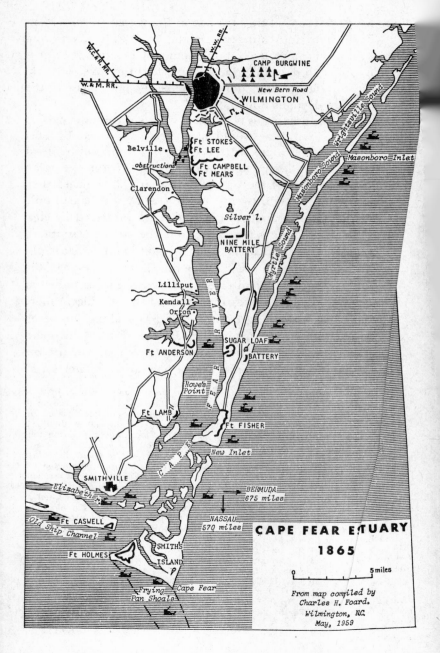

CAPE FEAR ESTUARY
1865

From map compiled by
Charles H. Foard.
Wilmington, N.C.
May, 1959

We have no record of the last span of the voyage of the "Mary Celeste," the thirty-four mile run up the Cape Fear River from Smithville to Wilmington. But the common practice was for a blockade-runner to dash into Smithville under the cover of darkness, remain until morning, and then make the final phase of the trip during the daylight hours.

A traveler beginning this northward voyage during the closing months of the Civil War would have been impressed by Fort Fisher, which had been erected across the bay from Smithville at the southern tip of a long tongue of land lying between the ocean and the eastern shore of the Cape Fear estuary. A great earthen mound, twenty feet high, twenty-five feet thick, and a half-mile long and studded with artillery emplacements, protected by electrically controlled mine fields, sealed off the strategic southern end of the peninsula from attack from any hostile force that might succeed in landing on the beach to the north, out of range of the fort's artillery. To this "land face" of Fort Fisher was joined at a right angle another such earthen mound, a "sea face," more than a mile long, extending from the land face along the beach almost to the end of the peninsula. To the rear of this giant shaped system of artillery works lay the Cape Fear estuary, the approaches to which were guarded by a half-dozen smaller forts.[2]

cited as Curtis, *Reminiscences*. As is often the case with memoirs, neither of these writers is concerned with exact dates. Waddell says the ship cleared for Nassau in August, 1863, but does not indicate just when the return voyage took place. Dr. Curtis the quarantine officer for the port who boarded the ship at Smithville, is even more vague, recalling the incident to have taken place sometime during 1864 or was after the yellow fever epidemic of 1862-63. The name of the ship is also somewhat elusive. Dr. Curtis does not give the name, while Waddell's "Mary Celeste" is not precisely corroborated by other sources: A leading Wilmington exporter, 1864 was sorry to hear of the loss of the "Mary Celestia," De Rosset and Brown Louis H. De Rosset, October 5, 1864, De Rosset Papers (group II), Southern Historical Collection, The University of North Carolina, hereinafter cited as De Rosset Papers (group II); while a "Mary Celestina" is listed as a blockade-runner in the *Official Records of the Union and Confederate Navies in the War of the Rebellion* (30 vols.; Washington: Government Printing Office, 1896) III, Ser. I, 122. A more recent investigation of blockade-running, furthermore, has produced a list of 111 of the "about 250" ships operating out of Wilmington, including a "Marie Celeste." North Carolina State Archives, *Colonel William Lamb Day: Souvenir Booklet* (Wilmington: Carolina Printing Co., 1962), hereinafter cited as Lamb. For other sources on blockade-running see notes 12-14.

2. *Lamb, passim*; John G. Barrett, *The Civil War in North Carolina* (Chapel Hill: The University of North Carolina Press, 1963), pp. 246-47, 266, hereinafter cited as Barrett, *Civil War in North Carolina*.

The elaborate system of forts that studded the mouth of the Cape Fear is an indication of the importance that the Confederacy attached to the Port of Wilmington, which for the latter half of the war was by far the most important Confederate door to the outside world.[3] For more than four years the project was under construction by the soldiers of the garrison, consisting of the Thirty-sixth North Carolina Regiment as well as several companies from the Tenth North Carolina; they were assisted by some five hundred laborers, some of whom were slaves, others conscripted yeomen from the back country. So much forced labor went into this undertaking that for years to come the construction of the forts would be poison in the memory of the plain people of the Cape Fear region.[4]

After passing Fort Fisher, there was little on the eastern shore of the river to command the traveler's interest. The peninsula grew wider as one moved northward until at last the ocean was lost from view. The country was sandy, unproductive, and sparsely settled. At this point one's attention would have been drawn to the other side of the river, as he would have been approaching the first of the great rice plantations that lined the western or Brunswick shore. There the very names on the boat landings brought to mind famous men and great deeds.

There was Howe's Point, for example, behind which had once stood the three-story mansion of Major General Robert Howe, who for two years had been in command of the Southern Department of the Continental Army during the Revolution. A few miles beyond Howe's Point one caught sight of the gleaming portico of Orton, the big house of a plantation employing two hundred slaves.[5] Years later novelists would create an image of

3. New York *Herald*, January 7, 1865, quoting the Richmond *Dispatch*, n.d.; New York *Herald*, February 23, 1865; Barrett, *Civil War in North Carolina*, p. 245.
4. As late as 1871, when the Conservatives were waging a campaign for a convention to upset the Reconstruction Constitution, Edward Cantwell found that in Sampson County the most telling blow that he struck against the convention was the argument that, if the Conservatives got their convention, the people of Sampson would find themselves back at work on the forts. Wilmington *Daily Journal*, July 2, 1871.
5. Thomas Miller to General Joseph Roswell Hawley, May 15, 1865, Joseph R. Hawley Papers, Manuscripts Division, Library of Congress, hereinafter cited as Hawley Papers.

the ante-bellum South that was to become a legend. Oblivious to the crudeness and brutality of the old society, these writers could recall its rare moments of beauty, remembering the shady verandas and mint juleps, forgetting the log cabins and drinking gourds. But the lovely mansion at Orton is a reminder that at the heart of each legend lies some particle of truth.

Orton plantation had been founded in 1725 by Roger Moore, and for three generations it had remained in his family. In subsequent years it belonged to various members of the rice gentry. One distinguished owner had been General Benjamin Smith, for whom Smithville was named and who had contributed twenty thousand acres of Tennessee land for the foundation of the University of North Carolina.[6] For such services, however, it was no easy matter for the voters of the state to confer an appropriate honor on a man who already had the distinction of being master of Orton. Upon being elected Governor of North Carolina, General Smith remarked that the Governor's Mansion was not "fit for the family of a decent tradesman."[7] Including the colonial period, there had been ten North Carolina governors by the time of the Civil War who had been residents of the lower Cape Fear.[8]

If a traveler up the Cape Fear had been of mind, by chance, to stop in for a visit at Orton, or at Clarendon, or one of the other great estates, he would not necessarily have found the owner and his family at home. One reason was the fact that these plantations raised mosquitoes on almost as grand a scale as rice. With the coming of the seasons of the fevers, some planters moved to special summer houses located on higher and healthier ground in western North Carolina.

Other planters had summer houses on the shore where the

6. Louis Toomer Moore, "Colonial Plantations of the Lower Cape Fear," p. 47. Contained in Ida Brooks Kellam *et al., Wilmington Historic Colonial City* (Wilmington: Stamp Defiance Chapter of the National Society Daughters of the American Revolution, 1954), hereinafter cited as Moore, "Plantations," and Kellam, *Wilmington;* James Sprunt, *Chronicles of the Cape Fear River* . . . (Raleigh: Edwards and Broughton Printing Co., 1914), pp. 60-64.

7. Benjamin Smith to General [James?] Willborn, July 12, 1811, Governor's Papers, Benjamin Smith, North Carolina State Archives; William Lord De Rosset, *Pictorial and Historical New Hanover County and Wilmington, North Carolina, 1723-1938* (Wilmington: published by the author, 1938), p. 6.

8. Kellam, *Wilmington*, p. 32.

prevailing seawinds kept the mosquitoes pushed back into the hinterland. George Moore, for example, in addition to Moorefield Plantation, had another place on Masonboro Sound. With the coming of the mosquitoes and the heat, this father of twenty-eight children would "call up fifty or more negroes, distribute household effects for summer use among them, then start the procession afoot along the road. . . . His family would accompany on horseback."[9]

Winter loneliness, like the summer fevers, drove the planter from his rural isolation for part of the year. Though Wilmington had fewer than ten thousand people, it was the nearest approach to a metropolitan center that was to be found in North Carolina and many planters owned town houses there.[10] For a few months each year they could amuse themselves by attending the balls, the opera, the cockfights, the theater, by gambling, by becoming involved in scandals, by fighting duels, and other aristocratic pastimes.

In their politics, a few planters had continued to adhere to the old Whig party long after it had become defunct as a national organization. As Unionists, these men had continued to work for sectional compromise right up until the firing of the first shot. The vast majority of planters, however, had not only become converts to the Democratic party, as the party of the militant slavery interest, but adhered to the ultra wing of that party. They succeeded in making the lower Cape Fear a stronghold of the secessionists. This may be seen in the election of February 28, 1861, in which the North Carolina voters rejected an act of the legislature, calling for a convention to consider the question of secession. New Hanover County, for example, despite the fact that it ranked tenth place in white population, nevertheless returned more proconvention votes than any other county.[11]

9. Moore, "Plantations," p. 53.

10. Wilmington *Herald*, August 2, 1865. (Appears also as *Herald of the Union* and *Daily Herald*, the title varying.)

11. Henry Judson Beeker, "Wilmington During the Civil War" (Master's thesis, Duke University, 1941), p. 34; Barrett, *Civil War in North Carolina*, pp. 3-5; Joseph Carlyle Sitterson, *The Secession Movement in North Carolina* (Chapel Hill: The University of North Carolina Press, 1939), *passim*.

A stranger arriving in Wilmington by blockade-runner during the closing months of the war would scarcely be prepared for what he found there. Having had such recent adventures with the fire of the Federal fleet, and in waters as lethal as gunfire, he would hardly expect to find the maritime commerce of Wilmington in a very prosperous state. Why then this virtual forest of masts and spars along the water front? The paradox of a port seeming to thrive on adversity becomes understandable when we take a look at the grand strategy for victory the Union was employing, the so-called "Scott Anaconda."

General Winfield Scott had visualized the role of the North in the war as that of a gigantic snake, or anaconda, which would wind itself about the South, closing one port after another by seizure or blockade, until at last the predominantly agricultural Confederacy, its foreign trade stifled, would no longer be able to equip its armies with military hardware. As a result of Union seizures, the Confederacy lost the use of a number of important harbors during the first year of the war. Others, such as Charleston and Mobile, while remaining in Confederate hands, diminished in importance until they virtually ceased to function as ports, as the blockade slowly tightened.

In Wilmington, however, Confederate foreign trade continued to flourish, the dangerous waters around Cape Fear inspiring more fear among Union naval officers than among local pilots who had spent their lives navigating these waters. It was only with the storming and capture of the Cape Fear forts that the work of the Anaconda was complete.[12]

As chief Confederate port, Wilmington was the home of many blockade-runners. The men on these ships sometimes demonstrated heroism, loyalty to their shipmates, and devotion to their cause. However, it was not from such noble sentiments that blockade-running derived its chief inspiration. This murderous

12. Alfred Moore Waddell, *The Last Year of the War in North Carolina* (Richmond: William Ellis Jones, 1888), p. 14; James Russell Soley, *Admiral* [David Nixon] *Porter* (New York: D. Appleton Co., 1903), p. 407; Barrett, *Civil War in North Carolina,* p. 244; Kellam, *Wilmington,* p. 29; Hugh T. Lefler and Albert Ray Newsome, *North Carolina: The History of a Southern State* (Chapel Hill: The University of North Carolina Press, 1963), pp. 435-36.

business had a motivating spirit that was far older and uglier than Confederate patriotism. It was simply a matter of cotton arithmetic, a branch of mathematics in which exporters were particularly proficient. Here is the way it worked: Down the Wilmington and Weldon Railroad came trains carrying bales of cotton. The Wilmington and Manchester line brought the cotton of "up country" South Carolina. Still other bales arrived from Piedmont North Carolina by way of the Wilmington, Charlotte, and Rutherfordton Railroad. Steam boats and flat boats, from up the river, unloaded mountains of cotton on the Wilmington water front, and still more came.

By 1865, if one offered a planter three cents a pound for his crop in hard money, he would have bought cotton before his arm was fully extended. Beyond the Gulf Stream in Hamilton, in Bermuda, and in Nassau, there were British buyers, men who were as eager to buy cotton at the equivalent of forty-eight cents as the planter had been to sell it at three. As the cotton famine grew more acute in Europe, buyers there would even pay as much as a dollar a pound.

This meant that a shipper could make about $200 on every bale that he sold, and a blockade-runner could carry from 650 to 1,000 bales. Then there was the return haul. Things that could be bought cheaply in the West Indies would bring fancy prices in the beleaguered Confederacy. "We can't tell about drugs," a Wilmington shipper advised his agent in Bermuda, "but would not send any more chloroform[;] it is hard to sell. . . . Walker Mears . . . thinks 'Essence of Cognac' would sell high."[13]

Seamen had to be paid a bounty, it was true. But a sailor's bounty, no matter how much unbridled joy it might purchase for him at "Whisky Lil's" in the "Dry Pond" neighborhood of Wilmington, represented only a small fraction of the operating margin of an export-import house. A shipper could clear a quarter of a million dollars, hard money, on a successful run to Nassau and

13. De Rosset and Brown to Louis H. de Rosset, November 8, 1864, De Rosset Papers (group II); James Sprunt, *Tales of the Cape Fear Blockade*, ed. Cornelius M. D. Thomas (Winnabow, N.C.: Charles Towne Preservation Trust, 1960), pp. 20-21, 68-69, hereinafter cited as Sprunt, *Blockade*.

back.[14] So let the "Mary Celeste" or any ship make that run successfully three or four times. Then let the Yankee broadsides blast her, send her splendid crew down to Davy Jones's Locker, because the shipper's fortune would already have been made.

Besides its special wartime significance, connected with blockade-running, Wilmington was also the normal peacetime market for a large hinterland. At Wilmington the river divided. The Northeast River, extending thirty or forty miles above the city, flowed through a region of large plantations. The main branch of the river, however, the Northwest Cape Fear, connected Wilmington with Fayetteville, 112 miles away, which for practical purposes was the head of navigation. On this branch of the river, particularly on the western bank, one would see an occasional plantation, with cotton replacing rice as the staple crop. Mostly though, the river flowed through a sparsely-settled wilderness, a pine forest rising out of lean, white soil. This was the great Piney Woods.

Here in these forests it appeared that time had stood still. The people that one occasionally met followed a mode of life that differed little from that of their pioneer ancestors, a fact that rarely failed to evoke an outburst of indignation from cultivated visitors. "I am certain there can be no lower class of people," wrote an observer in 1866.

They are generally without fixed home and without definite occupation. They are always thinly clad, their habitations are mere hovels, [sic] they are entirely uneducated, and many are hardly above beasts in their habits. Very few families have $50 worth of property of any kind. The men live most of the time in the woods, and generally keep

14. Sprunt, *Blockade*, pp. 20-21, 68-69; Robert Carse, *Blockade: The Civil War at Sea* (New York: Rinehart and Company, 1958), *passim*; Hamilton Cochran, *Blockade Runners of the Confederacy* (New York: The Bobbs-Merrill Company, 1958), *passim*. The destruction of maritime records was so extensive at the time Wilmington fell to the Federal forces that the exact volume of Confederate foreign commerce is difficult to determine. However, the Harbor Master of Wilmington, G. W. Williams, on the basis of his private memoranda, estimated the port cleared 270 blockade-runners between May 20, 1863 and January 16, 1865. Joshua T. James, *Historical and Commercial Sketch of Wilmington, N.C.* [sic] ([Wilmington?]: n.p., [1867]), p. 38.

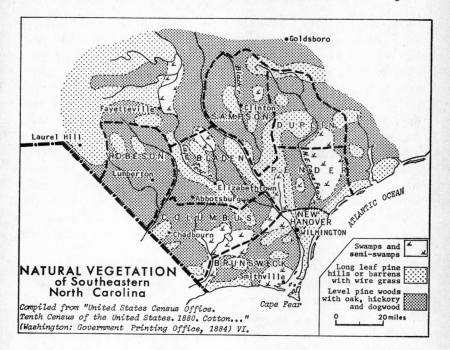

NATURAL VEGETATION
of Southeastern
North Carolina

Compiled from "United States Census Office.
Tenth Census of the United States. 1880. Cotton..."
(Washington: Government Printing Office, 1884) VI.

Swamps and
semi-swamps

Long leaf pine
hills or barrens
with wire grass

Level pine woods
with oak, hickory
and dogwood

0   20 miles

one or two dogs and own a cheap rifle. The women are slatternly and utterly without any idea of decency or propriety; they cultivate a little corn, and sometimes a patch of cow-peas, collards, or sweet potatoes.[15]

If we delete the writer's value judgments, what emerges from this account is a description of a mode of life that prevailed among countless backwoods whites and Indians of the early eighteenth century.

Piney Woods men spent their time hunting, trapping, and fishing, not so much to avoid work, as visitors often thought, but

15. Sidney Andrews, *The South Since the War: As Shown by Fourteen Weeks of Travel and Observation in Georgia and the Carolinas* (Boston: Ticknor and Fields, 1866), p. 177.

to supplement a not too conspicuous food supply. The small-scale, garden-type agriculture was determined not so much by the fact that the males loved liquor as it was by the limited amount of farm land. Scattered throughout the territory were low spots called "bottom," "bays," or "pocosins," which were rich enough to cultivate, though not always dry enough. But even in the wet ones, frost-resistant reeds grew which furnished year around grazing for livestock.

By all odds the most significant resources of the pines barrens came from the pine trees themselves. Besides lumbering, the area was responsible for a group of forest products called "naval stores," including tar, rosin, and turpentine. There, trees were tapped for crude turpentine which in turn was distilled into spirits of turpentine and rosin. The people of the pine forest also gathered dead, heart pine, or "fat lightwood," from which they extracted tar by means of a primitive kiln. However sterile the Piney Woods might appear to the stranger, its people floated enough tar, rosin, and turpentine down to Wilmington to make the city the world's greatest market for these products.[16]

In the more remote areas, the Piney Woods people might live as squatters. In other areas, where land titles were more clearly established, they sometimes lived in an almost manorial relationship with the gentry. A Confederate veteran from a prominent landed family, recalling his boyhood in the pine barrens, wrote that the people were permitted to live in the forests, cultivating as much land as they chose,

which rarely extends beyond a garden and a truck patch, the men fishing and hunting by day and night, the women hoe the little crops and raise poultry, the children gathering whortleberries and wild currants. These men are required to do three things [by the land owners]: first, they are to guard the [turpentine] orchards from fire, and if a small fire occurs, as it often does in the summer time by lightning striking

16. Thomas Gamble, "Pages from Wilmington's Story as America's First Great Naval Stores Port," *Naval Stores: History, Production, Distribution and Consumption*, ed. Thomas Gamble (Savannah, Ga.: Review Publishing and Printing Co., 1921), pp. 31-34; A. W. Schorger, and H. S. Betts, *The Naval Stores Industry: United States Department of Agriculture Bulletin No. 229* (Washington: The Government Printing Office, 1915), p. 3.

and igniting a resinous pine tree, they and their families must extinguish it. If it gets beyond their control they are to blow horns, summoning the neighboring tenants . . . ; secondly, they must once salt and care for the herd of cattle and drove of sheep belonging to the proprietor, carefully penning the sheep at night so as to protect them from dogs, wildcats and bears, which are found in those large tracks of unbroken forests. Thirdly, they must look out for the planter's honeybees, and when the cold weather sets in they must take the honey and carry it into the mansion for the use of the planter's family. They are obliged, under contract, to turn out when summoned to work the roads of the estate. These tenants find a ready market for all the game, poultry and berries they will carry into the plantation. Sometimes they spend a whole lifetime in this dwarfed but important relation to the proprietor. They form a distinct element in the organism of this large landed estate. They never mingle with more thrifty white people, while the negroes on the estate look down on them calling them most disdainfully, "poor white trash." Under the old regime this was the people who were unhappily affected by the plantation system, because they lived in the presence of and in close contact with service labor and lived and died with an emphatic protest against the decree which forced them to work. From this class all thru [sic] the coastal region, during the late Confederacy, sprang what was called the "buffalo" who cast in their lot with the federal troops as soon as any lodgment was made. They have not yet died out from among us but are still [a]live, utterly contemned by the better class of whites and distrusted by negroes.[17]

Travelers reacted against what they judged to be the misery of the people of the pine barrens. But they also disliked their backwoods eccentricity. The Piney Woods people lived in such isolation that their cultural patterns had digressed in some respects from people in more accessible communities. Unlike the inhabitants of more populated areas, they did not feel driven by custom to cut their hair, trim their beards, or to maintain their homes in an orderly, conventional way.

Even more shocking to cultivated visitors was their lack of a consistent pattern of Negrophobia in both their behavior and

17. James Battle Avirett, *The Old Plantation: How We Lived in Great House and Cabin Before the War* (New York: F. Tennyson Neely Co., 1901), pp. 70-71.

ideas. A cross-examining lawyer, for example, once asked a Piney Woods woman if she had ever given birth to a "bastard child whose father was a mulatto or negro?" "Never," the woman shot back, but indeed she had given birth to a "colored child"; and one can imagine the shudder of horror that passed through the Wilmington courtroom as she added that she would own the fact "as long as I live."[18]

Wilmington was the heart of the Cape Fear country, the place where all lines of communication began and ended, where the newspapers were printed, where people came to buy and sell and to amuse themselves. Nothing important could happen on the plantations, at the country crossroads, or in the lonely pine barrens that did not soon become a subject of conversation in Wilmington. A journalist, arriving in the city in 1864, found, as the Anaconda drew its coils tighter around the Cape Fear country, that the question which was probably of greatest concern to the people, the strength of the Cape Fear forts, was not considered a legitimate subject of conversation. The impregnability of the forts was an article of faith, the unquestioned assumption underlying all conversation.[19] "We are in daily expectation of the forts being attacked," an aristocratic lady wrote, "but there is perfect confidence felt in our ability to defend them. . . ."[20] The big question was, when would it begin?

On the day before Christmas, 1864, in the darkness before dawn, a brilliant flash for a split-second made the sea face of Fort Fisher blaze white, and the early morning calm was ripped by a shattering blast that smashed glasses on board ships out at sea and could be heard in Wilmington, thirty miles away. This was General Benjamin Butler's way of opening the siege of Fort Fisher, by exploding a powder ship. The fleet bringing the Cape Fear invasion force, consisting of 6,500 men under the command of General Butler,[21] had arrived four days before; but, while still three and a half miles off the coast, the Union men could hear

18. Wilmington *Herald*, October 13, 1865.
19. *Ibid.*, September 11, 1965.
20. Eliza Jane de Rosset to Louis H. de Rosset, October 28, 1864, De Rosset Papers (group II).
21. Barrett, *Civil War in North Carolina*, p. 264.

the thunder of a raging surf. They decided to stay a safe distance off shore and wait for a calmer sea.

An opportunity for a landing came on the night of December 23. In an effort to make a breach in the defenses of Fort Fisher, General Butler ordered the "U.S.S. Louisiana" to be loaded to the gunwales with high explosives to which a time-fuse was connected, and that she be cut loose and allowed to drift into the fort on a predawn flood tide. In the wake of the exploding powder ship, the invading troops braved the pounding surf only to discover that, however much damage the great blast had done to the military reputation of General Butler,[22] the sodded breastworks of Fort Fisher were quite intact. There was nothing for them to do except retreat to their ships.[23]

In Wilmington everyone knew that the repulse of the Christmas Eve attack was not the end, but the beginning of the battle for the Cape Fear. The two daily newspapers proclaimed fervently a call to arms, making each morning's issue a kind of journalistic equivalent of Pickett's Charge; and indeed it was not long before Confederate patriotism was put to a severe test. On January 13, 1865, the Union invaders, now commanded by General Alfred Howe Terry, were able to establish themselves firmly on the beach north of the land face of Fort Fisher.[24]

The editor of the *North Carolinian*, himself a native of Scotland, lashed out against rumors that the fort had fallen: "The Fort still holds out gallantly and gloriously beneath the same sacred emblem that led Catherine the Great to victory and empire —the cross. It now waves as defiantly as it did on Christmas Day, when the armada and army of the enemy were driven from our

22. A general who had served with Butler, and who, like Butler, was a Radical, wrote, following the powder ship fiasco, that Butler "is in some things a great man but he is no general. . . . He is everlastingly studying to create a sensation and everything he writes or does shows on its face that he has a theatrical consciousness. . . . He is finished as a commander in the field." Hawley to wife, January 12, 1865, Hawley Papers.

23. *The War of the Rebellion: A Compilation of the Official Records of the Union and Confederate Armies*, 128 vols. (Washington: Government Printing Office, 1895), XI, Ser. I, 228-29, hereinafter cited as *Official Records of the Armies*.

24. I. R. Hamilton to John Swinton, January 5, 1865, John Swinton Papers, Southern Historical Collection, The University of North Carolina.

shores in disgrace."[25] The editor of the *Journal*, a native of Ireland, was as virulent against these rumors as was his Scottish colleague: "The sensational reports about Fisher are entirely unfounded. Official information from General Whiting . . . , reports enemy's attack unsuccessful. Fresh troops are being sent to him, and we are confident they will hold it. P.S. [*sic*] January 16— 6 A.M.—Fisher capture at one A.M. this morning."[26]

Fort Fisher, key to the defense of the Cape Fear, had fallen. The other forts, guarding the various approaches to Fisher, were now useless to the Confederacy and were within a few days abandoned. In the Battle of Fort Fisher, the Confederates suffered more than two thousand casualties; including those captured, their losses totaling roughly one-fourth of their troops on the lower Cape Fear. The Union forces also had suffered more than a thousand casualties.[27] But with the capture of Smithville General Terry was able to begin replenishing his depleted ranks. Furthermore, he did not have to wait for his replacements to arrive from recruiting centers in distant northern cities. They came to him from the rice fields of the lower Cape Fear. Into Smithville they swarmed, shouting as they came, "God bless Massa Licum we'se free. . . ."[28] "Officers of the colored regiments are now recruiting for their commands," wrote a Yankee reporter from Smithville, and they "are meeting with great success."[29]

In the meantime, people in Wilmington continued to go about their individual affairs, as serenely as the circumstances would allow, and remarkably oblivious to the momentous events around them. It is true that the first assault on Fort Fisher had forced the Theatre to postpone the showing of "Hamlet" until after the holidays; but, faithful to the tradition that "the show must go on," that production was rescheduled for January 11.[30] The theater-goer's taste, however, did not generally run in such a serious vein. Most performances were either light comedy or

---

25. Wilmington *Daily North Carolinian*, January 16, 1865, hereinafter cited as Wilmington *Carolinian*.

26. Wilmington *Daily Journal*, January 16, 1865.

27. Barrett, *Civil War in North Carolina*, p. 280.

28. Curtis, *Reminiscences*, p. 35.

29. New York *Herald*, February 13, 1865.

30. Wilmington *Daily Journal*, January 11, 1865.

spectacles. Even during its twilight days, the old society showed more taste for amusement and diversion than for exploring its own soul.

One alert bookseller, apparently sizing up his inventory in light of the current military situation, offered a "variety of Confederate novels. Cheap for Confederate money . . . ,"[31] so little was he able to foresee what an enduring cultural legacy he was unloading with such rashness!

The historical events taking place during these days were so monumental that they tended to impress themselves in some way upon the most commonplace activities of ordinary people. For example, during the first assault on Fort Fisher, the Reverend L. S. Burkhead, of the Front Street Methodist Church, sat down to compose his Christmas sermon. But he found himself counting the shells that were being fired at the fort, which he calculated to be averaging forty per minute. It struck him how inconsistent it was to "preach the blessed gospel of *Peace* with the sound of *war* ringing in my ears."[32]

However, there were other anomalies in Wilmington that day. At an auction to be held on Exchange Corner, a Negro woman, three children, ages one, five, and seven, four mules, and a girl were scheduled to be sold. One cannot help wondering what inconsistencies came to the minds of these people that Christmas Eve,[33] as the thunder of their redemption rolled over the sand dunes from the ocean beyond Fort Fisher.

There were many things to remind people that this was no longer the white man's war of 1861, fought, as someone has said, by northern whites who wanted to keep slavery in the Union against southern whites who wanted to take it out. By 1865, the war was no longer an ordinary sort of war, with each side seeking only to eliminate the army of the other. It was as if the mad vision of John Brown had become a reality, and his spectral army

31. Wilmington *Carolinian*, February 20, 1865.
32. Reverend L. S. Burkhead, "History of the Difficulties of the Pastorate of the Front Street Methodist Church, Wilmington, N.C., For the Year 1865," *Historical Papers of Trinity College* (Durham: Trinity College Historical Society, 1909), Ser. VIII, p. 36, hereinafter cited as Burkhead, "Difficulties."
33. Wilmington *Daily Journal*, December 26, 1864.

had descended to earth, had been issued blue uniforms, and was now marching through the South, freeing the slaves and putting weapons in their hands.

The *Journal* reported that there were four thousand Negroes among the force of perhaps eight thousand that was now moving against Wilmington,[34] guided by Lem Brown and other local Negroes.[35] Such a force, by its very nature, was aimed not only against a rival army, but also against a rival social system. The slaves, the very "mud sills" upon which ante-bellum society rested, were being transformed into Union soldiers as that army moved.

Confederate Wilmington was quick to recognize the danger created by such an army marching on a city in which a large portion of the people were slaves. Who could say what lay behind the grinning mask that concealed Negro thoughts? Behind which fossilized smile was to be found the angry face of a Nat Turner; terrible eyes that seemed to ask if there could be blood enough in one city to wash away the wrongs of the ages? The city authorities acted swiftly: On Christmas Day mobilization was extended. Old men, previously considered beyond military duty, were armed and put on guard duty in the city. Boys ten to fifteen years old were likewise armed and given the task of guarding prisoners, in order to relieve older Confederates for other duties.[36] Before the week was out the Negro pass system had been stringently tightened.[37]

In retrospect it is not easy to understand the tenacity with which slaveholders clung to the maintenance of a system as conspicuously transitory as slavery must have appeared in January and February of 1865. Yet, despite the fact that liberating troops

34. *Ibid.*, January 16, 1865. The original invasion force had 6,500 soldiers, including two Negro brigades, and 2,000 sailors and marines. However, more than 1,000 of these men were killed or wounded in storming Fort Fisher. Though after the battle Union officers were reported to have had "great success" in recruiting local Negroes, it is not certain to what extent this may have made up for combat losses. Barrett, *Civil War in North Carolina*, pp. 264, 275; New York *Herald*, February 13, 1865.

35. Curtis, *Reminiscences*, p. 33.

36. Wilmington *Daily Journal*, December 31, 1864.

37. *Ibid.*, January 3, 1865.

were advancing unchecked up the Cape Fear valley, in Wilmington the recovery of runaways and the local slave trade were
pursued industriously. Even within a week of the capture of
Wilmington, the *Journal* published a notice of the capture of a
"woman named Betsy and her son Elias, belonging to Owen D.
Holmes," owner of Kendall, one of the great rice plantations.[38]
Later, when the Union forces were at Old Town Creek, only
eight miles below the city, the *Carolinian* was advertising the sale
of twenty-six Negroes on terms of "six months credit, purchasers
giving note and approved securities"![39]

Ante-bellum society was not characterized by much human
equality, even among whites. Considerable economic and social
differences came to exist between those who reaped the benefits
of slave labor and those who worked in competition with it.
Chronic peacetime inequality, however, was magnified by war and
inflation into grotesque proportions. After the fall of Fort Fisher,
food prices in Wilmington reached fantastic levels. People who
could afford ham might pick one up for $525, while the less af-
fluent could find salt pork offered for $6 a pound and corn for $40
a bushel.[40]

"You don't mean that *you* lack food to eat!" a lady wrote in a
fine hand to her husband, a Confederate officer stationed near
Wilmington. "I supposed that you mean people generally for
which I am truly sorry, but shall be greatly distressed if you lack
food yourself. Send me word what to send you and how, and it
shall promptly be attended to. . . ."[41] But for the "people generally," particularly wage earners, people with relatively fixed in-
comes, those left behind in the inflationary scramble, the matter
was not so promptly "attended to." On January 23, the *Journal*
commented editorially that "it appears to us that some steps
should be taken relative to the suffering many of the poorer class

38. *Ibid.,* January 17, 1865; Curtis, *Reminiscences,* p. 31.
39. Wilmington *Carolinian,* February 20, 1865.
40. Donald MacRae to Julia MacRae, January 18, 1865, and Julia MacRae to
Donald MacRae, February 2, 1865, Hugh MacRae Papers, Department of Manuscripts, Duke University, hereinafter cited as MacRae Papers.
41. Julia MacRae to Donald MacRae, February 2, 1865, MacRae Papers.
Emphasis in the original.

of this town are undergoing. We are informed that there are many who have neither food nor fuel. . . ." At the same time, the Clarendon Saloon could advertise that it "has always the best fare to be found in the Confederacy. No expense has been spared to furnish epicures the rarest delicacies of the season. Down stairs can be found all of the choicest brands of foreign and domestic liquors."[42] And on the southern horizon at each nightfall the fires of atonement burned closer.

"Darkness and gloom covered" Wilmington the day the Confederates began their withdrawal, an observer wrote. "Those immense fires on each side of town were fearful. Contrary winds blew the dense black smoke of both directly toward the town; and, when the . . . clouds met in the center, it seemed as if a black oppressive girdle encompassed the town."[43] Yet the next morning, February 22, 1865, horsemen wearing gray cloaks still dashed furiously up and down the streets. But there was not much time left. The Yankees were already across the river. The riders were part of the rear guard of General Robert Frederick Hoke's cavalry, and they were supervising the evacuation of the last Confederates. Suddenly, the men in gray were gone.

A group of Wilmington gentlemen gathered on the water front at the foot of Market Street. They were looking out over the river, at the strange army gathering on the other side, when their attention was drawn to a company of horsemen riding up from the south end of the city. They were Yankee scouts. One of them courteously arranged a meeting between Mayor John Dawson and General Alfred Howe Terry to work out formal surrender arrangements. Then the riders began dashing up and down the streets, rounding up Confederate stragglers. "Then came General Terry at the head of a column up Front Street, with the strains of martial music, and colors flying. Leaving the main column at Market Street, heading a squadron of splendidly equipped men mounted on superb chargers—every horse a beauti-

42. Wilmington *Carolinian*, February 20, 1865.
43. Catherine Douglas de Rosset Mears to Eliza Jane de Rosset, March 28, 1865, from copy in De Rosset Papers (group II) of original belonging to William Green de Rosset, Saratoga, Florida.

ful bay—he dashed up to the City Hall. . . ."[44] There General
Terry took formal possession of the city.

The city turned out to watch the Yankee parade. But they
were not really Yankees, these men, though they wore the Union
blue. They were Kentuckians,[45] men who would understand the
brooding fear that white Wilmington felt that day. The Federal
takeover might prove to be a polite arrangement between southern gentlemen. The columns marched on. There was the sound
of singing. Black men wearing blue uniforms had appeared.
"Christ died to make men holy, let us die to make them free," the
black soldiers were singing. The human "mud sills" of ante-
bellum Wilmington suddenly came alive and flooded wildly
through the streets. "The men danced in jubilation, the women
went into hysterics, then and there, on the sidewalks. And their
sable brethren in arms march passed, proud and erect, singing. . . ."[46]

An elderly white gentleman, "a very quite man who stood on
a street corner watching the column pass without a word until the
negro troops beside whom streamed a shouting mass of ex-slaves,
appeared. Then he turned away, and with both hands raised and
an indescribable expression of mingled horror and disgust exclaimed, 'Blow Gabriel, blow, for God's sake blow.' "[47]

On the following Sunday morning, the Reverend L. S. Burkhead was up before dawn. As pastor of the Front Street Methodist
Church, he had special duties to perform at this early hour.
Because, in his labors on behalf of this flock, he had ministered
both to the bond and to the free. As a matter of fact, about eight
hundred of his thousand communicants were Negroes; and it was
for the sake of his black sheep that he arose before dawn each
Sunday. In Wilmington, Sunday was not entirely a holiday for
Negroes; and the Front Street Church, alert to the particular
needs of all of its members, had established the custom of holding

44. Burkhead, "Difficulties," pp. 37-38.
45. Wilmington *Herald*, March 13, 1865.
46. Frank Moore, *The Civil War in Song and Story* (Chicago: P. F. Collier,
1889), p. 187.
47. Waddell, *Memories*, p. 57.

a sunrise service each Sunday morning for the convenience of the Negroes. Thanks to this arrangement, a Negro could render unto God all of his Sabbath-day obligations in time to prepare his master's breakfast.

But on this particular morning, the Reverend Burkhead had some misgivings. He was going to his own church to minister to his own flock, to be sure. But Wilmington was not the Wilmington of last Sabbath morning. It was not that he had failed to foresee that there would come such a day as this. On the contrary, ever since the fall of Fort Fisher, five weeks ago, he had labored to prepare his flock for this day, so that with the coming of the Union troops they would "possess their souls in patience, and . . . refrain from all extravagance. . . ." He had warned them that "Yankee chaplains—even colored chaplains—might labor to win their hearts and . . . persuade them to leave their own church and pastor. . . ." He had also felt that it was his duty to warn them that the "Confederates might possibly retake the City and if they were guilty of the commission of wrongs upon the whites they might expect in that case to be severly punished."[48] They had promised to be faithful; but, as a minister of the gospel, the Reverend Burkhead sometimes had been saddened by Negro promises.

Upon reaching the church, he found a Negro, whom he identified only as "Charles," reading the scripture lesson. Charles had chosen the Ninth Psalm as his text. "The whole congregation was wild with excitement, and extravagant beyond all precedent with shouts, groans, amens, and unseemly demonstrations."[49] Charles read:

> Thou hast rebuked the nations,
>> Thou hast blotted out their name
>>> forever and ever. . . .

> The enemy have vanished in everlasting ruins;
>> their cities Thou has rooted out;
>>> the very memory of them has perished. . . .

48. Burkhead, "Difficulties," pp. 39-40.
49. *Ibid.*, p. 44.

> For the needy shall not always be forgotten
> and the hope of the poor
> shall not perish forever.

The Negro closed the scripture reading by calling on the Congregation to go home and take down "dem Bibles and read and study ober dis morning lesson on dis de day of the jubilee."[50]

The Reverend Burkhead did not go forward to take his customary seat behind the pulpit. But during the singing of the next hymn, a Negro, in the uniform of a Union chaplain, arose, walked forward, and took his place in the empty seat of the pastor. "After another song and prayer, Charles rose and stated that there was a strange brother present who would like to make some remarks." The chaplain rose and began: "A few short years ago I left North Carolina a slave; I now return a man. . . . One week ago you were all slaves; now you are all free (Uproarious screaming). Thank God the armies of the Lord and Gideon has [sic] triumphed and the Rebels have been driven back in confusion and scattered like chaff before the wind. (Amen! Hallelujah!)" All that the Reverend Burkhead had feared was coming to pass. His people were opening their ears to the false prophets, and their feet were straying from the path. He then, a sadder man, "returned to the parsonage and took breakfast and thought over the wonders of the never-to-be-forgotten sunrise prayer-meeting, while the shouting and general demonstrations of joy at the jubilee were heard and seen along all the streets in the vicinity of the Front Street Church."[51]

The Union army left a garrison in Wilmington and continued its victorious sweep of the Cape Fear country. Fifty miles up the river lay the little village of Elizabethtown. It did not appear to be a very worthy military objective, so the Federal troops, after celebrating a kind of belated Halloween, a festivity that lasted several days and included some looting, marched on, without bothering to honor the community with a permanent garrison. They left behind them a dangerously bitter and humiliated man.

Neill McGill, Confederate officer, leader of the local Home

50. *Ibid.*, p. 42.
51. *Ibid.*, p. 43.

Guard, as respected by the substantial, Confederate planters along the western bank of the Cape Fear as he was feared by the Unionist in the wilderness beyond the river, had been forced to stand helpless while his property had been looted. McGill was a fighting man, and only blood would be able to extinguish the fire that now burned inside of him. But with whom would he fight? When the Yankees had been in Elizabethtown there had been entirely too many of them. His Home Guard would have been no match for the Yankee army. Now that they were gone there was no one left to fight. Well, almost no one. The day the Yankees left he had met Needham Bryan on the road coming out of Elizabethtown, and had told him "how the Yankees treated him and took his property," and that "Matthew Sykes was the very damn son of a bitch that was the whole cause of it, and if he ever returned he would be put through. . . ."[52]

Matthew Sykes, or "Matt" as he was called in the Piney Woods, was a strong Union man, and he came from a family of Union people. Back in 1861, when the Secessionist-Confederate party had won out, Matt had faced the universal dilemma of southern Unionists: would he fight against his own cause, or would he fight against his own neighbor? To the Unionists the idea of civil war was monstrous, but the most hideous of all civil wars is a war against kinsman and neighbor.

Like many another of his persuasion, Matt was willing to let the Secessionists have their war if they would leave him in peace. But they would not. They passed the conscription acts instead. He had to choose. Matt could find no way out of the dilemma, but he listened to the words of his father-in-law, who persuaded him to sign up for a short term in the Confederate army and thus avoid conscription.[53] The differences of the river folk had always been a matter of politics not of killing so he signed up with his Confederate opponents against the strangers who were then invading the South.

Matthew Sykes completed his term of service at Fort Fisher in June, 1864, and returned home to the Piney Woods. But

52. Wilmington *Herald*, October 28, 1865.
53. *Ibid.*, October 11, 1865.

things had changed at home since he had been away. Gone was the appearance of harmony that had prevailed during the first months of the war. The Secessionist-Confederate party had brought on war, and war had brought on misery; but not very evenly distributed misery. You could still buy the good things of peace if you had the money. But the people of the Piney Woods did not have the money. Then the casualty lists that were posted in Elizabethtown grew longer and longer in 1863 and 1864. During World War I, the United States with a military population of 100,000,000 lost 126,000 men. But during the Civil War, North Carolina with a military population of only 600,000 lost more than 40,000 men![54]

To the people of the back country, even more hateful than the casualty lists were the exemptions that were allowed under the conscription acts. If you owned twenty slaves or more, you did not have to go. Surely this war had something to do with slavery! If you had money enough to hire a substitute, you did not have to go.[55] The angel of death had been kind to the great plantations that lined the western bank of the Cape Fear, but had visited the cabins in the wilderness with savage cruelty.

People were bitter against the Confederate party when Matt came home. Some people were saying that it was a rich man's war and a poor man's fight. After all that had happened, what would the Confederates be able to say in reply to this? To devise a reply to this contention would take some time, to say the least; but, in the meanwhile, the Confederates sent to the Piney Woods the next best thing to a clinching argument, which was a few patrols of armed and mounted men to keep the discussion from growing too impolite while they were thinking of some likely answer.

Neill McGill's Home Guard had been formed to keep the back country under control. He and his men had ridden the lonely roads of the Piney Woods, investigating the Unionists and grumblers. The fact that Matthew Sykes was a Confederate

54. United States Bureau of the Census, *A Statistical Abstract Supplement: Historical Statistics of the United States, Colonial Times to 1957* (Washington: Government Printing Office, 1960), p. 735.

55. Confederate States of America, *Statutes at Large*, 1862, ch. 45.

veteran did not quell the suspicions of the Home Guard. Soon
Matt and his wife Catherine began hiding from this patrolling
cavalry. In the daytime this was easy enough. One could nearly
always get some warning of their approach. But late at night
there was danger of being surprised while asleep and seized.
Because of this Matt and Catherine began a practice that the
Heroes of America and other North Carolina Unionists called
"lying out," that is, sleeping in the woods.[56]

When the Union invasion of the Cape Fear came, Matt was no
longer a prisoner of the old Unionist dilemma. It was no longer
unthinkable for him to shoot the kind of neighbor who rode
nightly with the Home Guard. But what would happen to
Catherine, to her family, and to his family if the night riders
found out that he had gone over to the Yankees? No one could
ever tell what he did not know. So, without even telling Catherine, Matt disappeared. He volunteered for the Yankee army.
Having use for a man with his knowledge of the Cape Fear
country, they enlisted him as a guide. He took part in the victorious Union sweep up the valley of the Cape Fear. But, worried
because his family did not know his whereabouts, he soon asked
for leave to go home to "make provision" for Catherine.[57] He was
granted a week's furlough at home.

The last day of Matt's leave at home was Palm Sunday. On
Monday morning he would have to start back to camp. Matt and
Catherine should have followed their old practice of "lying out"
that Sunday night. The victorious Union army had swept on far
beyond Elizabethtown, and the Home Guard was again the
master of the back-country roads. Had not Catherine's niece,
Mary Edwards, heard Neill McGill say that "Sykes and the d----d
Yankees thought that they had possession, but he would show
them that they had not."[58] Also, it was only Friday that the
cavalry had ridden into Mitchell Dove's yard and had asked about
Matt.[59]

But Matt and Catherine did not "lie out" on Sunday night.

56. Wilmington *Herald*, October 13, 1865.
57. *Ibid.*, October 12, 1865.
58. *Ibid.*
59. *Ibid.*, October 18, 1865.

It was impossible that they could have known what had happened at Appomattox, Virginia, that morning, that Lee had surrendered the Army of Northern Virginia. News traveled slowly in the Piney Woods. They undoubtedly did feel a sense of confidence as a result of the triumph of their cause in the Cape Fear country. They may have decided not to "lie out" simply because it was raining Sunday evening.

In any event, they chose not to sleep in the wet woods that chill April night, but to spend the night at the house of Catherine's father, Elias Edwards. But Catherine did not sleep. While Matt slept, while her father and her sister, Lucretia, slept, Catherine sat tending the fire, watching, waiting, and listening as the rain fell outside. Yet, for all of her vigilance, Catherine did not hear them when they came. It may have been because she had her ears too tuned for the thundering hoofbeats of an approaching cavalry patrol, or it may have been because the rain thickened the night and muffled all footsteps. But two hours before light on the day Matt was to return to camp, one rider and two men on foot stole up to the Edwards' "double frame house." It was Mc-Gill and two of his men! Catherine did not see them until it was too late. She dashed to where Matt was sleeping, woke him, and led him quickly into a storage room, where she buried him in a pile of loose cotton.

In the meanwhile, her father had gone to answer the door. They asked for Sykes. "Which Sykes?" Edwards evaded. The men pushed into the house. They brought a blazing light into the storeroom. One of them, kicking through the pile of cotton, discovered where Matt was hiding. "Don't kill him!" Catherine screamed.[60] But the men seized him and a Home Guard private bound his hands with a piece of cotton rope. They started to lead him out into the rain. He was still in his "night clothes." Catherine said that she would get Matt's clothes. "The clothes he had on would do," one of the men had said, but they waited. While Matt was getting dressed, the Home Guard private, John McMillan, sat in front of the fire smoking. Elias Edwards asked

60. Wilmington *Daily Dispatch*, October 11, 1865, hereinafter cited as Wilmington *Dispatch*.

McMillan what they planned to do with him. Well, they would "do something with him; . . . They would give him a court martial."[61] Then they led Matt out.

Catherine and her sister, Lucretia, dressed quickly. Leaving their father behind, they hurried two and a half miles to Matt's home to get the help of his widowed mother, Unity Sykes. The rain had stopped and dawn was breaking when the three women found tracks, in the wet earth, of a horse and some men on foot. They followed the trail until it took them by the house of a neighbor, where they learned that McGill's party had been by there, but Matt had not been with them. The three women retraced their steps along the Elizabethtown road toward the Edwards place. The road led by low, swampy "bays." Matt was somewhere out there.

When they reached the Edwards place, they found Edwards had assembled a posse of about thirty kinsmen and neighbors. Tracking was no new art in the Piney Woods, and the Edwards posse soon picked up McGill's trail. They found the point where his party had left the Elizabethtown road. The trail now led them down "Shady Grove" road, a corduroy track through a "thick and wooded" quagmire known as "Juniper Bay." Coming upon "Piney Island" in the middle of the "bay," they saw it. Matt's horribly mutilated body was hanging from a small sapling, his feet almost touching the ground.

The Piney Woods people got the help of the Yankees. McGill and McMillan were captured, though the third man escaped. The two were tried before a court-martial in Wilmington, where the Confederate party and the gentry rallied to their defense. Their friends engaged two of the most distinguished lawyers in the Cape Fear country to represent them. But McGill and McMillan said nothing in their own defense. The killing of Matthew Sykes they neither admitted nor denied, though their lawyers denied the jurisdiction of the court.

However, the defense rested its case primarily upon the high character of the accused. Some well-known men appeared in court to bear witness to this, including John Dawson, Confederate

61. Wilmington *Herald*, October 11, 1865.

mayor of Wilmington and brother of a wealthy banker, as well as James Shackelford, exporter of cotton, lumber, and naval stores with offices in Wilmington and New York, who under the Confederacy had been chairman of the New Hanover County Court.[62] The defense attempted to impugn the character of the Piney Woods people who came to Wilmington to testify against McMillan and McGill, as well as that of the murdered man himself. But the military court was not impressed and sentenced the two men to death for murder.

Nevertheless, the families that had reigned on the banks of the Cape Fear for more than a hundred years were not to be frustrated by the court of a Yankee major. It would be no easy task to help the prisoners to escape, to be sure, since they were not only housed in the solid brick, Wilmington jail, but also they were under the constant surveillance of a Union sentry. Yet could mere brick and steel and a guarding soldier hold men who had friends so powerful as those of McMillan and McGill? A Union night-sentry was approached by an aristocratic young man with a proud military bearing.[63] There was some negotiation about the appropriate size of a bribe. Finally his acquiescence in an escape plan was purchased for $1,000, "or more."[64] He was to permit the prisoners to make a hole in the prison wall by removing the bricks with penknives. But the Union soldier did more than acquiesce. Using his bayonet, he helped the prisoners chip out the mortar from between the bricks.

62. *Ibid.*, October 24, 1865; Frank D. Smaw, *Wilmington Directory, Including a General and City Business Directory for 1865-1866* (Wilmington: P. Heinsberger, 1865).

63. That Colonel Alfred Moore Waddell negotiated this bribe is a supposition based on the following: (1) Because he was both an old Whig and a former Confederate officer, Waddell enjoyed a measure of confidence of both sides and sometimes served as an intermediary in delicate negotiations; (2) he describes in his *Memories* how he negotiated a similar bribe several months earlier; (3) as a legal representative of McGill and McMillan he was a logical person to make such an attempt, though to have avowed it afterwards, as he did the previous bribe, would have violated a confidential relationship with clients; (4) certain hints in *Memories*. For example, the book has no formal arrangement. Rather each recollection reminds him of another. Having just related the story of his having negotiated the Smithville bribe, he is apparently reminded of the part he played in the defense of McGill and McMillan.

64. Waddell, *Memories*, pp. 89-92.

The next morning the jailor found an empty prison cell, and a yawning hole through which both the prisoners and their guard had fled. On the floor there was a Union bayonet,[65] but its edge was slightly dull, having been used to free men who had murdered a Unionist.

65. Wilmington *Dispatch*, February 24, 1866. A year later Governor Jonathan Worth wrote President Johnson that petitions, "signed by most of our General Assembly and many of our most prominent citizens," urged that McGill and McMillan be granted a presidential pardon. Jonathan Worth to Andrew Johnson, January 22, 1867, Governor's Papers, Jonathan Worth, North Carolina State Archives.

II ⤬ *"Angels now are on de wing..."*

IT WAS LATE WHEN TOM SUTTON WOKE ON THE MORNING OF February 22, 1865. He and his companion had slept dangerously too long on Tom's comfortable feather bed. The two young soldiers hurried into their gray uniforms. Now they were in trouble and it was because of Tom's bed. During the retreat from Smithville, after the Confederates had evacuated the forts guarding the mouth of the Cape Fear, sleeping on the hard ground, Tom had thought more than once of the soft feather bed at his mother's[1] house in Wilmington.

Then, three days before, his regiment, the Fortieth North Carolina, had thrown up hasty defenses only four miles south of Wilmington. Two days had passed and nothing much had happened. Tom thought it ridiculous to sleep on the ground when he had a real bed so close at hand. Somehow he had managed to get an overnight leave, and took a friend along to share his good fortune. But they were not used to such luxury and had overslept. Now there were going to be some embarrassing questions asked when they got back to the regiment.

Jumping into their saddles, the two young artillerymen galloped furiously southward out of Wilmington, past the moss-laden cypress groves of Greenfield Plantation. But Greenfield, ordinarily bustling with military life, was curiously silent this morning. They thought that "things looked strange," but dashed on.

[1] In this account Sutton uses the phrase, "my parent." We should understand this to refer to his mother rather than to his father. He was writing for a newspaper, and a convention of that day made it a mark of good taste to avoid an unnecessary, direct reference to a lady in a newspaper.

Coming upon the Fortieth regimental positions, they found them completely deserted. There they learned that not only the southern defenses of Wilmington, but the city itself had been evacuated at midnight, while they had been asleep on Tom's feather bed.

To the south, beyond the horizon, were the relentlessly advancing Yankee columns. They turned their faces toward the north, where Wilmington lay. There a terrible spectacle greeted them. Great volumes of black smoke arose. But the smoke did not rise very high. It seemed thick and heavy, and spread out over the city in a continuous black layer. It looked like a funeral pall, Tom thought.

But there was not much time to think. They spurred their horses and bounded off to the north. Stopping long enough in Wilmington to say goodbye to Tom's mother and tell her that "the Yankees are coming," they were off again. They overtook the Fortieth North Carolina at the Northeast Cape Fear River, just as the engineers were getting ready to cut the pontoon bridge.

The black smoke that Tom Sutton had seen had come from burning rosin, turpentine, and cotton, which General Braxton Bragg had ordered to be destroyed. Why did the dying Confederacy show such a compulsion for destruction? Sutton asked himself this question as a youth, and twenty years later he still had not found the answer. Why, for example, had the Fortieth North Carolina been ordered to blow up Fort Caswell? "It was a beautiful place, erected at the outlay of so many thousands of dollars, and why destroy it? . . . the destruction of Caswell could not possibly retard the enemy's movements."[2]

Why indeed? It is ironic that the Cape Fear valley was laid waste by an army that could entertain no hope for victory and but little even for a negotiated peace. It is doubly ironic when one considers the fact that this policy of destruction came during the closing weeks of the war and was aimed at those things that otherwise would have brought immediate prosperity to the region with the coming of peace. The world market was famished for cotton and naval stores and would pay fancy prices for them. Had

2. Wilmington *Review*, October 22, 1884.

it been possible to market the rich hoard of these commodities that had accumulated around blockaded Wilmington during the last two years of the war, the ships of a half-dozen nations, deeply laden with the bounties of peace, would have crossed the Cape Fear bar, as if drawn by a powerful magnet.

General Braxton Bragg, however, in consultation with General Robert E. Lee,[3] who in turn was faithfully carrying out the policies of the Richmond government, treated this vast wealth as an ordinary military objective that must be defended or destroyed. When the Union army approached Wilmington, he ordered the bulk of the cotton and naval stores to be evacuated deep inland, and then destroyed the railroads over which these products might have found their way to market. In the area of the city, bridges, wharfs, and shipyards were burned as was the "extensive line of cotton sheds" on Eagle Island. The Confederate commander then ordered the burning of those commodities that he had been unable to evacuate from Wilmington, including one thousand bales of cotton, fifteen thousand barrels of rosin, and a "great quantity" of turpentine.[4]

So precipitate was the Confederate evacuation, however, that certain facilities of the Wilmington, Charlotte, and Rutherfordton Railroad, particularly in the area around Laurinburg, had escaped the desperate torch of General Bragg. But happily for Bragg this oversight was quickly corrected by a fellow West Point graduate, General William Tecumseh Sherman, who, though serving the opposite cause, was said to share with his southern colleague a certain professional affinity for a cheerful blaze.

To one of his commanders Sherman wrote: "En route break the railroad which is known as the Wilmington and Charlotte. . . . It is of little importance," he said of the line upon which much of Wilmington's peacetime prosperity depended, "but being on it, we might as well use up some of its iron." His

3. Don Carlos Seitz, *Braxton Bragg: General of the Confederacy* (Columbia: The State Company, 1924), p. 508.

4. New York *Herald*, February 25, 28, 1865; John G. Barrett, *The Civil War in North Carolina* (Chapel Hill: The University of North Carolina Press, 1963), p. 283, hereinafter cited as Barrett, *Civil War in North Carolina*.

troops then destroyed three-quarters of a mile of track, and a "large quantity" of new iron rails, and then burned the depot and railroad shops at Laurinburg.[5] Fortunately, however, anticipating the end of the war, Sherman reversed his railway policy and began the long process of rebuilding the lines.[6] But the flames stoked by fanaticism had swept the Cape Fear country; and, when they had finally burned themselves out in the northwest, the economy of the region was in paralysis.

Even naval stores, based on such a durable resource as the pine forest, had not escaped. Due to the destruction of the railroads, much of the existing stock could be marketed only by a long and circuitous route. Furthermore, during the winter season in which the Piney Woods people ordinarily would have been preparing virgin trees for tapping, or "cutting new boxes" as they called it, war had swept in upon them. Now the war had passed on, but so had the winter. With the coming of warm weather, they were too busy tending the old pine orchards to find time to open up new ones. Also most of the turpentine stills had been seized by the Confederate government,[7] probably for the sake of the copper used in their construction.

Before the war the people of the Cape Fear country had depended primarily upon two industries, naval stores and rice. If the former suffered damage as the result of war, the latter suffered almost total annihilation as a result of emancipation. No ante-bellum industry was more dependent upon compulsory labor than rice, with its heavy demand for backbreaking toil in disease-infested quagmires. "With the exception of small fields here and there, cultivated by negroes for themselves," rice production was virtually abandoned for eight or nine years after the war.[8] As late as 1872, a correspondent for the New York *Tribune* wrote that nowhere in North Carolina had he seen "so many evidences of

5. Barrett, *Civil War in North Carolina*, pp. 299-300.

6. Charles Lewis Price, "Railroads and Reconstruction in North Carolina, 1865-1871" (Doctoral dissertation, The University of North Carolina, 1959), p. 99.

7. The Wilmington *Herald*, June 10, 1865. (The title varies. February 28-May 27, 1865, it was called *The Herald of the Union*. Afterwards it was The Wilmington *Herald* or *The Daily Herald*. Hereinafter cited as Wilmington *Herald*.)

8. Wilmington *Review*, August 24, 1882.

poverty and ruin brought upon the Southern people by the war as along the banks of the Cape Fear. . . ."[9]

At the end of the war, not only was the output of commodities for export, such as naval stores and rice, almost at a standstill; but also the production of food supplies for the local markets was very slight. "Why is our market so bare?" asked a Wilmington newspaper in May, 1865. "What has become of all the farmers? Are they afraid of Wheeler's cavalry, or what is their reason for not bringing their produce, vegetables, etc., to market?"[10] As much as Wheeler's cavalry, the farmers and fishermen may have been afraid of semi-Confederate irregulars such as the "Ishmailite" band that Union gunboats had driven back into the Piney Woods.[11] And what did one actually see in the Wilmington market? There were full-grown, "full-bearded men, . . . standing behind a few bottles of dirty water intended to be sold for beer."[12]

It would seem that in March, 1865, the lower Cape Fear would have been an unlikely destination for many of the thousands of people who had been uprooted by war. The main industries of the area were virtually at a standstill; the railroads and shipping facilities were badly damaged; and, due to the unsettled condition of the back country, the distribution of food had almost ceased. Yet, on March 15, two steamers arrived in Wilmington from up the river loaded with refugees from Sherman.[13] Two days later, a local paper reported that three more steamers were momentarily expected in the city bringing refugees from Confederate conscription.[14]

Most of the dislocated people were not so fortunate as these, however. An "immense throng of white and black refugees" had to make the ninety-mile journey from Fayetteville to Wilmington

9. Wilmington *Morning Star*, October 15, 1872, quoting New York *Tribune*, September 22, 1872.

10. Wilmington *Herald*, May 23, 1865.

11. *Ibid.*, March 25, 1865; Thomas S. Phelps to General Joseph Roswell Hawley, March 25, 1865, Joseph R. Hawley Papers, Manuscripts Division, Library of Congress, hereinafter cited as Hawley Papers.

12. Wilmington *Herald*, March 27, 1865.

13. New York *Herald*, March 21, 1865; General Joseph Roswell Hawley to Captain Horace James, April 5, 1865, American Missionary Association Archives, Fisk University, hereinafter cited as Missionary Archives.

14. Wilmington *Herald*, March 17, 1865.

on foot.[15] Fleeing from the desperate Confederate Home Guard recruiting bands, who were beating the bushes of the back country for fresh meat for their heroic last stands; fleeing from the man-made famine that galloped northward with Sherman's foragers; fleeing from the vengeance of late masters, from the communities where they had been known as slaves, refugees of all description merged on the Cornwallis Road leading to Wilmington, where they presented "a most wretched and pitiable sight."[16] "I stood dumb before the great misery," a battle-hardened soldier wrote. "Actually and literally, every few minutes for hours my throat would choke and my eyes fill as I looked on."[17]

In Wilmington the doors of mansion and shack were thrown open until every house was filled.[18] But there were not enough houses. In a matter of days the population of the town had increased about two and a half times. An official report of the military government estimated that there were six to seven thousand refugees, white and Negro, one to two thousand wounded soldiers, 8,600 liberated Union prisoners of war, who were in "frightful condition," several thousand of them suffering from "jail fever," a contagious disease that even killed two of the physicians treating them.[19] Many refugees, especially freedmen, were forced to camp without shelter wherever in the city they could find a little space. The primitive sanitary facilities were by no means adequate. "In the rear of the buildings on Market Street," an editor wrote, "no person can pass without holding their [sic] breath . . . in these yards cows, pigs, cats, dogs and low negroes are altogether in this pen and in the rear of the best business houses in the city. It is the same wherever one goes."[20]

When one considers the shortage of food, as well as the sani-

15. New York *Herald*, March 21, 1865.
16. Wilmington *Herald*, March 23, 1865.
17. Hawley to wife, February 28, 1865, Hawley Papers.
18. Wilmington *Herald*, April 4, 1865.
19. *The War of the Rebellion: A Compilation of the Official Records of the Union and Confederate Armies*, 128 vols. (Washington: Government Printing Office, 1895), XLVII, Pt. I, Ser. I, 164-65, hereinafter cited as *Official Records of the Armies*.
20. Wilmington *Herald*, June 14, 1865. Further details are reported by Joseph G. Longley to M. E. Strieby, April 11, 1865, Missionary Archives.

tary conditions, that prevailed in Wilmington, it appears remarkable that the people escaped a major epidemic during the spring and summer of 1865, such as the yellow fever epidemic that killed 10 per cent of the native population in the fall of 1862.[21] But while there was no major epidemic, the city nevertheless suffered an appalling death rate during these days. Indeed, one of the first industries that the Union army revived in Wilmington was a carpenter shop needed to make coffins for the forty to fifty people who were dying daily.[22] How many people in the area finally fell victim to the battle wounds, the famine and pestilence left by war? The clerk who prepared the official report wrote: "During March about —— were treated in hospitals; —— died [*sic*]." But he never filled in the figures.[23]

There were many particular causes for the many deaths that occurred in 1865. But poor diet and bad sanitation were the underlying causes of most of them. Within a week of the occupation of Wilmington, the Union commander had created a Commissary of Subsistance and empowered the officer in charge to seize existing stocks of rice or other foods.[24] A relief committee composed of local citizens, was also appointed to decide which applicants for relief were the neediest.[25] Politics may have played some part in the advice that committees of citizens gave the Commissary as to which destitute persons most needed help. A former Confederate officer writes that Confederate veterans and their families received the highest priority.[26] Nevertheless, by the first week in July, the relief committee was distributing food to more than one thousand persons.[27]

Despite these measures, there continued to be reports of deaths which appear to have been connected with poor diet, though it is difficult to tell whether this was due to the total inadequacy of relief supplies or improper distribution. Even in the

21. Barrett, *Civil War in North Carolina*, p. 259.
22. Wilmington *Herald*, March 13, 1865.
23. *Official Records of the Armies*, XLVII, Pt. I, Ser. I, 165.
24. Wilmington *Herald*, March 23, 1865.
25. *Ibid.*, March 11, June 13, 1865.
26. Alfred Moore Waddell, *Some Memories of My Life* (Raleigh: Edwards and Broughton, 1908), p. 71.
27. Wilmington *Herald*, July 15, 1865.

fall, after conditions had generally improved, the daily animal-deaths of the poor were sufficiently commonplace that the press could report with little indignation that somebody came "upon the body of a likely looking negro girl laying [sic] in some pine undergrowth. . . . It was evident that she had crawled to the place of her death. . . . She was about twenty years of age, greatly emaciated and very nearly bare of clothes. The impression is that the girl died of sickness and want of care and nourishment."[28] There were no Confederate veterans in her family!

Besides the fact that the diet of the people was entirely too light, the chief threat of an epidemic came from the over-concentration of people in the Wilmington area and the inadequacy of the sanitary facilities there. To combat this danger the Union commander created a series of "contraband" camps in the area of Fort Anderson and on Smith's Island at the mouth of the Cape Fear. At one time these camps contained a total of eight thousand freedmen and other refugees.[29] Administered by Union army officers, they provided refugees a clean, orderly place to live until they were able to find work. The New England Freedmen's Aid Society even set up schools at the camps.[30] Nevertheless, a certain amount of diet-related illness continued to plague the contraband camps. Lieutenant John L. Rhoads, one of the officers in charge, attributed most of the sickness to the fact that the army supplied hardtack to the freedmen as a staple, instead of corn meal to which they were accustomed.[31] Undoubtedly corn meal would have brought about some improvement in the health of the "contrabands," since it was unrefined and therefore contained a wider variety of nutritional elements; but probably what would have helped more than anything else would have been to have increased the quantity of each ration. The whole concept of giving destitute people something for nothing was regarded by Union

28. *Ibid.*, October 17, 18, 1865.

29. Joseph Gregoire de Roulhac Hamilton, *Reconstruction in North Carolina* (New York: Columbia University Press, 1914), p. 148.

30. Samuel S. Ashley to Hawley, May 1, 1865, Hawley Papers.

31. Philadelphia *Inquirer*, August 9, 1865. This issue contains a highly detailed account of conditions on the lower Cape Fear by a correspondent who had just visited the area.

army officers as unwholesome if not socially dangerous. As a result, a policy had been established that, in order to insure that free assistance would not subvert individual initiative, rations should be sufficient "merely to sustain life."[32]

The year 1865 was a time when men died violently, when property fashioned by the toil of a lifetime vanished in a blazing hour, when people were uprooted and dislocated. But 1865 was also a time when governments disappeared, when institutions vanished, and when the loyalties of men were divided. Though February is the shortest month in the year, February, 1865, lasted long enough to see some startling shifts in the loyalties of men of the lower Cape Fear. A Wilmington merchant and publisher, H. H. Munson, for example, at the beginning of February was promoting the sale of fancy military apparel: Confederate army and navy buttons, military caps, vests, and gold lace.[33] Before the month was over, however, Munson, showing remarkable adaptability to a changing military situation, had shifted his enterprising efforts to the publication of *The Herald of the Union*, a newspaper in which the wearers of Confederate staff buttons received some very bad press.

There were other indications that the possibility of making a quick dollar, whether it might be stamped "C.S." or "U.S.," could greatly shorten and ease the travail that certain individuals experienced in transferring their loyalty from one government to the other. It would be interesting to know, for example, what sort of mixed feelings such a farsighted businessman as James Dawson experienced as he watched the Union troops march into Wilmington. For, his Confederate patriotism notwithstanding, the final demise of the Confederacy was not an unmitigated disaster for Dawson, and certainly not one that found him totally unprepared. In fact, on the economic level at least, Dawson could be said to have transferred his loyalty many months ago.

Like many others, Dawson had seen the mountains of cotton bales that the blockade-runners had been unable to move through

---

32. Office of the Chief Commissary, District of Wilmington, Order of March 25, 1865, Circular No. 1. Published in Wilmington *Herald*, April 11, 1865.

33. Wilmington *North Carolinian*, February 3, 1865.

the Federal fleet. But, whereas others had seen in this cotton glut the ruination of a cause, Dawson's patriotism had not blinded him to the possible personal opportunity that lurked in those high-piled bales. That cotton could be bought with Confederate money. Who but a Lincoln hireling would refuse outright the money behind which the honor of the country stood? Indeed Confederate money was backed by honor. But to a man with Dawson's practical turn of mind, the pessimistic war news must have suggested that the economic value attached to Confederate money might not survive military defeat, while the economic value attached to cotton most certainly would.

Dawson had the courage of his convictions. He converted all the Confederate money that he could lay hands on, and there was a good bit of it around, into cotton. One had to be discreet in such transactions, it is true. Working-class families in Wilmington were on the verge of starvation, and the bushels of dollars that speculators were dumping in the city were not increasing the amount of food that a man's weekly wage brought home. But Dawson had the sensitivity to store his cotton in inconspicuous places, lest his growing supply reflect upon his patriotism. After all, his brother, John, was the Confederate Mayor of Wilmington.

The world cotton famine came too late to help the Confederacy. But it did not come too late to help James Dawson. After the fall of Wilmington he sold his hoard on a soaring market for "not less than" $300,000, a transaction that made him perhaps the richest man on the lower Cape Fear.[34] Dawson used a portion of his fortune to found Dawson's Bank, and lived to enjoy all the honors commensurate with the dignified status of a bank president.

James Dawson and General Braxton Bragg had each found uses for a thousand bales of cotton that were as different as the new South was different from the old. To a man with such an aristocratic, ante-bellum mind as General Bragg, a thousand bales of cotton might furnish the means for offering a burning sacrifice to a dying cause. But to a man with the bourgeois mentality of James Dawson, such a quantity of cotton provided the means for

34. Wilmington *Review*, December 27, 1882.

making a bank president out of a commission house clerk. The morning-era of the Dawsons had dawned on the Cape Fear.

The quick conversion of such men as Munson and Dawson from the Southern Cross to the Stars and Stripes can be attributed to the requirements of their business interests. Yet many people transferred their loyalty in February, 1865, and some of these conversions are not so easy to explain. February began with crowds cheering the men in gray and ended with the crowds cheering the men in blue. Can heroes become villains and villians heroes during such a short month?

The Yankees did not think so. They had had some sobering experiences with the newly discovered loyalty of occupied southern cities. But, for some reason, within a few days of the Federal occupation, they lost some of the skepticism that they had had concerning the loyalty of the people in Wilmington. A New York *Herald* correspondent wrote that "the hypocritical Unionist, a rebel at heart, has too often played us false. . . . But in Wilmington there is not the least shadow of a doubt as to the loyalty of its citizens. Our soldiers filled with the experience of the past and coming with the minds prejudiced as to the sincerity of such sentiments are thoroughly relieved of all skepticism in the present case."[35] The official report that the army made to General Grant concerning the capture of Wilmington was stating the general opinion of northern observers when it said that "Union feeling is showing itself strong in the city."[36]

How does one explain this seeming change of loyalty? Were the crowds that cheered the Yankees simply a fickle mob willing to flatter any power that might pull cannon through the streets? Undoubtedly some loud hosannas for the Union were nothing more than the prudent enthusiasm of the conquered. At the same time, we must bear in mind that two cheering crowds were not composed of the same people. There was some genuine feeling for the Union in Wilmington. One can scarcely doubt, for example, the sincerity of the welcome that the Negroes gave to the

35. New York *Herald*, February 28, 1865.
36. *Official Records of the Armies*, XLVII, Pt. II, Ser. I, 560. Other Union observers drew the same conclusion. Frank Moore, *The Civil War in Song and Story* (Chicago: P. F. Collier, 1889), p. 187; New York *Tribune*, March 9, 1865.

Federal army. While one loyal Confederate wrote that "the Myers family are the only demonstrative white people in town," she then describes some pro-Union enthusiasm among other whites that might be considered "demonstrative."[37] Another native observer noted some partiality for the Union among the white poor.[38] It is easy to believe that their fervor was genuine. Caught in the spirals of Confederate inflation, they had grown as lean as the speculators had grown fat.

Yet the support they received from such groups does not explain why the Yankees thought that Union sentiment was particularly strong in Wilmington, as they could expect a few cheers from Negroes and laboring-class whites in almost any southern community. What appears to have been peculiar about Wilmington was the fact that the town was virtually united in its hatred for the chief, local representative of Confederate authority, General Braxton Bragg. Northern observers may have made the mistake of equating hatred for General Bragg with a hatred for the government and society that he had defended.

The people of the lower Cape Fear believed in 1865, as have certain historians since,[39] that General Bragg bungled the defense of the region. Fort Fisher represented a great investment of effort, it was a special object of local pride and seemed to offer the best prospect for turning back an invasion. Yet Bragg failed to commit his troops in the Second Battle of Fort Fisher.[40] Having failed to defend Fort Fisher, the highest achievement of Confederate engineering and the result of four years work by hundreds of men, General Bragg decided to conduct a token fight for Wilmington, the defenses of which were the result of a few days work by battle-weary soldiers.

37. Catherine Douglas de Rosset Mears to Eliza Jane de Rosset, March 28, 1865, from a copy in De Rosset Papers (group II) of an original belonging to William Green de Rosset, Saratoga, Florida.

38. Henry Judson Beeker, "Wilmington During the Civil War" (unpublished Master's thesis, Duke University, 1941), p. 110, citing an interview with William Yopp, hereinafter cited as Beeker, "Wilmington During the Civil War."

39. Joshua T. James, *Historical and Commercial Sketch of Wilmington, N.C.* [*sic*] ([Wilmington?]: n.p., [1867]), pp. 33-35, hereinafter cited as James, *Wilmington*; Barrett, *Civil War in North Carolina*, pp. 271, 279-80, 442.

40. Barrett, *Civil War in North Carolina*, pp. 271 ff.

A subordinate of Bragg on February 21 opened fire on the Yankees from the Wilmington water front with a single cannon, a move that seemed to add more to the possibility of the city being leveled by Union artillery than it added to the life expectancy of the local Confederate regime. It added even less to Bragg's popularity in Wilmington, however. The move delayed their advance overnight;[41] and, while the Yankees declined his invitation to shell the city, this delay enabled him to achieve some comparable results by the liberal use of fire.

When General Alfred Howe Terry, with some 6,500 troops, marched into Wilmington, perhaps the Confederates had so emptied the vials of their wrath against the seemingly incompetent General Bragg that they had little bitterness to waste on Yankees. In the meanwhile, General John McAllister Schofield, with part of the Twenty-third Army Corps, had arrived to take charge of the Department of North Carolina, including not only the troops under General Terry, but also some smaller forces that for some time had been occupying New Bern and the region of the sounds, as well as some others that were active in the mountain region.[42] Dividing the department into military districts, Scho-

---

41. New York *Herald*, February 25, 1865; Andrew J. Howell, *The Book of Wilmington* (n.p.: n.p., n.d.), p. 145, hereinafter cited as Howell, *Wilmington*; James, *Wilmington*, pp. 35-36. The Confederate commander's apparent blunders may have inspired the North Carolina Negro folk song, "Ol' Gen'ral Bragg's a Mowin' Down de Yankees":

III

Heah comes our troops in crowds on crowds
I know dat red an' gray.
But Lawd, what make dem hurry so
An' frow deyr guns away?

. . . .

V

Ol' Massa buzy duckin' 'bout
In de swamps up to he knees,
While Dinah, Pomp, an' Pete dey look
As if dey mighty pleas' Oh—, o— ee.

. . . .

Frank C. Brown (ed.), *North Carolina Folklore* (5 vols.; Durham: Duke University Press, 1952), II, 543-44.

42. The Department of North Carolina was becoming increasingly important to the Union, not only because of the Federal victories on the lower Cape Fear, but also because a major Northern army, some sixty thousand men under General

field placed a native of Richmond County, North Carolina, General Joseph Roswell Hawley, in charge of the District of Wilmington, consisting of New Hanover, Duplin, Sampson, Brunswick, Bladen, Columbus, Robeson, and Cumberland counties.[43] From the initial welcome that the federal forces received, one might expect that Hawley could look forward to governing a highly co-operative civilian population. But, as he and other Union men would soon discover, the people of the Cape Fear country were by no means united in a rejection of ante-bellum society.

It is not recorded whether or not it was a carpetbag in which Thomas M. Cook packed his belongings that day in 1864, when his employers, the publishers of the New York *Herald*, assigned him to cover the expected battle for Fort Fisher; but certainly at that time the young war correspondent had no idea of making his home among the people who were then at war against the Union. In February, 1865, however, when his journalistic duties brought him into Wilmington, along with the occupying troops, he was favorably impressed with the town.

The city had its faults. Cook mistrusted and disliked the black-skinned people, with their strange, almost incomprehensible speech, who thronged in such numbers through the streets; but this did not prevent him from making some good friends among the local whites. Not only did these new friends seem to be overwhelmingly loyal, but, like himself, they had also been Democrats before the war.[44] It was the good, loyal people in the middle that he liked, and he felt that the war had been caused as much by the extremists on one side as by those on the other.

At least one acquaintance that Cook made in Wilmington, furthermore, turned out to be a distinct benefit to him in his

---

Sherman, was then approaching North Carolina. Sherman reached Fayetteville, on the middle Cape Fear, March 11, 1865. Barrett, *Civil War in North Carolina*, pp. 281, 295, 311, and *passim*.

43. Beeker, "Wilmington During the Civil War," pp. 132-33.

44. For twenty-five years before the war, the Democratic vote in New Hanover County was approximately four times that of the Whig vote. North Carolina Historical Commission, *North Carolina Manual, 1913*, prepared by J. Bryan Grimes, R. D. W. Connor, *et. al.* (Raleigh: Edwards and Broughton, 1913), pp. 983-86.

career as a newspaperman. It was probably from the penitent
Confederate, H. H. Munson, that Cook learned of the splendid
opportunities that existed in the area for the newspaper business.
The war had created a newspaper vacuum throughout a large
part of North Carolina. So long as the railroads were disorga-
nized, only a local paper had a chance. Wilmington, as the largest
town in the state, offered the best base for a local circulation.
Later, as the railroads radiating from the city were reconstructed,
it would be possible to expand circulation into a vast hinterland.

Unfortunately for Munson, however, although he had capital,
printing equipment, and publishing experience, he was nevertheless embarrassed in his efforts to fulfill this journalistic need,
because of the handicap of his political past. Until the Federal occupation of Wilmington, when he had realized how mistaken he
had been, his editorials in the *North Carolinian* had served as the
bugle cry of the Confederate extremists in the Cape Fear region.
What he now needed, if he was to be of any further service to the
newspaper readers of that section, was a business partner whose
record of loyalty to the Union was of longer duration than his
own.

Thomas M. Cook was just the sort of business partner that
Munson needed; and for Cook, furthermore, a step from the
roving life of a war correspondent to an editorial desk and partner-
ship was just the sort of promotion that he needed. Together
the two men founded the *Herald of the Union*.[45] Thus in Wilmington Thomas M. Cook had found friends. He had found opportunity.

When Saul of Tarsus saw a blinding light and was converted
to Christianity, he proved to be the most resolute of the apostles
of the new faith. The sudden conversions made to the Union
cause in the Cape Fear country in 1865, on the other hand,
though consummated in the livid white light of burning turpentine, did not produce such steadfast proselytes. As a matter of fact,
it was only a short while before a number of them were showing
a lamentable inclination toward backsliding. The overwhelming

45. Wilmington *Herald, passim.*

enthusiasm that Wilmington showed for the Union at the time of the occupation soon gave away to various forms of Confederate resistance.

An early example occurred when the rector of the aristocratic St. James's Church, the Reverend Dr. Alfred Augustus Watson, later a bishop, omitted from the service the customary prayer for the President of the United States.[46] Such a pointed omission was sure not to go unnoticed by his strongly pro-Confederate parishioners. Nor did it go unnoticed by General Hawley, who commanded the District of Wilmington. An abolitionist who had returned to his native North Carolina at the head of a Union brigade, Hawley did not wait for a bolder slight against the federal government. Himself the son of a minister, he ordered the pews of St. James hurled into the street and the building converted into a military hospital.[47]

The Confederates did not repeat this particular form of resistance. Instead they confined themselves to a studied indifference to any manifestation of national patriotism. This attitude became so marked that Thomas M. Cook began to worry about the loyalty of the people of his home town. "This is a captured city," he admonished from his editorial perch on the *Herald*. "The people in it can be looked upon by the government only as rebel citizens. . . . This is all they can be considered until they manifest to the government they are friends."[48]

The neophyte Unionists did not allow this rebuke from their northern friend to go unheeded. John Dawson, brother of the highly successful speculator, was more repentant than most Confederates, having served as mayor during the war. Immediately, he advertised a "grand rally of the people." Just what transpired at this meeting has not been recorded. However, it is safe to assume that on this occasion there was no great sunburst of patriotic

46. Watson to Hawley, March 16, 1865, Hawley Papers.

47. Howell, *Wilmington*, p. 147; Ralph H. Gabriel, "Joseph Roswell Hawley," *Dictionary of American Biography*, ed. Allen Johnson and Dumas Malone (21 vols.; New York: Charles Scribner's Sons, 1928-37), VIII, 421-22, hereinafter cited as *D.A.B.*; undated sketch of the history of St. James's Church, De Rosset Papers (group II).

48. Wilmington *Herald*, March 9, 1865.

ardor, the "grand rally of the people" having been scheduled to take place in Dawson's office.[49]

The great Union victory at Appomattox, on the other hand, was the occasion for a thundering response in Wilmington. Unfortunately for the Union cause, however, the thunder all came from federal warships in the Cape Fear estuary, General Hawley having ordered a hundred-gun salute to be fired at sunset. The church bells of Wilmington, however, pealed dutifully, perhaps some of them responding to what had happened at St. James's.[50]

The Confederates might respond with sluggish indifference to Union rallies, but the murder of Lincoln was a different matter entirely. When the news reached Wilmington, a large number of Confederates and other whites gathered in the Theatre where they heard speeches condemning the murder and passed a resolution expressing their abhorrence and sorrow. Such a meeting presents an interesting study in human motivation. How did the Confederates actually feel on this occasion? There come times when, faced with the stark reality of death, men feel that all of the conflicts that pit man against man have shriveled into insignificance, and that at least for a brief moment all mankind stand shoulder to shoulder against the real enemy. Such a motivating spirit as this is one possible explanation for the speeches and resolutions, though not the only one.

One must bear in mind that the Confederate army was still in the field. The principal speaker of the day, furthermore, was Alfred Moore Waddell, a Confederate colonel who had only recently folded his gray uniform. Also, one must bear in mind, not what Lincoln has come to mean to the twentieth-century South, but rather what Lincoln meant to ardent Confederates in a captured southern city in 1865. Every cause needs a villain as well as a hero. Lincoln was the chosen villain of the Confederacy. Confederates believed that his very election in 1860 had justified war. For five years he had been held up as a more terrible alternative to all other evils: which would you have, conscription or Lincoln,

49. *Ibid.*, March 11, 1865.
50. *Ibid.*, April 15, 1865; Order of General Joseph R. Hawley, April 11, 1865, Hawley Papers.

the food tithe or Lincoln, hunger, misery, unequal war, or Lincoln? What could a few weeks of half-hearted lip service to the Union do to change this deeply-graven image of Lincoln as a symbol of things more terrible than war, famine, pestilence, and even death?

Perhaps the most accurate estimate of the motivating spirit of the theater meeting was made by Thomas M. Cook, who helped organize the gathering. He later said that it provided "a chance to escape the wrath to come."[51] According to this view, the meeting was essentially a reaction of the conquered in anticipation of an outburst of rage by the conquerors.

There was another reaction on the lower Cape Fear when Lincoln died, however, the reaction of the freedmen. Theirs was not an immediate response like that of the whites who had gathered in the theater. Few of them read newspapers nor were they so knowledgeable in the requirements of diplomacy and political expediency. In fact, one might ask what the death of a white stranger could possibly mean to the world of the dark people. Theirs was a world as narrow as bondage could fashion. Its horizons extended as far as the eye could see, beyond which lay the half-believed realm of hearsay. It was a world with more room for magical charms than for books.

If the man Lincoln was a stranger to the world of the freedmen, what of his political principles? Political concepts such as "Union," "loyal," and "Republican" could evoke almost nothing familiar in their experience. Yet on Easter, when the dark, muscular men and women in Wilmington saw the houses draped in black and heard that Lincoln had died by an assassin's bullet, they were stirred. He had set them free. Thus, while Confederate Wilmington was giving full vent to its prudent grief for the fallen prince of the black Republicans, there was a ripple of activity in the contraband colonies, in the railroad construction camps, in the turpentine forest, where by a curious miracle of Easter Lincoln was finding new life in the creative energies of the freedmen. Unprecedented things began to happen. Negroes

51. Wilmington *Herald*, June 16, 1865.

began to form "arrangements committees." Leaders began to emerge.

The reports of these activities must have made strange reading to a community accustomed to ante-bellum-type newspapers. Except for organizations with such well-defined and supervised activities as fire brigades and bands of musicians, regularized gatherings of Negroes in prewar days generally bore the suspicion of subversion. Even three months before, Negro meetings that elected committees and chose leaders would have been regarded as the darkest of conspiracies. Now these activities were being reported as casually as if they had been carried on by the American Bible Society.

As Negro leaders began to emerge, people began to learn new ways of referring to Negroes. In ante-bellum society Negroes had been most commonly referred to in the third person plural: "they" have been quiet and orderly of late, or "they" have been stirred-up. Even when one mentioned a Negro individually, the reference did not so much identify a person as it did property. There was Colonel Davis' Dicey, and Captain De Rosset's Brutus. But it was no distinguished person's "George" who led the Lincoln Memorial Procession on April 27, 1865. It was George W. Price, "Marshal on Horseback," if you please. And behind Price marched a half-mile-long multitude[52] that would have filled many times over the theater where the whites had gathered the week before to commemorate Lincoln's death. The death of Lincoln marked the birth of a Negro political movement on the lower Cape Fear.

In the activities occasioned by Lincoln's death, as well as earlier patriotic meetings, one can detect divergent attitudes which were the result of conflicting national loyalties. These attitudes are significant inasmuch as they foreshadow future lines of political cleavage. However, the problem of divided national loyalties itself was short-lived. In fact, in May, 1865, it evaporated as completely as Confederate military resistance. From then on it would have been hard to find a single person who did not recognize that the Civil War had settled at least two questions:

52. *Ibid.*, April 28, 1865.

the ultimate authority of the federal government and the abolition of slavery.

Yet there was another question on the immediate historical agenda that the decision of arms had not made at all clear: what sort of social order was going to be reconstructed on the wreckage of the ante-bellum South? In 1865, few people could have found the right words to have answered this question, or, for that matter, even to have posed the problem; though fewer still could escape answering it by their deeds. During the next three years, however, thinking men were able to work out theoretical solutions to this question. There were two of these, basically, though each had countless individual variations. During Reconstruction people were called "Radicals" or "Conservatives" depending upon which of these two basic solutions they preferred.

The answer to the southern question, as many Radicals saw it, was to extend the social order that then prevailed in the North all the way to the Gulf of Mexico and the South Atlantic. They wanted to see the plantation South converted into a vast domain of black and white yeoman farmers. To accomplish this, some would have favored the distribution of public land in the South as homestead. A few even favored the confiscation of the estates of the leading Confederates, and the use of the land to allot to each freedman's household "forty acres and a mule."

The image of the New South that came to the minds of the Conservatives, on the other hand, looked not so vastly different from the old one. The plantations would be restored, cultivated by the willing hands of Negroes. If slavery, the traditional means for inducing this willingness, was no longer a practical possibility, fortunately for the Conservatives it in no wise was the only way. Barring the confiscation of his lands, in time the planter would be able practically to dictate the terms under which his former slaves returned to work. Sooner or later each Negro would have to come to him and contract some sort of work agreement that took into account the fact that it was the planter who had the keys to the smoke house and the corn crib.

Long before they had acquired much understanding of the southern question, men were contributing to its ultimate solution by their deeds. When a hungry Negro, for example, decided to move out of a contraband camp, where rations were sufficient "merely to sustain life,"[53] and began to avail himself of the bounty of somebody's pine forest, it was not because he had heard that Thaddeus Stevens had a plan that would permit freedmen to possess large Confederate estates. More likely it was because he had heard that in Wilmington there was a white man who would give him salt pork and corn meal in exchange for tar. On the lower Cape Fear in a disorderly though direct way, Negroes were practicing what the Radicals preached almost before the Radicals could preach it.

The freedmen looked upon the Cape Fear country that now lay open before them in much the same way the first whites had looked upon it 150 years before. They noted, like the first European settlers, that they shared the land with another race, which was claiming prior possession. But, like the pioneers, the freedmen were more impressed by the possible danger posed by the other race than they were by the moral strength of its property claims. "They have no idea at all of trespass," wrote one indignant white, "one will go without leave and cut an ash heap[54] on his neighbor's land, strip his elm trees to bottom his chairs; cut down his maples to make his plow handles; tear down his grape vine to tie his raft; strip his red oaks for tan bark; and cut his bee trees wherever they are found."[55]

Barring a legal settlement of the land question by Congress, this was a situation almost certain to lead to racial antagonism because, in the sparsely-settled ante-bellum Cape Fear country, even some of the poorest whites had been able to own a little property. Indeed one of the strongest bonds that existed between the barefooted Piney Woods patriarch and the lowland rice planter was the fact that both had an interest in upholding respect for private property. The freedmen, on the other hand,

53. Office of the Chief Commissary, District of Wilmington. Order of March 25, 1865, Circular No. 1. Published in Wilmington *Herald*, April 11, 1865.
54. By means of some backwoods chemistry, they used wood ashes to make soap and commercial potash.
55. Wilmington *Journal*, June 19, 1868.

had certain common values reflecting the fact that they were a people with neither property nor traditions of property.

By poaching and squatting the freedmen and other refugees were winning for themselves an uncertain living. Such activities, however, involved too much disorder and conflict to serve as a permanent solution to the southern question. Sooner or later the federal government and the army would have to restore order; and, in a society characterized by sharply divergent interests, there was practically no politically neutral way that this could be done. If the government evicted the squatters and policed property against poachers, it would be laying the basis for a Conservative social order, founded on a plantation gentry and a submerged Negro caste. If, on the other hand, the government gave any kind of recognition to squatters' rights or undertook any other Radical settlement of the land question, it would be laying the basis for a more equalitarian society based on the family-size farms, and one in which the freedmen would have some vested stake in existing property relations. The question that the clash of arms had left unresolved would be decided by a clash between the Conservatives and Radicals for the control of the government and the army.

In general, the army and the government in 1865 were controlled by men who leaned toward a Conservative solution of the southern question. But in General Joseph Roswell Hawley, commander of the eight-county Military District of Wilmington, February until June, 1865, the Conservatives had an adversary of formidable proportions. An abolitionist and Free-Soiler, Hawley had extensive family connections both in his native state, North Carolina, and in his adopted home, Connecticut. He was well-educated and was a member of the Connecticut bar. As the owner and editor of a leading Connecticut newspaper, furthermore, he had had considerable experience as a publicist.

Moreover, Hawley's military experience had further increased his political resources. Not only was he something of a battlefield hero; but, as the commander of a brigade, he had had considerable administrative experience. Also, that he was a man of some political acumen is suggested by the fact that in 1866 he was elected governor of Connecticut and, upon the completion of his term, spent a total of thirty years in Congress.[56] Even the great intellect of Radicalism, Charles Sumner himself, would not have made such a dangerous antagonist to the Conservatives of the Cape Fear valley.

Shortly after Hawley took command of the District of Wilmington, the Radicals in Washington won an important round with the Conservatives when they succeeded in obtaining the passage of the act that created the Freedmen's Bureau, an agency that they hoped would be able to implement their program. The commissioner of the Bureau, who, unfortunately for the Radicals, was to act "under the direction of the President," was nevertheless to "have authority to set apart, for the use of loyal refugees and freedmen, such tracts of land within the insurrectionary states as shall have been abandoned, or to which the United States shall have acquired title by confiscation or sale, or otherwise, and to every male citizen, whether refugee or freedman . . . , there shall be assigned no more than forty acres of such land. . . ."[57]

However, under the constitutional system of government, with its "checks and balances," the passage of a particular law means little if the branch of the government charged with carrying out the laws, the executive branch or presidency, is in disagreement with that law; and neither Lincoln nor Johnson was anxious to carry out a Radical program. But the President is only the capstone of the executive branch, the laws often being executed by his local subordinates, such as army officers, treasury officials, or federal marshals. During Reconstruction, if the President seemed sluggish about executing a Radical law, sometimes a local federal official, who happened to be a Radical, would attempt to implement the law on his own initiative rather than wait for a directive from his chief in the White House.

Since the White House was cool to the idea of "forty acres and a mule," during the three weeks following the creation of the Freedmen's Bureau, Hawley and other Radicals on the lower Cape Fear discussed various ways they might carry out such a pro-

56. *D.A.B.*, VIII, 421-22.
57. United States, *Statutes at Large*, XIII, 507-9.

gram in the region. Together they devised a plan which they published over the signature of a treasury official who had probably been sent into the area to collect customs for the Port of Wilmington:

There appears to exist a most urgent demand for immediate action in relation to the abandoned plantations and land in this vicinity. Until some authorized agent, appointed under the recent act of Congress relating to abandoned land, appears for the purpose of assuming control, it seems an urgent military necessity that they should be occupied as far as possible, and put in the process of cultivation. After full consultation with the military authorities, the plan of leasing to active and reliable persons, white and colored, will for the present be adopted. Leases will be given to such parties for such amounts of land as they can give assurance of their ability to cultivate; also for turpentine and tar privileges. It will be required of all parties so leasing that every reasonable effort will be made to give immediate employment not only to freedmen and their families residing and remaining on said land, but to white and colored refugees, who have recently come within the federal lines. For the purpose of giving relief as far as possible to those in actual need, it is understood that the Commanding General has determined to take possession, as far as may seem necessary, of the present crops of rice [i.e., those harvested in 1864,] and other articles of food on said abandoned lands.

For the purpose of expediting this matter, it is hoped that truly loyal parties will bring and send in reliable statements of abandoned lands, their situation, extent and locality.

The local Treasury Agent for Wilmington, Ulyssas [*sic*] H. Ritch, Esq., will receive and act upon application for leasing the land in question.

> D.[avid] Heaton Sup. Sp'l Ag't Tr. Dep't
> [*sic*] Wilmington, North Carolina,
> March 20, 1865[58]

When was land "abandoned"? According to the Conservatives, no land was abandoned if there was somebody around who had a deed to it. A hungry freedman could convince General Hawley, however, that a piece of land was abandoned if it was growing up

58. Wilmington *Herald*, March 23, 1865.

in weeds. The latter interpretation worked a hardship on those planters who were having some trouble persuading their former slaves that it was time to begin the spring plowing. And which came first, "military necessity" or property rights? If a squatter was busy cultivating a crop on somebody else's land, would Hawley evict him? By no means. He would issue him a "lease." The question of the land title was a legal technicality, while the squatter was meeting a "military necessity."

Furthermore, like the freedmen, Hawley regarded property as abandoned if it were not physically occupied by the owners. In this sense of the word, many of the rice plantations during the season of the fevers had been "abandoned" each year for generations. "If a man owns two or more houses," a former southern officer sent word to the occupation authorities by way of a pro-Confederate native of New York, "he cannot be expected to occupy both—when they are as far apart as mine are—. . . ."[59] Thomas Cook also thought that the military government was applying too rigorously its policy of confiscation: "The government at Washington does not, in most cases, seem to understand property owners in the south [*sic*] not unfrequently [*sic*], on several residences. In this vicinity, for instance, we know of gentlemen, not a few, who have a winter town house, a residence on the sound for mid-summer, and a plantation residence in the country besides. Of course it is impossible for these gentlemen to occupy all of these residences at one and the same time. On the approach of our troops to this town some of them were vacant, and were taken possession of as 'abandoned.' "[60] The Bellamy family, for example, prominent members of the rice gentry, found that their handsome mansion in Wilmington had been converted into the headquarters of the Military District, with General Hawley himself as chief tenant.[61] Nevertheless the Bellamys were planning to return to Wilmington, a friend of the family sadly reported,

59. Donald MacRae to John C. MacRae, April 11, 1865, Hugh MacRae Papers, Department of Manuscripts, Duke University, hereinafter cited as MacRae Papers.
60. Wilmington *Herald*, August 2, 1865.
61. Donald MacRae to wife, March 2, 1865, MacRae Papers; William Lord De Rosset, *Pictorial and Historical New Hanover County and Wilmington, North Carolina, 1723-1938* (Wilmington: Published by the author, 1938), p. 37.

"the Dr. to practice medicine for the support of his family [,] the Yankees having made a poor man of him. . . ."[62]

A planter with a single piece of land might be able to escape Hawley's stringent decrees, particularly if his estate was small enough that he and his family would be able to cultivate it themselves, or if he were able to make some mutually satisfactory arrangement with some Negro tenants. But Hawley could be ruthless with the property of the gentry. On April 11, 1865, he signed a decree for the seizure of Orton, Kendall, Lilliput, and Pleasant Oaks plantations to be "set apart for the use of freedmen, and the destitute and refugee colored people,"[63] and sent an appeal to the "benevolent and liberal people at the North" for a shipment of "axes, shovels, hoes, (light and heavy) [sic] hammers, nails and a few plows. . . ."[64]

By seizing these four contiguous plantations, he turned over to the freedmen a tract of land stretching along the Cape Fear for more than five miles and extending deep into the wilderness. Though the Negroes occupied this land from April to September, 1865, when President Johnson issued a decree returning such property to the original owners,[65] it is not certain that they enjoyed any success as independent farmers. Of all types of real estate that land-hungry freedmen were seeking, rice paddies were probably near the bottom of the list. Nevertheless, the only rice reported to have been grown on the Cape Fear in 1865 was that in "small fields here and there, cultivated by Negroes for themselves. . . ."[66] Certainly 1865 was not a good year for southern agriculture.

When one reviews the policies of the Hawley administration, it is not surprising that a Conservative concluded that "probably no government official, who has ever been in command South [sic], rendered himself so objectionable to the Southern people, by his extreme Radical views, and his utter disregard of the feelings and conditions of the white population. . . ."[67] It was inevitable that

62. John C. MacRae to Donald MacRae, May 2, 1865, MacRae Papers.
63. Wilmington *Herald*, April 15, 1865.
64. Hawley to Captain Horace James, April 5, 1865, Missionary Archives.
65. United States, Bureau of Refugees, Freedmen, and Abandoned Lands, *Report of the Commissioner*, 39 Cong., 1 sess., pp. 4-5, 56-57.
66. Wilmington *Review*, August 24, 1882.
67. Wilmington *Journal*, April 7, 1868.

sooner or later such a characterization of Hawley would reach the Commander-in-Chief of the army, President Andrew Johnson.

Like Hawley, Johnson was a southerner with a Radical background, the two men having grown up in towns not a hundred miles apart. Like a rock Johnson had stood for the Union in 1861 when the Confederate flood tide was sweeping away Unionists all around him. But times had changed. Johnson was standing where he always had stood, a prewar Radical saying what would be appropriate on an east Tennessee stump; but history had swept on past him converting his Radicalism into its opposite. On June 21, 1865, General Hawley was relieved and a Conservative member of his staff, General John Worthington Ames, was given command of the District of Wilmington.[68] Radical military Reconstruction was at an end in the Cape Fear country, until 1867.

Estimates of General Hawley's administration were as different as Radicals were different from Conservatives. He was loved, he was hated, he deserved both. His edicts were at the same time compassionate and pitiless. Yet whether one thinks that his government decreed the Day of Jubilee or whether he thinks that it made grand larceny legal and petit larceny profitable, it nevertheless seems clear that Hawley did a great deal to get the prostrate economy of the Cape Fear region off the ground. His program of relief for the unemployed was inadequate, rations being enough "merely to sustain life."[69] But to persons willing and able to produce, he would issue "leases . . . for such amounts of land as they can give assurance of their ability to cultivate," or he would issue them "turpentine and tar privileges" for some tract of the Piney Woods.[70] Instead of defending men's rights to patches of weeds, he attempted to stimulate initiative by defending their rights to the fruits of their own labor.

In particular Hawley's policies helped revive the naval stores industry. This is significant because the prosperity of the Cape Fear country floated on turpentine. Before the war capital

68. United States, War Department, Army of the Ohio, Headquarters Department of North Carolina, "Special Order No. 98," June 21, 1865, Hawley Papers.

69. Office of the Chief Commissary, District of Wilmington, Order of March 25, 1865, Circular No. 1. Published in the Wilmington *Herald*, April 11, 1865.

70. Wilmington *Herald*, March 25, 1865.

invested in naval stores did not bring very quick returns, because almost all of it had to be buried in a long-term investment in land and slaves. In 1865, on the other hand, though there was very little money around, a little bit went a long way. Thanks to emancipation and the turpentine privileges issued by the military government, almost all of it went directly into wages and equipment such as stills. This brought about a quick return on capital and a steep rate of increase in production. One needed only to satisfy the military government that he had the means to employ a certain number of freedmen or Piney Woods men. They would then issue him a lease to a correspondingly large or small tract of turpentine land.[71]

The pine forests were soon humming with activity. Even before the railroads opened up, homemade barrels filled with tar were being loaded on crude log rafts lashed together with vines and floated down the creeks and rivers to Wilmington. Green hands were being trained. Barrels were being made. In anticipation of the flood of naval stores that would engulf Wilmington with the opening of the railroads, a newspaper reported that

the pine forests of Columbus County, and the Marion and Horry district[, in South Carolina,] swarm with laborers making turpentine and rosin. Everybody, white and black, who has nothing else to do which constitutes the majority of people this year has gone into this business because of the small capital it requires. The consequence will be that an unprecedented quantity of naval stores will be brought to market this fall. Here, of itself, is a business of vast extent. Wilmington already has the reputation of being the greatest naval stores market in the world. This winter it will be furnished with a greater amount of these staples than ever before.[72]

It would not be long before the magic hands of the Piney Woods folk and the freedmen would be transforming pine sap into virtual rivers of sparkling turpentine, while at the same time the rice planters would still be presiding over their solitary empires of weeds. The Conservatives for the time being had lost

71. *Ibid.*
72. *Ibid.*, August 7, 1865.

vital initiative in the economy of the lower Cape Fear. The drift of events in the spring and early summer of 1865, if allowed to continue, could have had far-reaching influence upon the shape of the social order that was being forged. The question that the clash of great armies had failed to resolve might well have been settled by men in their quest for salt pork and corn meal.

But, despite their poaching and squatting activities, hunger continued to dog the steps of the freedmen in 1865. Under slavery they had had at least the security of knowing where they could go for their next meal. Next meals were now sometimes long delayed. Yet once the Negroes had resolved to be free, it was a rare individual who cast longing glances back toward the flesh-pots of Egypt.

It is true that a number of stories arose at this time about Negroes who, like long-term prisoners, found it hard to adjust themselves to the responsibilities of freedom. Many whites liked these stories and savored them increasingly as their own nostalgia for the old master-slave relationship grew. They also loved songs in which Negroes, speaking in heavy dialect, seemed to share their own longing for the old plantation. "I lost my Massa When Dey Set me Free," was to become a favorite ballad on the lower Cape Fear.[73] But it is hard to find in real life the Negro who actually had these sentiments.[74]

On the contrary, the preference of Negroes for freedom was so universal and categorical that it became their guiding rule for finding their way through the baffling new world of politics. They came to look on the man speaking on a stump as good or bad, depending upon whether his words seemed to threaten freedom or whether they seemed to make it more secure.

In 1865, the Negro was not homesick for the old plantation. Nor was the most important thing in his life even that he was

73. Wilmington *Review*, September 14, 1882.

74. "I have visited 175 families," a missionary to the freedmen wrote from Wilmington, "and have found numerous cases of extreme poverty and suffering, . . . but I have not found a single instance of willingness to return to their former condition, although their wants are not as easily supplied *now* as *then*." Lucy S. Haskell to George Whipple, December 30, 1865, Missionary Archives. (Emphasis in the original.)

now sometimes hungry and usually threadbare. The important thing to him rather was that life seemed to unfold before him rich new possibilities. In fact, there was something about his life in the spring of 1865 that, strangely enough, made him think of molasses, the molasses that sometimes had been poured into the waiting tin plate of a slave as a sort of dessert when the main part of his meal was over. It was this kind of sweetness that now fell on his life like the rain from heaven. And in his exuberance he sang the song that Cape Fear Negroes came to love more than any other:

> I think I hear de Angels sing
> De Angels now are on de wing
> De Angels pouring 'lasses down
> Shoo fly! Don't bodder me.[75]

In 1865, a Negro believed that life's bounties came from heaven. A man could secure these for himself, so he thought, by cutting the bee tree he chanced upon, by harvesting the garden plot that he had planted, by distilling the pine gum that he had drawn. A white, on the other hand, at any rate a Conservative, thought that abundance came from certain property relationships, from dusty documents in county courthouses, from the force of arms and government which gives protection and special meaning to these pieces of paper. Before the year would be out, the Conservatives would have succeeded in re-establishing a system of property relations which would enable them to enjoy a portion of the bounty that heaven sent and the Negro gathered. But for the Negro there had never been a springtime like the spring of 1865.

75. Wilmington *Herald*, June 28, 1865. This song was said to have been brought to Wilmington by the crews of the blockade-runners who learned it from the stevedores on the water front at Nassau. Wilmington *Journal*, March 23, 1870. It created an immediate sensation after the war, but was still a favorite five years later. The Wilmington *Journal* of January 27, 1870, said that this "nonsensecal [*sic*] medley . . . salutes the ear in every public place." It was "immensely popular with the masses," and it "never fails to create enthusiasm in a theatre."

III ⇜ Ballots and Fence Rails

ON JULY 8, 1865, JUST TWO WEEKS AFTER GENERAL JOSEPH ROS-
well Hawley had been removed as commander of the Military
District of Wilmington, a Negro soldier was strolling through the
Wilmington Market Place, when he suddenly saw something to
remind him that he was a member of the Union army of occupation. He saw a man wearing the gray coat and brass buttons
of a Confederate soldier. This was a violation of "General Order
No. 9," which forbade anyone to appear in public wearing parts
of the Confederate military uniform. The soldier reminded the
man of the restriction and ordered him in the name of the Provost Marshal to remove the coat. The man declined to obey, saying that he had never heard of any such regulation. The soldier
placed him under arrest.

At this point, a Union officer, who had been watching the
episode, approached. But to the astonishment of the crowd in the
Market Place, instead of assisting the other Union army man in
his efforts to uphold the Military Government regulation, the
white officer seized the soldier by the collar, giving him "a continuous kicking until he reached the opposite side of the street
and then drove him to his regiment. . . ."[1]

There were other reminders that something had happened to
the Union army since that day in February when they had
marched through the streets of Wilmington singing the "John
Brown Hymn."[2] Sergeant John Benson, of the Sixth United

1. Wilmington *Herald*, July 4, 10, 1865.
2. Frank Moore, *The Civil War in Song and Story* (Chicago: P. F. Collier, 1889),
p. 187.

States Colored Troops, for example, went to the house of a white woman to arrest her on charges of having pointed a pistol at a Union soldier. Before his arrival, however, the woman had obtained the protection of some Union officers. Though the Sergeant succeeded in making the arrest, the officers prevented him from delivering the prisoner to the Provost Marshal. Whereupon Benson wrote a letter to the Wilmington *Herald* protesting the fact that it had been Union officers who had prevented him from carrying out his duty. It is significant that Thomas M. Cook, though a northerner, did not publish Benson's letter in the regular letter column, but rather as a paid advertisement.

But Sergeant Benson paid more than once for his advertisement protesting what was happening to the Union army: As a result of his letter, he himself was arrested, stripped of his rank, and imprisoned for "insolence to commissioned officers. . . ." Referring to the paid advertisement that he had accepted from Benson, Cook wrote that "a little wisdom will teach soldiers that their officers will not be insulted either in this manner or otherwise. . . ."[3]

What was, in fact, happening to the Union army? The simplest explanation is that the officer that President Johnson had put in command of the eight-county Military District of Wilmington, General John Worthington Ames, had more sympathy for southern Conservatives than he had for Negroes. But General Ames was not the only officer that was beginning to take a friendlier view of his late enemies. The Conservatives were proving to be good diplomats. They no longer looked on Yankees as one, undifferentiated, hostile mass. Rather they had discovered that many northerners had views that were not vastly different from their own, men for whom the conflict had ended at Appomattox. The war had abolished slavery, but not menial jobs nor the need for servants. Was it unreasonable for the white South to expect that these jobs would continue to be performed by those qualified by generations of experience? Surely there was a "place" for the Negro, in which he was more than a slave but less than an equal.

Yet four years of war and differences in environment were

3. Wilmington *Herald*, August 16, 1865.

reflected in some corresponding differences in northern and southern views. The conservatism of the northerners was less pronounced and consistent than that of the southerners. It was sometimes debased by an admixture of radical democratic idealism. But with the passage of time, the views of many Union officers in the South became increasingly like those of the southern Conservatives.

From the beginning of the occupation certain federal officers were accepted into the charmed circles of the Conservative middle class or of the gentry. Other officers, those "associated with the colored troops," were pointedly excluded.[4] Those who became involved in a web of genteel social relations, sometimes including marriage, gradually came to accept the views of their civilian friends. Eventually certain of these men were so thoroughly converted to the southern variety of Conservatism that they became involved in local politics, allying themselves with Confederate veterans.

"The true soldiers," beamed the *Journal* in 1868, "whether they wore the gray or the blue, are now united in their opposition . . . to negro government and negro equality. Blood is thicker than water."[5] The social process by which many Union soldiers came to accept the views of their former enemies was characterized by a Negro leader as the "cake and wine" influence.[6] It may have been some consolation to the men who had worn the gray to know that their Conservative women folk, in the parlors and bedrooms of Wilmington, were enjoying more success in upholding the basic values of ante-bellum society than they themselves had had on the ramparts of Fort Fisher.

However, the importance of Union army officers and their political opinions was beginning to diminish. As rapidly as he could, President Johnson was taking the army out of the business of government. In the Cape Fear country in July, for example, General Ames restored full power in the City of Wilmington to the same group of officials that had been in control when federal

4. Philadelphia *Inquirer*, August 9, 1865.
5. The Wilmington *Journal*, April 17, 1868, Hereinafter cited as Wilmington Weekly *Journal* or Wilmington *Daily Journal*.
6. Wilmington Weekly *Journal*, July 13, 1865.

troops took the city.[7] Before winter the ante-bellum county courts had begun to meet again. William Woods Holden, the provisional governor appointed by Johnson, called a convention, to be elected under prewar franchise restrictions, which would create a permanent state government.

The Convention of 1865, meeting in Raleigh in October, created the constitutional framework for presidential Reconstruction, 1865-68. Though scarcely a revolutionary body, out of deference to Johnson the delegates repudiated the war debt of Confederate North Carolina. By abolishing slavery and repealing the Ordinance of Secession, however, they were only acknowledging on paper that which Sherman and Grant had already accomplished in fact. Perhaps the most serious shortcoming of the convention was its failure to recognize the fact that there would have to be adjustments made in the process of government and in the operation of the courts that would bring the constitution into line with the momentous events that had taken place since 1860.[8]

Early in 1866, a presidentially reconstructed legislature, chosen in essentially the same way that unreconstructed legislatures had been chosen for thirty years, assembled and began to write a series of laws called collectively the "Freedmen's Code," or the "Black Code," in which they sketched a Conservative view of the sort of Negro-white relations upon which the New South would be founded. The Black Code established a labor system founded upon contracts drawn between planters and "persons of color." These were to be in writing and legally binding on both parties.

At first glance, it would appear that such a labor system constituted a marked departure from ante-bellum slavery. It is important to note, however, that, while legally-binding contracts have made possible a good deal of individual freedom in the modern world, this has been to the extent to which such contracts have been negotiated between persons at least equal before the law, and to the extent to which each party has sufficient mobility to enable him to sign or not sign the contract as he sees fit. But the

7. Wilmington *Herald*, July 17, 22, 24, 1865.
8. North Carolina, *Ordinances of the Convention*, 1865-66, ch. 1, 2, 18, and *passim*.

Black Code did not spell out this sort of relationship between whites and "persons of color."

The harsh vagrancy statute, for example, seemed to take away from the Negro much of the mobility that emancipation had given him.[9] What sort of protection could a Negro expect from a legal contract, furthermore, if his testimony against a white man was not admissible in court? Even slavery might be described as a sort of contractual arrangement in which all the terms are laid down by one party, but are legally binding on the other.

Two of the statutes were drawn with a view, substantially, to protecting a white man's property from a Negro's misery, entailing a rigorous definition of trespass, and the theft of such items as fire wood.[10] If a court could be satisfied as to a Negro's "intent" to steal livestock, moreover, he "shall be punishable in all respects, as if convicted of larceny, even though such animal may not have come into actual possession of the person. . . ."[11] Still another law, forbidding Negroes to use seditious language, was as vague in defining the offense as it was explicit in detailing the punishment.[12] The men who wrote the Black Code could scarcely have failed to foresee that in the reconstructed South Negro convicts would perform a number of the jobs previously done by Negro slaves.

Only one legal step now remained in order to put the new system to work: To transfer the Negro from the jurisdiction of the courts of the Freedmen's Bureau to that of the civil courts. "There now exist, under the laws of this State," Governor Jonathan Worth announced, "no discrimination in the administration of justice to the prejudice of free persons of color." Thus reassured, the head of the state Freedmen's Bureau turned all cases to the civil courts.[13]

The Black Code was the legal definition of the Conservative

9. North Carolina, *Public Laws*, 1866, ch. 42.
10. *Ibid.*, ch. 60.
11. *Ibid.*, ch. 57.
12. *Ibid.*, ch. 64.
13. Worth to General John Cleveland Robinson, July 12, 1866, and Robinson to Worth, July 13, 1866, Governor's Papers, Jonathan Worth, North Carolina State Archives; United States War Department, Bureau of Refugees, Freedmen and Abandoned Lands, *Report of the Commissioner*, 39 Cong., 2 sess., p. 734.

social order. In some communities, however, the Conservatives did not wait for such a legal definition before taking steps toward establishing their pattern of Reconstruction, and in most cases they owed more of their success to the pugnacity of some local militia officer than to the craft of some lawyer. County militia companies, or county police, had been authorized by General John McAllister Schofield, commander of the Department of North Carolina, at the end of the war, as a means of stopping the depredations of the various armed bands of troublemakers that were disturbing various parts of the state.[14] In the Cape Fear region such companies were formed in Bladen, Brunswick, Columbus, Duplin, New Hanover, Robeson, and Sampson counties.[15] These units were formed very quickly, the military government apparently making little effort to scrutinize their political composition.[16] As a result, the companies were filled with men who had had the most recent military experience, the Confederate veterans and members of the Home Guard. They were generally commanded by former Confederate officers.

Duplin County provides an example of the Conservative social order being established locally by the county militia or police, months before the Black Code was written. Peace reigned in the county in the spring and early summer of 1865. In fact, one would not immediately have seen the need for a company of police. In contrast to the rice country, the freedmen in Duplin

14. David Schenck Diary, May 31, and July 24, 1865, David Schenck Papers, Southern Historical Collection, The University of North Carolina; "Friend" to Catherine (McGeachy) Buie, March 2, 1865, Catherine (McGeachy) Buie Papers, Department of Manuscripts, Duke University, hereinafter cited as (McGeachy) Buie Papers; John C. MacRae to Donald MacRae, April 3, 1865, Hugh MacRae Papers, Department of Manuscripts, Duke University, hereinafter cited as MacRae Papers; *The War of the Rebellion: A Compilation of the Official Records of the Union and Confederate Armies*, 128 vols. (Washington: Government Printing Office, 1895), XLVII, pt. III, Ser. I, 79, 396, 490, 587, hereinafter cited as *Official Records of the Armies*.

15. *Official Records of the Armies*, XLVII, pt. III, Ser. I, 549-51; *Wilmington Herald*, May 13, December 15, 1865; Philadelphia *Inquirer*, August 9, 1865.

16. A member of the Police Guard was required only to take the presidential oath of allegiance, which did not raise the question of past allegiance, and to swear to help "preserve the peace, prevent crime, . . . and obey all lawful orders of the United States Military authorities." A copy of the oath, used in Robeson County, is contained in the (McGeachy) Buie Papers.

had not deserted the plantation; and spring found them absorbed with the crops, just as they had been at this season of the year for many generations. But while the freedmen worked with plow and hoe, the police drilled with saber and pistol, instruments that might influence the division of the harvest if not the cultivation of the crop.

The showdown came in Duplin in July when the freedmen "laid by the crops," that is to say, when they had brought the crops to the point where cultivation was complete, so that the fields could be left unattended until the harvest. The "laying by of the crops" raised some fundamental questions in Duplin in 1865: Did these crops belong to the men who had produced them, or did they belong to the men who held titles to the land? If they belonged to both and were to be divided, then who was to get how much of what? These were questions that had never been answered before.

The freedmen were not adverse to yielding a small share of the harvest to the Almighty, or His worldly representatives, He having made the rains fall; but many of them had trouble grasping just what part the men with the deeds had played in cultivating cotton. Nor did this matter become any plainer to them when the Union army issued a circular upholding the Conservative position that all existing land titles remained valid.

In fact, when shown this circular, some of the Negroes drew a strange conclusion: Instead of concluding that their former masters were entitled to a portion of the crop, some of them resolved that the freedmen themselves were entitled to deeds to the land. Surely it would be a smaller matter to obtain such papers than it was to raise a crop of cotton. "Some of them," wrote Captain J. N. Stallings, head of the Duplin County police, "are declaring they intend to have [l]ands, even if they shed blood to obtain them. Some of them are demanding all of the crop they have raised on the former master's lands, and in some cases, so obstinate are they in these demands, that I have had to arrest them before they would come to terms."[17]

Captain Stallings does not mention just what means he em-

17. Wilmington *Herald*, October 11, 1865.

ployed to induce arrested freedmen to "come to terms."[18] But in July a series of crimes, attributed to his organization, including four murders, brought about an investigation by a Negro detachment of the Union army, led by two white lieutenants at least one of whom was a Radical. Despite the fact that it was the head of police to whom the crimes had been attributed, Captain Stallings claimed that he had not heard of any killings taking place in the county until he himself was arrested on charges of murder, along with more than a dozen others.[19]

But it was one thing for a Radical lieutenant to gather testimony, witnesses, and arrest suspects, and quite another matter entirely to obtain a conviction in a conservative military court. General Ames, who within a week after assuming command of the Cape Fear country had granted both himself and the Wilmington city post commander thirty-day leaves, was just returning from his visit home. He ordered Captain Stallings and six others released "on parole." Lieutenant Loftin, whom a wounded freedman had identified as a member of the detachment that had shot him, the general ordered to be confined, not to jail, but to a hotel room in Wilmington. The other prisoners were released on bond within the limits of the city.[20]

No one was ever brought to trial for the Duplin County murders, nor is there any indication of further inquiry into the matter after General Ames returned from his furlough. Captain Stallings, who a subordinate said had given orders to shoot Negroes who had committed theft,[21] continued to be a prominent leader in the region for many years, as a law enforcement officer, as a Baptist minister, and as an editor of the Clinton *Caucasian*; and the Union army interfered no further with the establishment of the Conservative social order in Duplin County.

18. However, in Sampson County where similar conditions existed, a local Unionist wrote Governor Holden that the county police were coercing Negroes "to go back & serve their old masters & if the negroes refused . . . , they were hung by the thumbs until they promised to do so." Quoted in a letter from Major Clinton A. Cilley to Captain Edwin C. Latimer, August 14, 1865, Governor's Papers, Holden, North Carolina State Archives.

19. Wilmington *Herald*, September 29, 1865.

20. Philadelphia *Inquirer*, August 9, 1865.

21. *Ibid.*

In other parts of the Cape Fear country, the activities of the Conservatives attracted less attention, but the final results were scarcely different. The Brunswick County estates that General Hawley had seized and turned over to the freedmen were now, on orders from President Johnson, returned to their owners.[22] The confiscated town houses were likewise returned; and, according to one report in the fall of 1865, house rents were higher in over-crowded Wilmington than they were at that time in New York City.[23] The ante-bellum county courts had begun to meet again and thereby to give the dignity of civil authority to the filibuster-ing of the militia bands. Squatters were evicted. Trespass, poach-ing, and other petty offenses against property were ruthlessly suppressed. In an effort to make the use of force a Conservative monopoly, the county police began ransacking Negro homes in search of weapons.[24]

Once the practice of raiding Negro dwellings became estab-lished, however, the police and militia by no means confined themselves to a search for arms. They began seizing "stolen" property as well.[25] Since the Negroes had owned no property at the end of the war when they were freed, the police felt justified in assuming that any property they found in the possession of a

22. United States, War Department, Bureau of Refugees, Freedmen and Abandoned Lands, *Report of the Commissioner*, 39 Cong., 1 sess., pp. 4-5, 56-57. Conservatives argued that, with the Homestead Act, the principle of "land for the landless" was already incorporated into American law, and that, if the freedmen wanted land, they only had to take advantage of the provisions of that act. How-ever, Allen Rutherford, the Radical superintendent of the district of the Freed-men's Bureau covering the lower Cape Fear, wrote in his annual report for 1866 that "I know of no Freedmen in this District who have availed themselves of the benefit of the [Homestead] act, although a number of inquiries have been made on the subject by Freedmen who wished to do so, but who could not afford the outlay required to carry them from here to the States where the lands are located." United States, War Department, Bureau of Refugees, Freedmen and Abandoned Lands (Record Group 105), North Carolina General Orders . . . Monthly and Annual Reports, Annual Report for 1866 of the Superintendent of the Southern District of North Carolina, Wilmington, October 29, 1866, National Archives, here-inafter cited as Annual Report of the Freedmen's Bureau, Wilmington District, 1866.

23. J. D. McLaulin to George Whipple, September 14, 1865, American Mission-ary Association Archives, Fisk University, hereinafter cited as Missionary Archives.

24. Philadelphia *Inquirer*, August 9, 1865.

25. Wilmington *Herald*, September 29, 1865.

Negro was stolen unless the Negro could prove otherwise in court or in some cases to the satisfaction of the raiding officers.[26]

Draft animals were perhaps the most important type of property that was in the hands of freedmen in 1865. Only land was more essential to a man's productivity. The possession of horses and mules had been radically redistributed as a result of the sweep of war over the Cape Fear region. This reallocation of draft animals had come about as a result of a practice of the Union troops, particularly those of Sherman.[27] They would seize a horse or mule from some farm they passed, use him until he was lean and sore from the harness or saddle, and then either give him to some freedman or abandon him and seize a fresh animal.[28] A good many horses and mules fell into the hands of the freedmen who were able to restore them to health in time for the spring plowing.[29] By this more or less accidental process, the Union army brought about some redistribution in economic power, taking from the "haves" and giving to the "have-nots."

If the Negroes were to become the "mud sills" of the New South, not only was it necessary for the Conservatives to stop them from squatting on the land, but also they needed to relieve them of draft animals or any other property that they may have gleaned from the trail of Sherman or from the plantations of their former masters. Indeed the "Place" of the Negro in the New South was such a poor bargain, that, in order to put him into it, they had

26. United States, Congress, Joint Committee on Reconstruction, *Report of the Joint Committee: Part II, Virginia, North Carolina, South,* Reports of the Committees, Vol. II, 39 Cong., 1 sess., 1866, p. 272, hereinafter cited as Joint Committee, *Report.*

27. John G. Barrett, *The Civil War in North Carolina* (Chapel Hill: The University of North Carolina Press, 1963), pp. 297-98, 312.

28. Jonathan Worth to Andrew Johnson, January 15, 1866, Governor's Papers, Worth, North Carolina State Archives, hereinafter cited as Worth Papers.

29. Not all of this livestock fell into the hands of freedmen: Despite being a Unionist my great-grandfather, John McNeill of Robeson County, known as "Honey John," found himself without draft animals in the spring of 1865, as a result of a visit by Sherman's foragers. However, he recovered one good three-year old horse, which had deserted the Union army at a high-tail gallop after having thrown a soldier who had accidentally ridden him over one of Honey John's bee hives. From some Indian friends who were gleaning the trail of Sherman, he obtained a second horse, a lean and wicked, sore-backed brute that he significantly christened "General Sherman." Thanks to these two horses, he was able to raise a crop in 1865.

to reduce his bargaining position virtually to the power of his bare hands.

The Conservative police companies undertook this task cheerfully. They began a continuous search for "stolen" property. Given the prevailing conditions of transportation and communications, it would have been a stupendous task for the police to have discovered the original owner of some mule or piece of furniture, found in the possession of a freedman, and to have returned this property to him, the owner being perhaps a planter in South Carolina or Georgia. But men with so little sympathy for wrongdoers as the police were not to be stymied by such problems. If they could not find the original owners of "stolen" property, they nevertheless managed to find ways of disposing of it.

It should not be supposed, however, that raiding police officers kept for themselves all the property they seized. On the contrary, they sometimes took their friends along with them on raids that they might share in the emoluments of law enforcement. "A tour of pretended duty is then turned into a spree," a Union officer complained. "Houses of colored men have been broken open, beds torn apart and thrown on the floor, and even trunks opened and money taken."[30] The tactics employed by the police and their friends may have added zeal to the search for stolen property. They did not make it any easier, however, for a freedman to convince raiding officers that he had obtained some particularly desirable possession in an honest manner.

In October, 1865, John Andrews, a freedman, was arrested with "a piece of iron he could not account for."[31] The following month six Negroes were brought before the mayor's court in Wilmington charged with having thirty-five barrels of rosin. The mayor could find no evidence that the rosin was stolen, so the prisoners were discharged. But, because the Negroes had not proved to his satisfaction that they were the rightful owners, the court retained the rosin.[32] In later years, the whites of the Cape Fear were to detect what they felt was a defect in the character of

30. Joint Committee, *Report*, p. 272.
31. Wilmington *Herald*, October 17, 1865.
32. *Ibid.*, October 17, 1865.

the Negro: Whereas, a system of values shared by the whites placed a strong emphasis on the quest for property, the Negro seemed to lack this. He seemed to be more strongly motivated by the pursuit of momentary pleasures. The whites marveled at this and attributed it to what they regarded as his primative and childlike nature.[33]

The Conservatives greatly reduced the bargaining power of the Negro by seizing the property that he had acquired since freedom. But they still had to deal with the fact of the freedman's mobility, which gave Negroes a certain power to bargain. For example, when the Conservative order was established in Sampson County, a number of Negroes deserted the plantations, crossed over into the adjoining county, Bladen, and began work in the turpentine forests. When time came to break the land again, in February, 1866, some Sampson County planters found themselves hard-pressed for labor. A number of them appeared at the February term of the Sampson County court, and requested that the court bind out to them some of their former slaves as "orphans."[34]

It was very difficult sometimes for a freedman to prove that he was neither a minor nor an orphan. He might assume, for example, that, if he appeared to be full-grown and was earning the wages of a full hand, that these facts made him a man rather than boy, even though he was not sure of his actual age. A Negro was frequently even less sure, however, that both of his parents were living. Under slavery the entire family unit had been weak. One ordinarily knew who his mother was, though frequently it had not been his mother, but some elderly slave, who had cared for him as a child. The maternal tie was not necessarily strong and may have been broken entirely by a sale, rental, or assignment to separate duties. The paternal tie was even weaker, a slave frequently not knowing who his father was. Consequently, when a planter went before a court composed of other planters with problems like his own, and alleged that a certain freedman, a former slave of his, was only twenty years old and that one of his

33. Wilmington Weekly *Journal*, June 19, 1868.
34. Joint Committee, *Report*, p. 270.

parents was now dead, facts that would make him legally an orphan, it would be very hard for the freedman to prove otherwise to the satisfaction of such a court.

"Several hundred" freedmen, many of them seized in the Piney Woods of Bladen County, were declared "orphans" and bound out to their former masters by the Sampson County Court of Pleas and Quarter Session during its February term of 1866. One "orphan," bound out to work for his former master without wages, had been living in the pine barrens with his wife and child, earning full pay as a turpentine hand. The action of the Sampson County court served to bring to the surface a fundamental difference between northern and southern Conservatives: The northerners sympathized with the efforts of the southerners to make property safe from the leveling encroachments of squatters and poachers, and from the Radical efforts to invalidate certain land titles. But their sympathy ended at the point where it appeared that the southern Conservatives might be trying to add another chapter to *Uncle Tom's Cabin.* The Union army suddenly came to life. They marched into the area and broke up the Sampson County orphanage.[35]

Though the Union army in this instance relieved many individual benefactors of their protégés, it would be a long time before Sampson County would be relieved of this particular form of philanthropy. As late as 1872, a planter near Clinton was offering a twenty-five dollar reward for the recapture of two escaped "orphans." "I hereby forbid anyone employing them," he proclaimed in an advertisement, "or giving aid or comfort in any way to them upon penalties of law."[36]

By the end of 1865, Presidential Reconstruction was complete. The Conservative social order had been established. Its success depended upon the stability of its foundations. Would the Negroes, the "mud sills" of that society, accept their place? Some

35. *Ibid.,* pp. 270-71; Annual Report of the Freedmen's Bureau, Wilmington District, 1866. A similar use was made of apprenticeship laws in New Hanover, Brunswick, and Robeson counties, but here too "apprentices" were set free by the army. Jonathan Worth to General John Cleveland Robinson, October 30, 1866, and Robinson to Worth, October 30, 1866, Worth Papers.

36. Wilmington *Daily Journal,* March 5, 1872.

Conservatives felt that the place of the Negro represented a sufficient improvement upon his previous position as a slave that he would accept it or he could be persuaded to accept it. The big problem, as they saw it, was outside influences; and the sight of Negro troops, marching through the streets of Wilmington, arms in hand, was having a disturbing effect.

In this connection, as early as June, 1865, Colonel Alfred Moore Waddell wrote to William Woods Holden, who had been appointed provisional governor by President Johnson, that the occupation of Wilmington by Negro troops endangered the lives of the white population. Indeed the effect of their presence on the "negro inhabitants is growing worse every day, and unless there is a change . . . it will inevitably result in a *massacre*." He charged that there were "daily outrages" carried out by these soldiers or Negro civilians instigated by them. . . ."[37] These "daily" outrages of the troops in Wilmington seem to have escaped the notice of that city's daily paper, though the senior editor, Thomas M. Cook, had considerably more antipathy towards Negroes than did Waddell. Yet Cook sounded a warning of his own concerning the effect of the troops on the Negroes. "We are slumbering on a volcano," he wrote, ". . . the general eruption is likely to occur at any time."[38] These sentiments were embodied in a petition, signed by Mayor Dawson and other prominent citizens, and sent to President Johnson.[39]

Despite these dire warnings by Conservative leaders, there is almost no evidence of disorder in Wilmington during June and July of 1865. Nevertheless there was more behind this alarm than hysteria,[40] because it was a time when both the Conservatives and

37. Waddell to Holden, June 18, 1865, Governor's Papers, Holden, North Carolina State Archives, hereinafter cited as Governor's Papers, Holden.

38. Wilmington *Herald*, July 10, 1865.

39. John Dawson *et al.*, "Petition . . . ," undated but apparently written in reaction to events taking place in late July, 1865, Andrew Johnson Papers, Manuscripts Division, Library of Congress, hereinafter cited as Johnson Papers.

40. Governor Holden in fact received one report, originating with a Negro informer in Wilmington, of "a conspiracy among the colored race to murder all the whites (the old slave owners) [! *sic*] to get their lands & homes (they say they have made themselves) as soon as our troops leave." This report was recorded by C. C. Emerson and copied by John Dawson in a letter to Holden, August 12, 1865, Governor's Papers, Holden.

the Negroes were becoming aware of the vastly different con-
clusions each had drawn concerning the meaning of the war.
Also, in neighboring Duplin County, this was the time when the
county police had begun raiding Negro homes and committing
murders. Was this the work of an irresponsible marauder band or
was it a foretaste of what Wilmington Negroes could expect now
that the military government had turned over the city government to the local Conservatives? Just what kind of "place" must
the Negroes accept in order to avoid a conflict? It was probably
with such questions as these in mind that a group of Negro
leaders engaged the Wilmington Theatre and invited Colonel
Waddell to present his views to a mass meeting of Negroes. Waddell's Whiggish views, stressing distinctions of education and property rather than those of race, were not typical of the
Conservatives of the Lower Cape Fear, certainly not of the gentry;
but they formed a possible bridge by means of which the Negroes
and Conservatives might reach an understanding.

"It would be unjust and a mistake to suppose," began Cape
Fear Conservatism's most talented spokesman, "that the white
people among whom you were born and raised, with whom you
played when you were children . . . , have all at once turned to be
your enemies, because those of you who were formerly slaves have
suddenly been set free." It was not necessary that the war should
end the old cordiality that had existed since childhood between
the bond and the free in Wilmington. But it was necessary that
the Negroes lend an ear to their old friends rather than to the
strangers. It was also necessary that the Negroes recognize
squarely what emancipation meant and what it did not mean.

"I understand that some ignorant and misguided colored
people, more particularly in the country, [Duplin County?] are
under the impression that they are not only free, but that the property of their former owners will be taken and given to them. Of
course, this is a cruel mistake, and most of you know better than
to be misled by such extravagant ideas." Also, the "constitution
of the United States leaves such questions as, who shall vote, or
who shall sit on a jury, or be a witness . . ." to the states, and it
was a stubborn fact that North Carolina was not likely to extend

these rights to the Negro minority. But emancipation did mean at least five things to the Negro: (1) he was no longer a slave, (2) he had a right to acquire property, (3) he could earn wages, (4) he could seek an education, and (5) he was free in his choice of religion.

The Negro throng in the Theatre showed Colonel Waddell the same scrupulous courtesy that he had extended to them, clapping warmly at the appropriate places in his speech.[41] They were undoubtedly touched by his references to the old ties of Negro-white friendship that had been forged by the games of small boys not yet aware of the distinction in human condition that pit man against man, ties that had sometimes even endured into manhood as an occasional bridge over the chasm dividing the bond from the free, the black from the white, so that even a slave society could have a certain sense of community. Yet at the same time, with his characteristic logic and eloquence, Colonel Waddell had made it unmistakably clear that, despite war and emancipation, that chasm which they had come to know as men still yawned deep and wide before them. Essentially what he was telling them was that they had become ante-bellum "free" Negroes. But they did not want to be "free" Negroes. They wanted to be free men. And they wanted it so badly that they were willing, if necessary, to shatter the few warm ties that united the two peoples of the Lower Cape Fear.

Despite the decorum and good manners which the Cape Fear folk of both worlds characteristically show on such occasions, the Negroes overwhelmingly rejected Waddell's terms for coexistence. Yet the Negroes and whites had lived together so intimately for so many generations that it was not necessary for the Negro to record his rejection of the "free" Negro status by some act of violence or even by some pronouncement. The slightest change in the minute details of his behavior was all that was needed and the whites knew exactly what he meant. The name which the Conservatives gave to this subtle change of attitude was "insolence," and Negro "insolence" was about the only tangible cause

41. *Ibid.*, July 27, 1865.

they could offer for the rising tide of fear that engulfed them in June and July of 1865.

Despite reports that the psychological change taking place among the Negroes had brought the city to the brink of upheaval, a Yankee journalist visiting Wilmington in early August had some trouble detecting any Negro behavior that appeared to be insolent to him. He concluded that he was "inclined to think that any serious manifestations of the feeling in question are not very numerous. This, however, is a point on which Southerners are naturally sensitive. They perceive insolence in a tone, a glance, a gesture, or failure to yield enough by two or three inches in meeting on the sidewalk."[42] But the Wilmington whites were reading the signs correctly. The almost imperceptible change in the minutiae of Negro conduct, so insignificant to the Yankee journalist, actually foreshadowed a clash between two conceptions of the postwar society.

Colonel Waddell was right about the effect of the troops on Negro civilians, the Conservatism of General Ames notwithstanding. There was room for more than one slip between the intent with which an order might be issued from the District Headquarters and the way that order might be actually carried out by a Negro corporal in the Wilmington Market Place.[43] Negro civilians were conscious that the troops were a source of strength to them; and, after the pillage and murders by law enforcement officers in an adjoining county, Duplin, during the past week, the Negroes in Wilmington were not inclined to submit to the restoration in the city of the same administration as had existed under the Confederacy.

Given these conditions, it did not require a very consequential issue to bring about a collision. On August 1, Samuel Wycoff, a policeman, became involved in an affray with a Negro soldier,

42. Philadelphia *Inquirer*, August 9, 1865.

43. John Dawson *et al.*, to William Woods Holden, August 3, 1865, Governor's Papers, Holden. Indeed, the first day that power was restored to the civil authorities in Wilmington, a Negro sergeant arrested the Chief of Police, charged him with carrying a weapon unlawfully, and led him a prisoner before a hooting throng of Negroes to the Provost Marshal who promptly discharged him. "Petition to Johnson," July, 1865, Johnson Papers.

later adjudged "mentally deranged." Both men were wounded, Wycoff receiving some cuts from the soldier's bayonet, and the soldier a bullet wound from Wycoff's pistol. But the incident touched off an explosion of Negro anger against the Conservative authorities. One Negro soldier opened fire on the wounded policeman, who was then seized by a guard detail, which probably no longer had legal authority to arrest a civilian, and hauled before the provost marshal, who discharged him after a hearing. Whereupon an angry crowd of Negro soldiers and civilians surrounded the city hall.

The Union provost marshal ordered the soldiers away. At the same time a posse organized by Mayor John Dawson, brother of a prominent speculator and banker, attacked the crowd with clubs, dispersing and disarming the demonstrators. This attack was a tactical blunder that the Conservatives in Wilmington would not soon repeat. During the following night armed bands of soldiers and civilians attacked the police as they made their rounds, mortally wounding Thomas DeVane, a Confederate veteran. With the coming of morning, August 2, 1865, the entire police force, municipal government, and mayor resigned. The first restoration of the Confederate-Conservative regime in Wilmington had lasted just nine days.[44]

The Union army promptly restored the Dawson administration a second time, giving the mayor what was described as a "*carte blanche* in regard to the soldiers." Dawson in turn increased the police force from fifty to one hundred men, and increased their pay from a dollar a day to fifty dollars a month,[45] and requested the governor to send Spencer rifles or navy revolvers "with which to arm the police and other citizens."[46] This force was recruited by the new chief of police, Confederate Major General Robert Ransom, who picked men with military experience as Confederate soldiers.[47] The new police force immediately

44. Wilmington *Herald*, August 3, 4, 5, 1865; Philadelphia *Inquirer*, August 9, 1865.
45. Wilmington *Herald*, August 5, 8, 1865.
46. John Dawson *et al.*, to Holden, August 3, 1865, Governor's Papers, Holden.
47. Joint Committee, *Report*, p. 271.

began the task of disarming the Negroes, a job they carried out so scrupulously that they jailed one Negro for carrying a club down the street. To further strengthen their regime, the Conservatives began forming additional military companies, especially in the Wilmington area. By mid-December, 1865, in New Hanover County, they had a full regiment of eight companies commanded by Confederate officers.[48]

Thus, Presidential or Conservative Reconstruction was made possible by the resuscitation of virtually the entire Confederate military establishment on the lower Cape Fear. But the Union army's ironical policy of giving General Ransom's Confederate veterans a *"carte blanche"* in dealing with Negro soldiers, continued to be a source of difficulty. It was possibly connected with a mutiny of Negro troops against white officers in September, 1865, in which one officer and one soldier were killed.[49] It was certainly connected with an effort by Negro soldiers to set free city prisoners in February, 1866. Following the latter outbreak, however, the Negro troops on the Lower Cape Fear were replaced by whites.[50] As the size of the Confederate-Conservative military establishment increased, that of the Union occupation force diminished. By the end of Presidential Reconstruction in 1868, the federal garrison in Wilmington consisted of only fifty-three men.[51]

By the beginning of 1866, the Conservatives held in their hands very nearly the entire mechanism of ante-bellum political and military power. Their legislators were now in a position to pass laws that would be enforced by Conservative militia companies; and offenders would be tried before Conservative judges. Now when a court of the Freedmen's Bureau ruled that some freedman was entitled to a piece of property that had been taken from him or was entitled to some back wages that he was claiming,

48. Wilmington *Herald*, August 5, 8, December 15, 1865.

49. *Ibid.*, September 25, 1865.

50. John Robert Kirkland, "Federal Troops in North Carolina During Reconstruction" (Master's thesis, The University of North Carolina, 1964), p. 45; Wilmington *Dispatch*, February 19, March 24, 1866.

51. Joseph Gregoire de Roulhac Hamilton, *Reconstruction in North Carolina* (New York: Columbia University Press, 1914), p. 239.

they could ignore the ruling or reply to it with curses.[52] The Union army had come and gone, yet the faces of authority were virtually unchanged in the Cape Fear country. But something was wrong. The Brunswick County militia, for example, had been successful in evicting squatters and terrorizing trespassers, but not in growing rice. The fields were growing weeds, and the Negroes were running free. The Conservatives had not reconstructed the economic and social foundations of the old society.

In contemporary terms, it has become customary to refer to political leaders who govern with an uncommon degree of brutality as "strong men." More often than not this characterization falls considerably short of the truth, since the typical "strong man" stands almost alone at the head of some unstable and unpopular regime. Similarly the measures employed by the Conservative leaders following the Civil War did not result from their strength, but from their efforts to compensate for their underlying political weakness. In the Cape Fear valley, for example, they enjoyed virtually no support among the Negroes, who comprised almost half the population. The war, furthermore, had deepened the divisions among the whites so that the Conservatives did not have their unanimous support. Also, if the Conservatives failed to win broad popular support, they failed even more seriously to partially reconcile their opponents. As a result, they attempted to make up by cruelty and violence for their lack of a secure political foundation.

Two thousand years ago a Christian missionary from Tarsus proclaimed a faith in which there was neither "Jew nor Greek . . . bond nor free . . . ," and never since has it been quite as easy for men to live at peace with the world of cruelty and violence. Yet the reality of a universal ethic, one that would unite all of mankind regardless of race or social condition, has remained always beyond man's grasp, a vision too elevated for men to live by, but too stirring to be forgotten. Like the ancients, the men of the modern world have been able to realize no more than a limited,

52. William Birnie to Captain Allen Rutherford, November 22, 1867. United States War Department, Bureau of Refugees, Freedmen and Abandoned Lands (Record Group 105), North Carolina, Vol. 147: Subdistrict Lumberton, National Archives.

provincial ethic, one that unites the people of like race or social condition. But against the barbarians from outer darkness, one must be prepared to use violence.

In the mid-nineteenth century, the Americans living in the northern and western states were not divided between the bond and the free, nor were they separated by other deep chasms of social condition or race. Because they enjoyed this high degree of social unity, they also shared a body of ideas concerning right and wrong, a common ethic, which, though not eliminating cruelty and violence from their dealings one with another, at least did not make these unhappy aspects of human relations a conspicuous feature of their society.

Nowhere was this more manifest than in their local political institutions. Because the interests and ideas that united them were stronger than those that separated them, the political "ins" could exchange places with the political "outs" by a noisy but essentially peaceful process. Once in control, furthermore, a local administration could not only enjoy extremely broad support from an essentially unified people, but also it could half-placate its opponents in the boisterous give and take of politics. As a result, the hand of authority did not lie heavy on the land.

It was natural that northerners, irrespective of political party, should be influenced by the social values and political customs of their home communities. Yet when they crossed the Mason-Dixon line, heading south, without realizing it they passed beyond the frontiers of some of the ethical assumptions of their native villages and towns. In the Cape Fear valley, for example, a hungry Negro, who owned nothing, whose friends and great-grandparents had owned nothing, would not necessarily share their view that property was sacred and that it would be more honorable for a man's family to remain hungry than it was for that man to violate the hallowed perches of somebody's chicken coop.

Nor would a respected Conservative leader such as the Reverend J. N. Stallings, who as a Duplin County police captain had given orders to shoot without trial Negroes who had committed theft,[53] share their assumption that petty larceny was a minor offense, often born of misery, and not worth a human life; because larceny was an offense against property, and it was primarily property that made the way of life of the Reverend Stallings' kind of people different from that of the freedmen. In his dealings with his own kind, the Reverend Stallings was undoubtedly governed by many of the same considerations controlling human relations in any Yankee village. But against the black-skinned barbarians, he was prepared to use the saber and the pistol.

Northern ideas concerning the art of government also received some rude jolts in the South. The armed and mounted bands, as they thundered over the country roads establishing the Conservative authority, did not behave much like a gathering of neighbors at a New England town meeting; and some northerners watched these activities with an attitude of moral outrage,[54] suggestive of the way that certain mid-twentieth-century Americans might look on a particularly scandalous election in Latin America or Southeast Asia. The men General Ransom picked for the Wilmington police force, for example, were not likely to remind a Yankee observer of his village constable back home. "The policemen are the hardest and most brutal looking and acting set of civil or municipal officers I ever saw," an officer of the Freedmen's Bureau complained. They were a terror "to everybody . . . certainly to all the colored people or loyal men."

He once saw a Negro woman "in charge of two stout police. I waited, and they were laughing at her and she was rather noisy—intoxicated I should think. They stayed there on the street, in all twenty minutes or a half an hour; when I stepped down upon the pavement and approached them, I heard a sharp rap which could be heard a square. The policeman felled the woman senseless to the ground with his baton. She was a slight woman, hardly able to handle a boy twelve years of age."[55]

The methods of punishment, furthermore, that were employed south of the Potomac sometimes offended Yankee sensibilities. For example, in Wilmington one Saturday afternoon,

53. Philadelphia *Inquirer*, August 9, 1865.
54. *Ibid.*
55. Joint Committee, *Report*, p. 271.

March 17, 1866, Lieutenant Colonel William Henry Harrison Beadle was returning to his office from lunch. He saw a gathering of angry Negroes around the courthouse. The New Hanover Court of Common Pleas and Quarter Session, meeting inside, had just sentenced some Negroes to be flogged; and, at this very moment, Sheriff Samuel R. Bunting was laying on the stripes. The crowd around the courthouse was in an ugly mood. Colonel Beadle was an officer of the Bureau, and the freedmen were his responsibility. He conferred quickly with another Bureau officer. They then sent an orderly inside "to direct the sheriff to delay the whipping," as flogging might be a "partial continuation of the 'slave code.' "[56]

The chairman of the court, William A. Wright, "satisfied the officers that the laws of North Carolina did not discriminate against the negro, in cases of petit larceny, and that the white man would be whipped for the same offense." The Yankee officers were not appeased, however. To them the "infliction of stripes, on either a white man or Negro, was a relic of barbarism...."[57] Nevertheless, with President Johnson as their commander-in-chief, the squeamishness of local Bureau officers could not long delay the course of Conservative justice. It was almost with ante-bellum casualness that a paper could report during the following month that the "court transacted very little business yesterday, with the exception of the cases of five freedmen for larceny. They were all convicted and sentenced from twelve to thirty-nine lashes each, upon their bare backs."[58]

Not only were Union officers sometimes finicky about the use of the cowhide, but also they were sometimes revolted by a practice of southern courts of sentencing men to be branded with a hot iron. On April 5, 1867, Lieutenant Colonel R. F. Frank wired General Daniel Edgar Sickles, commander of the Second Military District, which included North and South Carolina, and obtained permission to prevent Sheriff Bunting from branding Nicholas Carr.[59]

56. Wilmington *Herald*, March 20, 1866; Wilmington *Dispatch*, March 20, 1866.
57. Wilmington *Dispatch*, March 19, 1866.
58. Wilmington Weekly *Journal*, April 28, 1866.
59. Wilmington *Post*, April 6, 1867.

During the latter half of 1865 and throughout 1866 the most conspicuous resistance of the Conservative order continued to be an occasional, spontaneous outburst of Negro violence against Black Code justice. At the same time, there were increasing signs that the opposition was beginning to assume more consciously political forms. Within a week after the second restoration of the Confederate-Conservative regime in Wilmington, for example, a crude advertisement appeared in the *Herald* informing the "brothers of the U. [*sic*] League" that, because of bad weather, their meeting would be held in a room over "Mr. James M. Bremmer's store."[60]

There are only scraps of information available concerning the early history of the Union League in Wilmington, but it was established there as early as April, 1865, "Union League number one" and "Union League number two" having taken part in the Lincoln Memorial Procession. Initially the League seems to have consisted of a handful of obscure Union sympathizers who got together from time to time to sing patriotic songs to the accompaniment of a "band of music."[61] But as early as July, 1865, we find them petitioning the Wilmington city government to appoint Negroes as policemen and as inspectors of fuel. The authorities not only refused, but appeared rather shocked at such a suggestion.[62]

In the meanwhile the freedmen were being goaded by events into taking more resolute political action. By the late summer of 1865, the Conservatives had made their conception of the place of the Negro clear. Furthermore, President Johnson and Governor Holden seemed intent on consolidating the unstable Conservative regimes.[63] Indeed when Governor Holden proclaimed that the election of a state convention would be carried out substantially according to ante-bellum rules, it must have appeared to some Negroes that the frontiers of Negro freedom were going to be defined by men who had found little to criticize

60. Wilmington *Herald*, August 12, 1865.
61. *Ibid.*, August 15, 1865.
62. John Dawson *et al.*, to Holden, July 12, 1865, Governor's Papers, Holden.
63. Holden to Mayor and Commissioners of Wilmington, July 15, 1865, Johnson Papers.

about slavery. In any event, Governor Holden's call for a convention produced one unexpected result: A meeting of Negroes in New Bern proclaimed a convention of freedmen, the first of its kind in the South,[64] which was to meet in Raleigh the same time as the constitutional convention. A committee of freedmen published the following call in Wilmington:

> Freedmen of North Carolina, Arouse!! [sic]
> Men and Bretheren
> These are the times foretold by the Prophets, "when a Nation shall be born in a day," the good time coming [sic]. Four millions of chattels, branded mercantile commodity [sic], shake off the bands, drop the chains, and rise up in the dignity of men.
> The time has arrived when we can strike one blow to secure those rights of Freemen that have been so long withheld from us.[65]

The proclamation went ahead to set forth the same procedure for selecting Negro delegates as Holden had laid down for the white men's convention: Each county was to hold a convention of freedmen. These conventions would send as many delegates to Raleigh as that county had had representatives in the legislature.

Governor Holden was going ahead and organizing civil government as it always had been under the state constitution of 1835, the Negroes having no political existence. But the situation was not as it always had been. No longer were the Negroes bound to the parochial isolation of separate plantations. They could now unite the strength of their millions just as the whites could. In the Cape Fear valley, for example, the Negro convention would carry the authority of nearly as many supporters as the white convention. In New Hanover County and Wilmington it would carry more.

September, 1865, saw a swelling crescendo of political activity that culminated in the two conventions in Raleigh. Since, as the Conservatives saw it, the Negroes did not exist politically, many of the local activities of the freedmen were beneath the notice

---

64. Sidney Andrews, *The South Since the War: As Shown by Fourteen Weeks of Travel and Observation in Georgia and the Carolinas* (Boston: Ticknor and Fields, 1866), p. 121, hereinafter cited as Andrews, *South Since the War.*

65. Wilmington *Herald,* September 8, 1865.

of the press.[66] But in New Hanover County and Wilmington it was hard to ignore the fact that the body politic was now twins. The Conservatives, meeting September 12, in the city hall, pledged their "hearty support to the administration of Andrew Johnson," though it is not clear from the newspaper accounts exactly what happened to a proposal by Thomas M. Cook to put the body on record as opposing secession and slavery.[67]

But there was no lack of opposition to these propositions the following night, when the freedmen assembled at the Front Street Methodist Church for a rally. Though this church probably had the greatest seating capacity of any auditorium in the city, it could not accommodate the throng. Those who could not crowd in flooded over to First Presbyterian, a few blocks away, and organized a second rally. In a general revival atmosphere, the dark-skinned men and women prayed, sang "old time Methodist" hymns, and heard political speeches.[68]

On September 21, the white electors of New Hanover County assembled to select delegates to the constitutional convention. The meeting did not show the political unanimity for which the South was to become renowned. There were in fact six different factions represented, each with its own ticket. Besides the "Independents," there were the "Independent Voters," and the "Independent Citizens." Also there were the "Loyal League," the "Regular," and the "People's" tickets. The "Regulars" showed the greatest strength, with 156 votes, and thereby succeeded in electing William A. Wright, chairman of the New Hanover court, as delegate to the constitutional convention. The "Loyal League," on the other hand, made a poor showing, its strongest candidate receiving only twenty-five votes.[69] The white Unionists alone were not going to be able to offer very serious opposition to the Conservative order.

That night a surging mass of freedmen converged on the city hall. The first to arrive packed the hall, while the throng in the street outside clamored for admittance. The meeting was "one of the largest gatherings of the kind ever before in the councils in this

66. Andrews, *South Since the War*, p. 121.
67. Wilmington *Herald*, September 13, 1865.
68. Wilmington *Herald*, September 13, 15, 1865.
69. *Ibid.*, September 22, 1865.

city . . . ," the *Herald* admitted, and the attendance would have been even larger had not a last-minute misunderstanding diverted a portion of the crowd to Front Street Methodist Church. Such a meeting must have been a strange experience for many of the freedmen. Not only were political concepts novel, but the very act of attending large meetings of Negroes was new to most of them. Perhaps they were not yet free, but the thousand isolated little worlds of bondage had merged into one big world that was now spread out before them. For the first time they were getting to know their own people. What kind of people were the Negroes anyway?

Many freedmen must have been surprised at some of the people they saw at the city hall. For example, of all the speakers that might have been picked to give the address of the evening, it would have been hard to have found a person who looked less appropriate to the occasion than the individual sitting in the speaker's chair. The speaker appeared to be a handsome white youth.[70] Nor did the young man appear to be a Yankee. His genteel manners and proud self-confident air were marks of the Cape Fear gentry.

Appearances were both revealing and deceiving. The speaker, John P. Sampson, was a native of Wilmington, though he had just returned from studies in the North. He had also served for a time as the editor of a Cincinnati newspaper. He was somewhat older than he appeared. Yet, while he shared much with the gentry, he shared something more important with the dark throng seated and standing before him. Like them he was not yet free. He was the son of a slave.[71]

Sampson's father had been owned by the wealthy, landed Sampson family of Sampson County, farther up the river, and had come to Wilmington at the age of eighteen, accompanied by his owner, who arranged a carpenter's apprenticeship for him there. In Wilmington the fair-skinned young slave had made his home, married, and formed friends among the light-tan demi-world of the Cape Fear gentry. Sampson's father was supposed to have been

---

70. Thomas M. Cook initially referred to him as "Mr. Sampson," apparently mistaking him for white. Wilmington *Herald*, September 23, 1865.
71. *Ibid.*

a Negro, a slave, and a carpenter. But he had neither looked like a Negro, behaved like a slave, nor spent money like a carpenter. In fact, if the real source of the Sampson family's income had come from work on the carpenter's bench, the father must have been a craftsman indeed, the census of 1860 evaluating his property at $35,000.[72]

For many years the Sampsons had known what it was like to be no longer really slaves, yet not quite free. Now, as John P. Sampson stood at the rostrum of the city hall, he faced a teeming multitude of people in such a position. His world, like their's, had grown in 1865.

There was probably not one Negro in the city hall who had not in some way suffered from the submerged place of the Negro, so all-pervasive and manifold was this political fact. Yet, in his address, Sampson concentrated on a single aspect of the problem, the denial of the right to vote. He called upon the federal government "for the immediate, unconditional, and universal enfranchisement of the black man in every state in this union . . . ," without which Negro "liberty is a mockery. . . ." The Democrats were claiming that it would be unconstitutional for the federal government to "declare universal suffrage," Sampson continued, leaving most of his listeners behind. They were right. But the "constitution cannot be above the people" because it was the people who created it. The constitution would have to be amended.

Discussing arguments that were being used against Negro voting, Sampson was on ground more familiar to his audience. Probably a few freedmen had heard the phrase, "Anglo-Saxon," in connection with some assertion of Negro inferiority. But Sampson thought that belief in the racial superiority of the Anglo-Saxon to the Negro was an opinion founded upon ignorance. Because the Anglo-Saxon, he explained, used to wear a "brass collar on his neck and the name of his Norman master marked on it."[73]

72. James H. Brewer, "An Apocalypse on Slavery: the Story of the Negro Slave in the Lower Cape Fear Region of North Carolina" (Doctoral dissertation, University of Pittsburgh, 1949), p. 176.

73. Wilmington *Herald*, September 23, 1865.

A week later John P. Sampson sat with the New Hanover County delegation facing a large plaster of Paris bust of Lincoln, enshrined in a bracket over the pulpit of a Negro church. One hundred and seventeen delegates representing forty-two North Carolina counties had gathered for the first freedmen's convention. Like Sampson, all except twelve of these men were native-born North Carolinians, but only a handful had such a genteel upbringing as his. Clad in the "cheapest homespun," and "awed by the very atmosphere" of the capital, though Raleigh was a town of hardly five thousand people, these men reflected both the weakness and the strength of the freedmen. Scarcely one-quarter of them could read and write, and some of these not well. They conducted the proceedings of the convention, furthermore, in "a language that no Northern white man can understand."[74]

Yet the homespun of these unlettered men clothed no small measure of dedication. Many of them had not found it easy to come to Raleigh. At the rallies of hungry freedmen, there had to be a widespread sense of commitment if the collection plate was to yield the price of a railroad ticket. Nor had it always been safe or prudent to come. In communities where there were federal troops one could get a military pass guaranteeing safe conduct, it is true. But where the Conservatives were in firm control, it had sometimes been necessary for a delegate simply to disappear during the night and show up in Raleigh a few days later; and he would have to return home the same way.[75]

Not only did most of the other delegates differ from Sampson in their appearance, but also in certain of their ideas. They did not share his preoccupation with the right of the Negro to vote. In fact, they devoted a considerable part of their efforts, not toward composing Radical demands to present to Conservative governmental bodies, but rather toward using the authority of the convention to give some immediate purpose and direction to the lives of uprooted freedmen. In a series of resolutions, the convention urged the freedmen not to flock to the cities, but to strive for land, for education, for friendly relations with their

74. Andrews, *South Since the War*, p. 131.
75. *Ibid.*

white neighbors, for co-operation with other freedmen, and to observe marriage.[76]

The freedmen's convention did, however, compose an address to the constitutional convention that had assembled across town. The phrasing probably made Sampson wince, as the address observed certain subservient formalities designed to increase the possibility that the Conservatives would give it a hearing. Also the address did not spell out all of the demands for full citizenship, but rather was confined to requestion certain attributes of citizenship. It asked that the protection of the law be extended to the persons and property of freedmen, that the state provide for Negro education, regulate the hours of labor, and abolish all laws "which make unjust discriminations on account of race or color. . . ."[77]

The constitutional convention received the address of the freedmen with courtesy, though there is no indication that the document influenced the deliberations of its delegates. Had they been willing to consider the propositions that some 35 per cent of the people in the state considered their essential rights, they would have created a government that might have brought considerable stability to North Carolina. But the Conservatives were attempting to consolidate their position by repression rather than by reform and compromise. They were thus able to preserve the political and judicial system in its ante-bellum purity.

But underneath this frozen institutional crust, the river of political change flowed relentlessly. The simple mechanics of

76. Emancipation may have made Negroes more aware of the potential for human dissension and tragedy that had been contained in the servile mating and marriage patterns. Perhaps the experience of James McCullum was one that was all too familiar to Negroes in 1865. Unlike many slaves, McCullum had been formally married. But after two babies were born, his wife, Emily, and the children had been sold away. He never expected to see them again. After four years had gone by, McCullum remarried and two more children were born. But when Emily and her children were set free, they found their way back to him. McCullum then asked the Court of the Freedmen's Bureau at Lumberton to decide which of his marriages was legal. He felt that it was the first one. William Birnie to Captain Allen Rutherford, November 22, 1867. United States War Department, Bureau of Refugees, Freedmen and Abandoned Lands (Record Group 105), *North Carolina, Vol. 147: Subdistrict Lumberton*, National Archives.

77. Herbert Aptheker (ed.), *A Documentary History of the Negro People in the United States* (New York: The Citadel Press, 1951), p. 546.

political action, for example, once a near-monopoly of the whites, were now being assimilated by the Negroes, who were rapidly becoming a meeting-going people. The fact that they were excluded from participation in government at all levels did not prevent Negroes, at almost any country crossroads, from electing chairmen or setting up finance committees for their local organizations. The whites might laugh at the "pints of order"[78] raised at meetings of the freedmen, or joke about the chairman whose plea at a rally for "peace and harmony" was transformed in the ears of some of his listeners to a request for "peas and hominy"; but the Negroes were learning some basic political know-how, and the Black Codes were not stopping them.

The first freedmen's convention had created a permanent, state-wide organization, the Equal Rights League, which, disclaiming all secrecy, maintained a public address in Wilmington after January 3, 1866. One of the first projects of the new organization was an effort to establish a Negro press. The need for a Negro paper had been brought home to many freedmen when the newspapers in some parts of the state refused to publish their call for a convention until it was too late for Negroes in the community to elect delegates and raise money for their trip.[79]

Immediately after the convention, the Equal Rights League launched at Raleigh the *Journal of Freedom*, a paper which survived long enough to get out a few issues in October, 1865. The following month James Sinclair, the Radical white minister from Robeson County, made a second attempt when he announced the publication of the *Southern Freedman* in Wilmington.[80] Wilmington offered a better prospect for local circulation, since the city's Negro population was somewhat greater than the entire population of Raleigh, and also a comparatively large number of educated Negroes resided there. Nevertheless Negro poverty and illiteracy were too great in 1865 for such a paper to survive even in Wilmington. It would require two years of broadening ties

78. Wilmington *Daily Journal*, July 24, 1869.
79. Andrews, *South Since the War*, p. 121.
80. Wilmington *Herald*, November 13, 1865. Several issues of *Journal of Freedom* are in The University of North Carolina Library.

with white Radicals before a paper even partially friendly to Negro rights could be successful in the Cape Fear valley.

In 1866 the violent methods the Conservatives employed to strengthen their local control on one side of the Mason-Dixon Line helped elect Radical congressmen on the other. As a result, their authority in the South was struck down by a Radical Congress, which in 1867 passed the Reconstruction acts restoring military authority in the South and making return to the Union contingent upon each state's writing universal manhood suffrage into its constitution.

The Reconstruction acts and the prospects for Negro voting came as good news to a group of dissident white political leaders in North Carolina. They had been soundly defeated when they had backed Alfred Dockery against Jonathan Worth in a race for governor, and their future prospects were poor with the existing electorate. Upon the passage of the first Reconstruction act, March 2, 1867, they sent out a call to Negro leaders and to their own followers throughout the state; and before the month was out a convention had met, and the Republican party had been founded in North Carolina.[81]

In the meanwhile, General Edward Richard Sprigg Canby, Commander of Military District Number Two, consisting of North and South Carolina, ordered a new registration,[82] which, if carried out according to the Reconstruction acts, was sure to bring about an important shift in the locus of political power. On one hand the acts banished from political life most ante-bellum officeholders by the stipulation that anyone who had ever taken an oath to uphold the Constitution, which many prominent persons had done in order to qualify for some civil or military office, and had subsequently engaged in a rebellion had thus disqualified themselves to vote and to hold office. Perhaps 10 per cent of the whites in North Carolina were in this way disfranchised.[83] On the other hand, Negroes were now to be included in the electorate, a

81. Hamilton, *Reconstruction*, pp. 240-43.

82. Second Military District, General Order Number 101, October 18, 1867, Worth Papers.

83. William A. Russ, Jr., "Radical Disfranchisement in North Carolina, 1867-1868," *The North Carolina Historical Review*, XI (1934), 279, and *passim*.

development which about doubled the number of voters on the lower Cape Fear.

In the election of 1867, many members of the governing class of the old society were forced to take a back seat. If a candidate had some practical knowledge of public life, it was likely that he had gained that experience in one of the free states. Some of the men running as delegates to the Constitutional Convention were Union army veterans, newcomers to the Cape Fear country. All, Conservative and Republican alike, were strangers to the political life of the region.

The strategy of the Conservatives was to conduct a quiet campaign in areas with a heavy Negro population. The Conservative *Journal*, for example, did not even publish a complete list of Conservative candidates. They reasoned that an exciting and noisy campaign would serve to dramatize to the Negroes their new right of suffrage, while, with more sedate electioneering, the Negroes, out of ignorance or apathy, might let election day slip by without voting.[84]

Conservative strategy underestimated the growth of political consciousness among the freedmen that had taken place during the past two years. The Republican campaign in support of a constitutional convention was successful in all of the counties of the lower Cape Fear, although Columbus County elected a Conservative, the Reverend Haynes Lennon, as its delegate to the convention.[85] Of the thirteen delegates elected by seven Cape Fear counties, eight were men little known outside their home communities and who would not reappear in the political life of the region.[86] Two others were Republican leaders of local prominence: O. H. Hayes, delegate from Robeson, was a Union army veteran who had opened a mercantile business in Shoe Heel following the war.[87] He would remain a local party spokesman throughout Reconstruction. Edwin Legg, delegate from Bruns-

84. Wilmington Weekly *Journal*, November 9, 15, 1867.
85. Raleigh *Sentinel*, May 1, 1868.
86. These were the Reverend Haynes Lennon, Joshua L. Nance, A. W. Fisher, F. F. French, Alexander Williams, Sylvester Carter, J. W. Peterson, and Samuel Highsmith.
87. Wilmington *Post*, November 2, 10, 1867.

THE FIRST NEGRO VOTES IN THE CAPE FEAR COUNTRY
November 19-20, 1867

County	Percentage of the population "colored"	Percentage of the electorate Negro	Percentage voting for convention
Bladen	48%	51%	68%
Brunswick	43%	50%	70%
Columbus	35%	38%	53%
Duplin	43%	45%	78%
New Hanover	58%	63%	73%
Robeson	45%*	48%*	71%*
Sampson	39%	40%	59%

The issue of the convention was generally a test of party strength, though not a strict one. Columbus County, for example, though voting for a convention, elected a Conservative delegate.
*Figures concerning the racial composition of Robeson County tend to be capricious and unreliable due to the large Indian population.
Sources: North Carolina, *Journal of the Constitutional Convention . . . 1868* (Raleigh: Convention Printer, 1868), p. 117.
United States, Census Office, *Ninth Census of the United States: 1870. Population* (3 vols.; Washington: Government Printing Office, 1872), I, 53-54.

wick, was a Union veteran who had settled after the war in Smithville where he became proprietor of a "shebang [?]."[88] For a number of years he would stand at the head of the Whiggish faction in the Republican party of his adopted county.

By all odds, however, it was predominantly Negro New Hanover that sent the most able delegates to the convention: Abraham H. Galloway, an aristocratic mulatto originally from Brunswick County, a quick-witted debater who had gained some political experience in the abolitionist movement in Ohio, whose political views lay somewhere between the Whiggish and the Radical Republicans; General Joseph Carter Abbott, a Union army veteran with Whiggish opinions, who had had years of experience as a newspaper man and in practical politics, and who since the war had become a lumber magnate on the lower Cape Fear; and the Reverend Samuel Stanford Ashley, a Radical, originally from Providence, Rhode Island, who was said to have served without compensation as the superintendent of the teachers employed by the Freedmen's Bureau for the Southern District of North

88. Wilmington *Star*, November 23, 1867; Wilmington *Daily Journal*, March 21, 1868, June 2, 1870.

Carolina.[89] Though generally presumed to be white, Ashley once became the subject of a newspaper controversy in which the *Journal* undertook to prove that he was a Negro,[90] a proceeding of which the minister did not deign to take public notice.

It is perhaps fortunate for North Carolina that her legal profession was poorly represented at the convention that met January-March, 1868. As a result the convention leaned heavily upon the legal talent of a few men who had obtained their training in the courts of the free states, where a more advanced concept of justice, punishment, and civil liberty prevailed. Unfortunately, however, the convention presents a sharp contrast between the great mass of delegates, who were inexperienced in matters of law and politics, on the one hand, and, on the other, a group of about a dozen men who were competent to discuss some of the more difficult political and legal questions involved in writing a constitution.

The three representatives from New Hanover County were among the small group of active delegates who largely dominated the life of the convention. At the outset the convention adopted a procedure whereby the problems to be covered by the constitution were divided into thirteen general areas,[91] and the chairman was empowered to appoint committees to study each area and to make recommendations to the convention. Ashley was made chairman of the Committee on Education, while Abbott served as chairman of the Committee on Finance. While in his work with the committee studying local government Galloway was generally overshadowed by Albion Winegar Tourgée, he nevertheless presented the recommendations of the committee in respect to the state's chief city, Wilmington.[92]

89. Wilmington *Post*, May 3, 1868. For further information about Galloway and Abbott, see below, Chap. IV.

90. Wilmington Weekly *Journal*, May 29, 1868.

91. (1) Preamble and Bill of Rights, (2) Governor, (3) Legislature, (4) Judicial Department, (5) Finance, (6) Internal Improvements, (7) Counties, Cities (local government), (8) Corporations other than Municipal, (9) Punishments and Penal Institutions, (10) Militia, (11) Education, (12) Suffrage and Eligibility to Office, and (13) Homesteads. North Carolina, *Journal of the Constitutional Convention . . . 1868* (Raleigh: Joseph W. Holden, Convention Printer, 1868), pp. 43-44.

92. *Ibid.*, pp. 66, 268, 339-41, and *passim*.

On March 16, 1868, as the capitol bell sounded, the delegates signed a document that was to remain the basic law of North Carolina for nearly a century to come. Some of the innovations that the new constitution introduced were manhood suffrage without property qualifications or racial restriction, removal of all religious proscription from officeholding except the disbarment of atheists, providing for the popular election of county officials, broadening the system of public schools, and softening the penal code, changing official penal theory to include the idea of reforming offenders, and reducing the number of capital offenses. These sweeping constitutional changes were not so interesting to the Conservative press, however, as was the discovery that several delegates had overcharged the state in reporting their travel expenses. In a final comment on the convention and its work, Conservatism's most influential voice, the *Sentinel*, predicted that true North Carolinians would blush "that a set of apes and hybrids should be holding a brutal carnival in her halls of legislation. . . ."[93]

When the convention delegates returned home to the Cape Fear country in the latter part of March, 1868, an ugly political clash threatened. In April there would be an election in which the voters would ratify or reject the new constitution and decide the composition of the legislature. The Conservatives were no longer putting their hopes on a quiet campaign and Negro apathy. They had different plans: "Quite an excitement was created on our streets Sunday morning," the Conservative Wilmington *Morning Star* wrote March 24, 1868, "by the discovery of a number of mysterious notices that had been during the previous night, posted up at several prominent points in the city. They are supposed to have emanated from the headquarters of the somewhat notorious 'Ku Klux Klan,' what ever that may be [!].[94] . . . that a 'Ku Klux Klan' *may* be in operation here, we are not prepared to deny. . . . We are living in revolutionary times, and we are not surprised to hear of

93. Raleigh *Sentinel*, March 18, 1868.

94. These words are written tongue in cheek. Of course the *Star* knew what the Ku Klux Klan was. In this very same issue they reprinted an article from the Montgomery *Advertiser* telling how the organization was scaring Radicals in Alabama. Three days earlier, furthermore, they had reprinted a similar article from the Memphis *Avalanche*.

the organization of 'Grand Armies of the Republic,' 'Constitutional Alliances,' or 'Ku Klux Klan.' "

If intimidation is to be an effective political tactic, behind it must be the physical means for inflicting harm. The Conservatives in the Cape Fear region were not lacking such means. There was hardly a county in the region in which they did not have a company of militia, and in New Hanover County they had a full regiment of eight companies. Federal troops in the Cape Fear country, on the other hand, had been reduced to a token force, despite the fact that they were supposed to be supervising the local civil authorities. There were only fifty-three Union soldiers in Wilmington and eighty more in Fayetteville.[95] Furthermore a number of the federal soldiers in Wilmington were not only Conservatives, but were active in the local Conservative campaign.[96]

It would have been unwise for the Conservatives to have used their local militia openly in the ratification campaign. The Duplin County murders in 1865, and the Sampson County "orphan"-hunting in 1866, had both brought about the intervention of the federal government. This intervention had not been very forceful, but it nevertheless seems likely that, had the campaigns by the local militia units been continued, in the end somebody might have been punished. On the other hand, it was not likely that local militia commanders would be held responsible for the activities charged against the Ku Klux Klan. It is possibly for this reason that thirty-year-old Colonel Roger Moore, a prominent member of the gentry, a distinguished Confederate cavalry commander, and currently a regimental staff officer of the New Hanover County militia, went to Raleigh and took an oath to the Ku Klux Klan after which he was appointed "Chief of the Division of the Ku Klux Klan in Wilmington," said to be "made up of the best blood in the South," including many Confederate veterans who had served under Colonel Moore in the Third North Carolina Cavalry.[97]

95. Hamilton, *Reconstruction*, p. 239.
96. Wilmington Weekly *Journal*, April 17, 1868.
97. William Lord De Rosset, *Pictorial and Historical New Hanover County and Wilmington, North Carolina, 1723-1928* (Wilmington: published by the author, 1938), p. 30.

A campaign of fear was soon underway, with no small amount of co-operation from the press:

A solitary horseman clad in the habitments of the grave, was seen, about 1½ o'clock [*sic*] this morning making a rapid circuit of that portion of the suburbs of Wilmington known as Dry Pond.[98] The horse was represented to have been of unusual size, and the rider had the appearance of a skeleton rather than a man. Our informant says that the ghostly horseman stopped at his house, drank four buckets of water, and said he was a little thirsty, not having had any water since he was killed at Fort Fisher. Was he Ku Klux? Or, what does it mean?[99]

A few days later the *Star* announced that some five hundred people had called by its offices to view the Ku Klux Klan drinking cup that was on display there. The paper described the cup as being made from a human skull "elegantly set in lead."[100]

The *Daily Journal* soon joined the campaign to publicize the Ku Klux Klan:

Terrible was the phantom seen in the alley near the Post Office Thursday night last. A skeleton, with a winding sheet drawn about his dry bones, seated upon a snow-white steed, whose nostrils emitted streams of flame with a strong odor of brimstone, was seen just before the heavy rain burst upon the city. Detaching his skull from its natural position on his shoulders, the skeletton, phantom, Ku Klux, or whatever it might be, rapped upon the window of the Post Office and in desperate haste inquired for the mail for Fort Fisher. A considerable crowd being attracted by this unusual sight, the Ku Klux exhibited evident sign of uneasiness, and in an explosion like the report of a pistol vanished. It is useless to say that the frightened darkies who chanced to be near the spot took to their heels. As they departed in their indecent haste these words reached their ears as if borne by the wind:

The Ku Klux are abroad! The Avenger Cometh with the Night when man sleepeth! Beware! The hour is near at hand![101]

98. Dry Pond was a strongly Republican neighborhood, predominantly Negro but also including many laboring class whites. The Republican slate for the legislature was known in Wilmington as the "Dry Pond Ticket." Wilmington *Morning Star*, March 27, 1868.

99. *Ibid.*, March 28, 1868.

100. *Ibid.*, April 3, 1868.

101. Wilmington *Daily Journal*, April 18, 1868.

Indeed the hour was near at hand. This yarn was published with only slight differences by both of the Conservative dailies in Wilmington on Saturday, April 18, 1868. On the following Tuesday an election would begin in which the voters would not only ratify or reject the new constitution but also decide whether the county governments and the state legislature were to be Radical or Conservative.

One might well expect that Conservative strategy would be based on a rather thorough understanding of the Wilmington Negro, the Conservative leaders having spent their lives in this community. Yet geographical proximity does not always lead to mutual understanding where people are divided by differences in social station. In this instance, the Conservatives had a mental image of the Negro that did not consistently help them to foresee the reactions of actual Negroes. The previous November their imaginary Negro had been too apathetic and ignorant to vote in a quiet election, while the actual Negro had buried them under a *déluge* of Republican ballots. With the ratification campaign, they now based their strategy on the image of a superstitious Negro who would flee in terror at the sight of a white sheet.

But once again the actual Negro behaved otherwise. On the morning of April 18, the press had warned that the "Avenger Cometh with the Night when man sleepeth." Yet, with the coming of night, not much sleeping was done by anyone. By means of a noisy barrage of gunfire, patrolling bands of Negroes served notice on all concerned, that the raids General Ransom's police had made on their homes, in search for hidden weapons, had not been entirely successful.[102] Nor, furthermore, were the Negroes totally helpless in cases where they had no conventional weapons. At least one of these bands was patrolling the streets armed with fence rails.[103] During the course of four tempestuous nights, April 18-21, 1868, these patrolling bands ended the career of the Ku Klux Klan in Wilmington.

With this new turn of events, the *Star* and the *Journal*, which had scarcely been able to contain their amusement at the antics

102. *Ibid.*, April 21, 1868.
103. *Ibid.*, April 24, 1868.

of the Ku Klux Klan, suddenly ceased to find the spectacle of political intimidation entertaining. "One of our most respectable citizens," exploded the *Star* on April 21, was halted at eleven o'clock at night by a "party of negroes, and after being asked several impertinent questions, was ordered to pass on. The gang of negroes numbered about a dozen, and was acting in concert under the direction of one of their party. . . . We call on our authorities to put down at once this riotous parading at night of the streets by large parties of men. It is a violation of our city ordinances, and is becoming an unbearable nuisance."

When the votes were counted three days later, the Republicans had won four of the seven counties of the lower Cape Fear, carrying Wilmington two to one.[104] But within another week, the appeals of the Conservative press for law and order had achieved some results, and the *Star* could report on April 30 that "the militia guard was patrolling the streets last night. We hardly think the 'men and brothers' [Negroes] were as energetic in their efforts to find the Ku Klux, as they were on previous nights. Perhaps gentlemen can go to their homes without being halted by strolling bands of vagabond negroes.

What has become of the Ku Klux? Nothing has been heard of them lately!"

Colonel Roger Moore had doffed his white robes, and once again put on his militia uniform, but not for long. Colonel Moore's militia and General Ransom's police force would not long survive the kind of legislature that the men with the fence rails had sent to Raleigh.

104. Racial lines appear to have been drawn more sharply in this contest than they had been in the election of the previous fall:

Percentage of the population "colored"	County	Percentage of Republican ballots cast
58%	New Hanover	62%
48%	Bladen	57%
45%	Robeson	56%
43%	Brunswick	51%
43%	Duplin	39%
39%	Sampson	46%
35%	Columbus	34%

Sources: J. Bryan Grimes *et al.* (ed.), *North Carolina Manual, 1913* (Raleigh: Edwards and Broughton, 1913), pp. 987-90; Raleigh *Sentinel*, April 28, 1868; Wilmington Weekly *Journal*, May 1, 1868.

IV ⤳ *Politics, Carpetbaggers,*
and Negroes

DURING THE NINETEENTH CENTURY THE BULL ALLIGATOR WAS
the herald of spring in the Cape Fear country. When people
heard his bellow in the night they knew that grass was beginning
to appear in the low grounds along the river. In Wilmington one
would soon be awakened at dawn by another reminder of the
changing season, the horn of the cowherd. Beginning in the
spring the town's Negro cowherd, George Mack, would walk
through the city at daylight blowing his horn. At houses along
his way there would be cows waiting behind the gates or coming
running to meet the herd. Mack would open each gate and let
the cow which lived there join her friends in the street. The
cattle would then continue on their way out of the city to the
pasture lands, following the sound of the herdsman's horn.

The call of the bull alligator and the summons of the cow
horn meant that oysters would soon disappear from the city
market, along with the sides of venison, the sweet potatoes, chest-
nuts, and possums. But there would soon be turtle eggs; the shad
were beginning to run; and the Piney Woods folk would soon be
bringing in huckleberries and plums. By the spring of 1868 many
of the hateful reminders of war were disappearing. Food was
again plentiful and people had money with which to buy it. The
brisk sale of tar, turpentine, and cotton at good prices was bringing money into the port. Railroads were being renovated and
new lines constructed. Jobs were not hard to find.

There were no longer many soldiers and sailors on the streets of Wilmington. Most people had not been sorry to see them leave, as the city had been heavily populated by military personnel for a long time. During the war the existence of large numbers of Confederate navy personnel and the crews of blockade-runners had not exalted the prevailing moral standards. In fact the city had reminded a Yankee journalist who arrived there in 1865 of "Sodom and Gomorrah."[1] Yet, despite his faith in the edifying effects of the Union occupation, he scarcely could have believed that the amusements of his fellow Yankees were converting Wilmington into a Sunday school. Indeed in 1865 the general picture of economic stagnation in the business district of the city had been relieved by only one prosperous enterprise, the thriving sin-mill of "Gentle Annie" Mansfield, on the corner of Front and Chestnut streets, where she, her staff, and clientele resolved their alcoholic differences with boisterous quarrels and bloody combat.[2] But, as a result of prosperity coming and soldiers leaving, the moral climate of the community had improved; and by 1868 Wilmington was beginning to assume a normal peacetime appearance.

However, peace had not brought prosperity to the rice industry. It had brought rather ruin and decay. Across the river from Wilmington there had once been golden fields; stalks bent heavy with grain had stretched away to the south as far as the eye could see. Now opposite the thriving port there were only ruined dikes, canals clogged with water weeds, and fields reclaimed by a tangled jungle-like growth.[3] In fact the total yield of some twenty-five plantations, stretching along the river for twenty miles, was estimated at only 32,000 bushels for the 1867-68 harvest.[4] This was less rice than the combined yields of two plantations, Kendall and Orton, before the freeing of the slaves.[5] For the rice planter peace had not ushered in the Day of Jubilee.

1. Wilmington *Daily Herald*, July 17, 1865. (This paper originated as *The Herald of the Union*, but began appearing shortly thereafter as *The Wilmington Herald* or *The Daily Herald*, hereinafter cited as Wilmington *Herald*.)
2. Wilmington *Herald*, June 23, 1865.
3. Wilmington *Post*, May 14, 1875.
4. *Ibid.*, October 2, 1867.
5. Wilmington *The Daily Journal*, December 1, 1875, hereinafter cited as Wilmington *Daily Journal* or Wilmington Weekly *Journal*.

Increasingly people were now shifting their attention from war and military matters back to the old peacetime channel of politics. With the adoption of a new constitution early in 1868, North Carolina had been readmitted to the Union. The state was no longer a "conquered province." Now it was to the voters, rather than to the military authorities, that one must appeal if he did not like the way things were being done.

But politics were not like they used to be. Not only had the electorate in the Cape Fear country roughly doubled in size, but political methods had become coarser, less gentlemanly. Political processions carried blazing pitch-pine brands through the streets of villages and towns. Tar barrels burned at mammoth out-of-door rallies, the thick, heavy smoke spreading like a funeral pall over the hopes of the Conservatives, and reducing everyone present, Negro and white, to a common, egalitarian blackness. These dark throngs were now The People, to whom one must appeal if he wished to hold office. "Sheriff Fennell's carriage driver" had even been nominated one gentleman exclaimed. "Meetings every night, and such howlings[,] oh my."[6]

One such gathering was a meeting of the Republicans of New Hanover County, which the *Star* disdainfully characterized as "the great unwashed, who a few days since, assembled in convention amid the sands of Dry Pond,"[7] where they had nominated candidates. This development had not been reassuring to Conservatives. In the first place it was not customary for the political leadership to the lower Cape Fear to gather in such places as Dry Pond, a community of Negroes and working class whites in the southern part of Wilmington that was so low and poorly drained that the term "Dry" was more hopeful than descriptive.

Secondly, and more serious, was the lack of familiar figures on the "Dry Pond ticket."[8] The *Star* could undoubtedly have for-

6. A. E. Wright to Julius Walker Wright, June 3, 1870, Murdock-Wright Papers, Southern Historical Collection, The University of North Carolina, hereinafter cited as Murdock-Wright Papers.

7. Wilmington *Morning Star*, March 21, 1868. (This paper began as the *Evening Star*, changing to *Morning Star* a few months later, hereinafter cited as Wilmington *Star*.)

8. Wilmington *Star*, March 21, 1868.

given the delegates to Dry Pond for being "unwashed" had they shown any willingness to recognize the tried and proven political talent of the Cape Fear. But they did not. Previous conventions, for example, had often looked to the Ashe family when they wanted a suitable candidate for the North Carolina lower house.

Early in the eighteenth century when North and South Carolina were still one province, John Ashe had been elected to the provincial assembly. His descendants for the next six generations, a period of a century and a half, had each in turn taken their seat in the lower house of the legislature. It had become almost as commonplace for the Ashe family to have a seat in the North Carolina House of Commons as it was for other aristocratic families to have an hereditary pew in St. James's Church. In 1795 furthermore, when Governor-elect John B. Ashe had died before he could assume office, his father, Samuel Ashe, had been elected to serve in his stead.[9] In the dynastic give and take of the eighteen-century aristocracy, it had apparently been the Ashes' turn to furnish a governor. In 1868, the heir-apparent to family honors, moreover, was a particularly capable individual, Samuel A. Ashe, who would later achieve some distinction as a historian. But the customary public honors were not awarded to the Ashe family in 1868.

Bypassing families having century-old ties with North Carolina public life, the Dry Pond convention selected three candidates for the legislature whose names were not reassuring to seasoned political observers of the lower Cape Fear. The most prominent of the three was a Union general, Joseph C. Abbott. "Can the 'C' in his name stand for 'carpet bag,'" the *Star* chortled.[10] To this kind of political scurrility General Abbott had been known to reply that when he had arrived in Wilmington it had not been with a "'carpet bag' but with a brigade."[11] And indeed he had. In fact he had won a citation for "gallant and meritorious conduct" as a brigade commander in the storming of

9. Wilmington *Daily Journal*, September 9, 1873.
10. Wilmington *Star*, July 22, 1868.
11. Wilmington Weekly *Journal*, July 3, 1868.

Fort Fisher.[12] What were the qualifications of this man, unheard of on the Cape Fear before 1865, elected to the legislature in 1868, from whence he was elected to the United States Senate?

Joseph Carter Abbott was born in 1825 in Concord, New Hampshire. He was a graduate of Phillips Academy in Andover, Massachusetts; studied law and was admitted to the New Hampshire bar in 1852; was owner or editor, at various times, of three New England newspapers; served on the New Hampshire state committee of first the Whig, then the Know Nothing party, which transformed itself into the Republican party. He served once as Adjutant General of New Hampshire and, just before the war, was appointed to a commission to adjust the United States—Canadian boundary.[13]

In the spring of 1865 he served as Post Commander of Wilmington, where he "made many warm friends by the uniform courtesy and urbanity he displayed in his social intercourse with the people, and the justice tempered with moderation and kindness with which he discharged his official duties."[14] His wife, who had joined him in Wilmington, undoubtedly contributed to his popularity. This devout Christian lady became active in a relief campaign during the typhoid epidemic of June, 1865, until she herself contracted the disease and died with it.[15]

It was probably while serving as Post Commander of Wilmington that Abbott became aware of the business opportunities that then existed in the Cape Fear country. Along with other sorts of famine existing in the area, there was a famine of capital and credit. The planters had never had much free cash, but their holdings in land and slaves had once provided them with considerable credit resources. With the end of the war, however, their investments in slaves evaporated as completely as any investments they may have held in Confederate bonds. It is true that the land

12. Captain E. Lewis Moore to General Joseph Roswell Hawley, January 25, 1865, Joseph R. Hawley Papers, Manuscripts Division, Library of Congress, hereinafter cited as Hawley Papers.

13. *Biographical Directory of the American Congress* (Washington: Government Printing Office, 1950), p. 759; Wilmington *Post*, October 23, 1881.

14. Wilmington Weekly *Journal*, September 20, 1865.

15. Hawley to Major C. A. Carleton, June 18, 1865, Hawley Papers; Wilmington *Herald*, June 13, 1865.

was still there, but land without labor was of questionable value, and free labor was not anxious to retrieve rich fields from overgrown pestholes. How much money could one borrow with a wild quagmire as security? A planter was lucky if he could even pay his taxes. Money and credit were scarce. Land was going begging. A little bit of capital went a long way in the Cape Fear country just after the war.[16]

Abbott happened to have some capital.[17] With it he was able to buy three thousand acres of good timber fifty miles from Wilmington, on the Wilmington, Charlotte, and Rutherfordton railroad, in the midst of the pine barrens. He hired freedmen and Piney Woods men, built a sawmill, which was soon turning out 100,000 board feet of lumber a month, and laid out the town of Abbottsburg. The enterprise prospered, so he expanded his operations to include a woodworking shop that manufactured laths, molding, window blinds, fence pickets, and broom handles. Later he further enlarged his business with a plant for the manufacture of boxcars and other railroad rolling stock. Eventually he was employing at Abbottsburg 150 men, fifty mules and oxen, a locomotive and eleven cars.[18]

According to the standards of the 1860's and 1870's, Abbottsburg was a large-scale and up-to-date enterprise, though it perhaps did not loom large in the total economy of the lower Cape Fear. But Abbottsburg came to be a symbol of progress and bold enterprise, a source of pride to the people of the region. A traveler wrote that the

country from Mears' Bluff to Abbotts looks anything but inviting. . . . [But at] Abbottsburg everything changes. The low one story houses with two rooms, where even the whitewash brush is unknown, which you have been used to seeing since you left Wilmington, your eyes rest upon residences unrivaled upon this road from Wilmington to Charlotte, for elegance and comfort. . . . There is a factory where they

16. Even as late as 1869 money was being lent for 36 per cent per year on the lower Cape Fear. A. E. Wright to Julius Walker Wright, January 30, 1869, Murdock-Wright Papers.

17. Wilmington *Post*, April 8, 1868.

18. Wilmington *Daily Journal*, March 30, 1872, April 11, 1873; *Post*, October 9, 1881.

build cars and everything else in the carpenter line. This factory is said to have the most complete woodworking machinery south of the Potomac.[19]

Though the Conservative *Journal* might have unkind things to say about Abbott's politics, Abbottsburg was another matter.

The most noticeable feature, to the businessman at least, on the lower line of the Wilmington, Charlotte, and Rutherfordton railroad, is the pretty little town of Abbottsburg. Eight years ago there was not so much as a log cabin there. It was one vast pine forest. . . . But the modern Aladdin, the everlasting Yankee, has touched it and the Genie of enterprise has converted the pine forest into a beautiful and blooming town. The busy hum of the saw has taken the place of the moaning music of the pines. . . .[20]

At Abbottsburg the people of the Cape Fear country might see an image of their own future, just as at Orton plantation they might see an image of their crumbling past.

If Joseph Abbott had stayed out of politics, or better still had entered politics as a Conservative, his name would have been entered in the historical annals of North Carolina as the benign and public-spirited gentleman who helped infuse new life into the war-prostrated Cape Fear country. But for the rest of his life, in victory and in defeat, Abbott would continue to adhere to the party that he had helped to found. In 1868, he accepted a place on the Republican legislative ticket which eventually carried him to the United States Senate. In the meanwhile, in the midst of weed-covered fields, there was probably more than one Conservative gentleman who, abandoned by his servants, was having an opportunity to reflect upon his century-old family heritage of public service, upon the fact that there had been few times in his life when it would have been more convenient to have accepted, say, a seat in the United States Senate, a seat which the hustling entrepreneur of Abbottsburg did not really need. That "cahpet bagger!"

There was one name appearing on the Dry Pond ticket, in the

19. Wilmington *Post*, July 2, 1875.
20. Wilmington *Daily Journal*, April 11, 1873.

election of 1868, that must have appeared puzzling to some people along the lower Cape Fear. It was the name of Abraham H. Galloway. Was it possible that some member of the old and well-connected Galloway family had accepted the Radical nomination for the North Carolina Senate? Was this Abraham H. Galloway from the Brunswick County gentry?

A local reporter for the *Star* had encountered this individual the previous fall, and his report had not been encouraging to *Star* readers: "The colored folks had a torch-light and general jollification last evening. . . . About 11 ½ o'clock, the procession halted in front of the market house, and after loud calls for 'Galloway,' somebody climbed up on top of the market house, and 'spoke his piece.' We heard a few of the 'passing remarks'; and what we did hear was not very conservative in its teachings."[21]

Galloway was, and yet was not quite, one of the Brunswick County Galloways. Though he was a man of fair complexion, he had been born of a black-skinned mother, a woman who was a Galloway family slave.[22] A miracle of this kind was particularly troublesome to the ante-bellum South because it has happened more than once. After becoming senator, Abraham Galloway explained the paradox, posed by the contrast between his and his mother's complexion, by saying that it was only charitable to characterize himself as an "Indian," his mother having been property of such a distinguished Conservative family.[23] Members of the legitimate lines of the Galloway family took no public notice of the senator's bitter jibes.

Galloway differed from a number of the aristocratic mulattoes on the lower Cape Fear in the deep enmity that he seemed to hold toward his owner-relatives. One can only suppose that he was treated much more as a slave than as a son. In any event he had fled from the Cape Fear country in 1857, escaping to Ohio, where he became a militant abolitionist.[24] One source holds that with

21. Wilmington *Evening Star*, September 25, 1867.
22. Wilmington *Daily Journal*, July 20, 1869.
23. Wilmington Weekly *Journal*, July 30, 1869; *Daily Journal*, July 20, 1869.
24. Wilmington *Daily Journal*, July 20, 1869; Herbert Aptheker (ed.), *A Documentary History of the Negro People in the United States* (New York: The Citadel Press, 1951), p. 499.

the outbreak of war, he served in the Union army.[25] Certainly the end of the war found him in New Bern, North Carolina, a town that had been occupied during the last three years of the war and in which there were a number of politically conscious and vocal Negro leaders.[26] While other aristocratic mulattoes were trying to discover some basis for compromise between their white and Negro relatives,[27] Galloway was fighting uncompromisingly for Negro rights.[28] It was this vigorous and persistent defense of the Negro, besides his own considerable gifts, that had swept him into a position of leadership by 1868.

If one examines the actual political position which Galloway took, during the five years of life remaining to him after the war, it is not apparent why his contemporaries regarded him as being "of exceedingly radical and Jacobinical spirit."[29] He favored heavy taxation of large estates, but opposed confiscation.[30] As did most Republicans, he favored the popular election of judges,[31] but opposed the efforts of the more radical Tourgée wing of the party to repudiate ante-bellum debts. He regarded the question of state debts as one of honor, and on this issue he "would vote as every *honest* North Carolinian would vote."[32] Thus, while his belief in consistent political democracy made him a Republican, his defense of traditional American ideas of property rights further identified him as a moderate Republican.

Why then did people of his own day regard him as a Jacobin? Perhaps it is because they had heard him speak from on top of the Wilmington Market House, because they could see with what passion he lashed the gentry, notwithstanding the fact, or perhaps even because of the fact, that they were his kinsmen; and he knew his enemy well, knowing just which thrusts were sure to draw

25. Sidney Andrews, *The South Since the War As Shown by Fourteen Weeks of Travel and Observation in Georgia and the Carolinas* (Boston: Ticknor and Fields, 1866), p. 125, hereinafter cited as Andrews, *South Since the War*.

26. Wilmington *Herald*, September 15, 1865.

27. *Ibid.*, July 27, 1865.

28. *Ibid.*, September 8, 1865.

29. Andrews, *South Since the War*, p. 125.

30. Wilmington Weekly *Journal*, September 27, 1868.

31. *Ibid.*, February 21, 1868.

32. *Ibid.*, February 28, 1868. (Emphasis in the original.)

blood. The teeming multitude in the street below would not fail to see that his subtlest allusion to his own fair skin was a cruel stab aimed at the most delicate hypocrisy of the elite classes. "Disgraceful," the *Journal* exploded, "a state senator boasting of his mother's shame and his own bastardy."[33]

Yet for all of his polemical roasting of the gentry, Galloway was and remained very much a product of the class that he so hated. Though he had escaped to Ohio in 1857, he had never freed himself of the psychological attributes of a gentleman of the lower Cape Fear. He shared their chivalrous deference toward women, and their fragile sense of honor. He had the irrational and reckless courage characteristic of a member of a hereditary military caste. In reply to an attack on the floor of the Senate by W. H. S. Sweet of Craven, for example, Galloway threatened to "hold the Senator from Craven responsible for his language, outside of this Hall . . . that if hereafter the Senator from Craven insulted him, he would prove to him the blood of a true Southron."[34] Galloway frequently carried a gun. Undoubtedly his life was sometimes in danger. There was always danger to his brittle dignity. In any event the *Journal* characterized him as the "pugilistic 'Indian Senator.' "[35]

Despite a number of dangerous confrontations, Galloway died a natural death in 1870, following his re-election to the Senate. It was with a sigh of relief that the *Journal* breathed, *Mortuis nil nisi bonum*, "of the dead nothing but good,"[36] as an obituary for a man whose tortured soul, like the legendary storm finch, could find fulfillment only in adversity and strife.

In the twentieth century, politicians have lost few elections by making appeals in the traditions of the ante-bellum establishment. This was by no means the case, however, so long as Negroes voted in large numbers. When the Negro voter thought of the Old South, a shady veranda and a leisurely mint julep were not necessarily the first recollections that came to his mind. During Reconstruction, in fact, a politician usually stood a better chance if he

33. Wilmington *Daily Journal*, July 20, 1869.
34. Wilmington *Weekly Journal*, April 2, 1869.
35. Wilmington *Daily Journal*, July 20, 1869.
36. Wilmington *Daily Journal*, September 2, 1870.

were not too closely identified with the old society. In the Cape
Fear country the first elections based on universal manhood suffrage elevated to public office a group of men who were not associated with the old regime by virtue of the fact that they were
practically strangers to the region. The *Journal* charged that most
of the Cape Fear counties, including New Hanover, Sampson,
Brunswick, Bladen, Cumberland, Harnett, and "probably others"
were "entirely under the control of carpet-baggers."[37]

The men that the *Journal* thus classified under one epithet in
actuality could stand more separate treatment. They included
economic conservatives such as Joseph C. Abbott, men whose
"radicalism" began and ended with their belief in the right of all
men to participate in politics and enjoy equality before the law.
There were others, such as Captain E. M. Rosafy, who studied
strange languages and spread perhaps even stranger doctrines
among the Negroes of Brunswick County.[38] Indeed one Conservative wrote that in that county Rosafy had attempted to "organize
a new party—somewhat after the creed of the communists of
France. . . ."[39] He urged his followers to sign a pledge stating
their belief in the "universal fatherhood of God, in the common
brotherhood of man and in the oneness of the American
nation. . . ."[40]

The newcomers also included sharp tricksters such as J. E.
Eldridge who, elected as sheriff of Bladen County, absconded with
eight thousand dollars in public funds, a sum which had to be
replaced by his fellow-Republican sureties;[41] and Joseph G. Longley who was suspected by his colleagues of profiteering with provisions intended for famine relief.[42] Because of the uniform
disdain which they held toward all carpetbaggers, the Conservatives sometimes failed to make such ordinary distinctions as
differentiating between radicals and conservatives, between men
of honor and thieves.

37. Wilmington Weekly *Journal*, August 7, 1868.
38. Wilmington *Post*, March 18, 1883.
39. Wilmington *Daily Journal*, May 17, 1876.
40. *Ibid.*
41. *Ibid.*, August 3, 1870.
42. J. D. McLaulin to M. E. Strieby, September 9, 1865, American Missionary
Association Archives, Fisk University.

One of the most influential of the newcomers to the lower Cape Fear was George Zadoc French. While the concept of a classical carpetbagger type may be an abstraction that lacks flesh and blood historical reality, at the same time, French corresponds closely to the ideas that many people have held concerning northern Republicans who settled in the South after the war. A sharp-witted New England Yankee in his mid-thirties, who during the war had engaged in the dubious occupation of an army sutler, he had arrived in Wilmington literally with the wagon trains of the Union army. Indeed the captured city had hardly stopped smoking before French had taken over an abandoned store building and was industriously selling tobacco, liquor, clothing, and "Yankee Notions" to the soldiers.[43]

Yet, despite the reputation of sutlers for sharp practices, the business was not all gain. With the arrival in Wilmington of nine hundred destitute Union officers, just released from Confederate prison camps and having "barely sufficient clothing left to cover their nakedness,"[44] French, who was more "accommodating than sutlers are generally credited with being,"[45] lent them money and accepted their IOU's in lieu of cash for his goods. Five months later he had received payment for only about one-third of the four thousand dollars in cash and goods that he had thus advanced to soldiers on their way home.[46]

There are other indications that the "accommodating" sutler was a man with no simple personality. He could sell "poor whisky and tobacco to soldiers at remunerative prices"[47] or, before a cheering crowd on the occasion of Wilmington's first postwar Independence Day, he could intone that "all men are created equal, that they are endowed by their Creator with certain unalienable rights," to which the Army-Navy Glee Club responded with "*E Pluribus Unum.*"[48] There was in fact a genuine strain of idealism in French, though of a very practical Yankee sort; so

43. Wilmington *Herald*, March 7, 1865.
44. Wilmington *Herald*, March 3, 1865.
45. *Ibid.*, August 4, 1865.
46. *Ibid.*
47. Wilmington Weekly *Journal*, December 18, 1868.
48. Wilmington *Herald*, July 6, 1865.

that in dreaming of a better world, he seldom forgot to think of ways of improving the particular condition of the dreamer. If, upon seeing nine hundred suffering men, his humanity had gotten the better part of his business judgment, this was not a lapse that would occur often in his life. The ideals that he held had made fortunes spring from the stony soil of New England, and that same heritage would surely not bankrupt George French.

He proceeded to apply his talents at the spot where the final impulse of war had thrust him, in Wilmington. By the fall of 1865 he was retailing civilian goods and was marketing cotton and naval stores of back country people for a commission,[49] with apparent success. Two years later French, who never believed in hiding his light under a bushel, admitted that he had the largest stock, the widest assortment of goods, and the lowest prices of any merchant in North Carolina.[50]

But no mercantile business would contain the amazing energies of George French. With the postwar collapse of real estate prices, he was drawn into land speculation. The obstacle to restoring the productivity, and hence the value, to land was the lack of the capital needed for hiring free labor. French hit upon the idea of allowing a family, willing to clear a tract of his land and prepare it for planting, to cultivate the tract for three years free of rent.[51] He also became involved in local schemes for building railroads.[52]

Of all of his business activities none evoked from him more enthusiasm than the plantation that he bought at Rocky Point on the Cape Fear above Wilmington. The preoccupation of French with this estate, however, does not at all seem to be the case of a successful bourgeois parvenu trying to play the gentleman. Quite the contrary. Far from trying to imitate the gentry, this hustling young man who had made his appearance so recently on the Cape Fear was brash enough to presume to teach lessons in farming to his neighbors, men whose families had been supervising plantations along the river for more than a century. The

49. Wilmington *Dispatch*, October 20, 1865.
50. Wilmington *Star*, September 23, October 10, 1867.
51. Wilmington *Post*, August 13, 1867.
52. Wilmington Weekly *Journal*, May 14, 1869.

estate that was to become the focal point of his boundless ambition he appropriately named Excelsior, and, perhaps foreshadowing a bold departure from ante-bellum agriculture techniques, he organized the enterprise as the Excelsior Plantation Company, with himself as president and his brothers, who had now joined him on the Cape Fear, as directors.

Neighboring planters might stand by helplessly as their fields reverted into the primeval swamps that their ancestors had reclaimed for rice in the eighteenth century; but George French, who by Cape Fear standards was almost totally devoid of ancestors, was nevertheless managing, despite this deficiency, to make Excelsior hum with activity. He believed in fertilizer. So did many other people. But French carried his belief to extremes that some citizens found offensive. During the evening hours, for example, when people in Wilmington used to like to sit on their verandas and enjoy the cool breezes, the insufferable Yankee would have his sewerage cart on the streets collecting the harvest of fertilizer that the city contributed to Excelsior, "dragging the filthy load through our public streets before anybody has thought of retiring to rest."[53]

George French's zeal for fertilizer eventually led him to a source of supply if not richer at least more accessible than Wilmington night soil. He discovered limestone deposits on Excelsior Plantation,[54] where he opened quarries and began manufacturing lime. Outstripping his own need for fertilizer, he was eventually employing 110 hands in this operation and was doing a brisk business supplying lime to the local market.[55] He thus pioneered in an industry that would figure large in the economy of the lower Cape Fear in the twentieth century.[56]

Whether fertilized by lime or by the energy of George French, the crops planted at Excelsior grew rapidly and well. In 1872, for

53. Wilmington *Daily Journal*, September 25, 1869.
54. *Ibid.*, February 6, 1874; Mattie Bloodworth, *History of Pender County, North Carolina* (Richmond: The Dietz Printing Co., 1947), p. 88.
55. Wilmington *Review*, September 29, 1884.
56. Duncan Peter Randall, "Geographic Factors in the Growth and Economy of Wilmington, North Carolina" (Doctoral dissertation, The University of North Carolina, 1965), pp. 98-100.

example, he was credited with having produced the first ear of green corn of the season to appear on the lower Cape Fear.[57] This was an important achievement for the New Englander because he had already launched another industry which would eventually help revitalize the economy of the region, the production of early fruits and vegetables for the northern market. He "has already shipped eight-hundred bushels of peaches and will begin picking his grapes soon," the *Journal* reported;[58] and the following year the same paper noted the shipment of sixty barrels of radishes from Excelsior to New York.[59] Edited by a former state leader of the Ku Klux Klan,[60] the *Journal* rarely had any kind word for northern-born Republicans, but in the case of French the paper conceded that he was "one of our very best farmers and he has done wonders at the famous Excelsior Plantation."[61]

It might appear that a man with such varied business activities would have little time for anything else. But this was not the case. Admitted to the aristocratic New Hanover Agricultural Society, this raucous carpetbagger was soon taking an active part on a committee that was studying ways of reactivating the rice industry and of promoting the production of peanuts.[62] He devoted even greater energy to the activities of the more plebeian Patrons of Husbandry, or Grange.[63]

In his political behavior French angered many of his fellow whites. He acted as if he were oblivious to what was to them an obvious fact, that on the lower Cape Fear there were two worlds and each had its prescribed place. He, on the other hand, did not regard Negroes as a distinctly different sort of human beings; but rather he saw them primarily as voters to whom he must appeal whenever he desired political influence, an attitude that many whites regarded as unprincipled or dangerously demagogic.

57. Wilmington *Daily Journal*, June 8, 1872.
58. *Ibid.*, July 7, 1871.
59. *Ibid.*, April 21, 1872.
60. Joseph Gregoire de Roulhac Hamilton, *Reconstruction in North Carolina* (New York: Columbia University Press, 1914), p. 461, hereinafter cited as Hamilton, *Reconstruction*.
61. Wilmington *Daily Journal*, February 13, 1873.
62. Wilmington *Weekly Journal*, December 25, 1868.
63. Wilmington *Daily Journal*, March 13, 1874.

Yet French was largely successful in his efforts to win the support of the Negroes. In their stumbling ascent from the prudent silence of bondage, they were drawn toward the man who could say the right words for them. George French was such a "slick talking man," one of his Negro supporters once remarked, that if he should ever happen to be "away from home and get strapped, he could preach his way back without the slightest trouble."[64] Some Negroes in Wilmington once even formed a "George Z. French Baseball Club."[65] He served for a time as chairman of the New Hanover County Republican party, as a member of the Wilmington Board of Aldermen, as Mayor pro tem of Wilmington; and he was elected to the legislature in 1870 and in 1894.[66]

French would live to see the day when predominant opinion throughout America would identify freedom with the privileges of men who were successful, rich, and had white skin. Considered as an individual, he himself was just such a man. But politically he was identified too closely for his own good with men who were unsuccessful, poor, and who had dark skin. When he was seventy, a white-supremacist mob dragged him through the streets of Wilmington with a rope around his neck, and drove him from the community in which he had made his home for more than thirty years and where he had pioneered in establishing two major industries.

Throughout the Cape Fear country during Reconstruction, the political assets of the Republican leaders are not usually hard to detect. French and Abbott combined a certain personal popularity with success in business, while Galloway owed his prominence almost entirely to his gifts as a popular orator and to his sharpness in debate. There were others, usually disaffected members of the gentry having a Whiggish background, whose family homes were an asset even in Republican circles. In the Cape Fear region Republican leaders of this type included Edward Cantwell, members of the Russell family of Brunswick and the Dockerys of Richmond County. The latter were important in

64. Wilmington *Post*, January 29, 1882.
65. Wilmington *Star*, May 10, 1868.
66. Wilmington *Post*, August 9, 1867; Wilmington *Daily Journal*, August 6, 1870; Wilmington *Star*, November 7, 1894.

Republican circles of southeastern North Carolina because their home county was in the same congressional district as most of the counties of the lower Cape Fear.

Since Republican leaders were men of such varied origin, it is not surprising that the party organization had no definite philosophy. The opinions of party leaders, however, fall into two rough groups, the Radical views of the popular leaders and the Whiggish views of the Republican businessmen. The differences between these two philosophies were not such as to preclude co-operation. The Radicals believed that all men, black, white, rich, or poor, should be equal before the law. Men holding to the old Whiggish tradition, on the other hand, believed that wealth, power, education, and talent are connected by a natural law. Just as ocean tides are drawn by the invisible bonds of the moon, so are wealth, power, and education drawn toward the person of ability; and, while the hand of man may momentarily interrupt this natural relationship, in the long run the stronger hand of nature will prevail.

It may be seen from this, that though the Whiggish Republican might regard the democratic ideas of the Radicals as naïve, at the same time, these were not ideas that he felt could threaten his position. Furthermore, he did not feel compelled to stridently assert his gentility or to ascribe special qualities to his white skin. His ideas were generally not so offensive to the democratic-minded plain people as those of the Conservatives who, in the Cape Fear country, did not always show Whiggish restraint and rationality. The *Journal* was capable of asserting that a projected demonstration by the Republicans "will bear about the same resemblance to *our* demonstration that a corn shucking or a bull-dance does to an important day in the House of Lords!"[67]

By and large, throughout the Cape Fear region in 1868, the candidates that the Republican party advanced, both Whiggish and Radical, were men of real standing in their own party. This was by no means true, however, for the original slate of candi-

67. Wilmington Weekly *Journal*, August 24, 1868 (emphasis in the original); Thomas B. Alexander, "Persistent Whiggery in the Confederate South, 1860-1877," *The Journal of Southern History*, XXVII (1961), 305-29 *passim*.

dates that the party advanced for the municipal government of Wilmington. In fact, when one considers that these men were nominated immediately following a sharp political conflict over the ratification of the new Constitution, the names appearing on the ticket appear to have been curiously chosen indeed. In order to write a Constitution based on the principle of universal manhood suffrage, the party in the opening months of 1868 had braved a storm of abuse from the more vocal classes and from most of the state newspapers. Yet immediately afterwards its leaders secured the nomination of men to govern North Carolina's principal city whose selection could have pleased few of the voters in either party.

Despite the fact that Wilmington had a Negro majority, despite the fact that the overwhelming majority of the Republican voters there were Negroes, despite the fact that a number of the more competent Negro leaders had settled in Wilmington, the original Republican ticket did not include the name of a single Negro. Furthermore, it included the name of only one white man, George Zadoc French, in whom the Negroes had some special interest. Bypassed were the most active spokesmen for civil rights, for mass education, for the Freedmen's Bureau, and the other popular speakers of neighborhood rallies.

What kind of men did the Republican leaders pick to administer Wilmington? With one exception, they appear to have been men who in a political sense owed nothing to the multitude in the streets, though a number of them owed at least a portion of their livelihood to patronage provided by the Republican machine in Raleigh and Wilmington. French was the only one of the nine candidates who enjoyed personal popularity.

Joseph H. Neff, for example, the successful Republican candidate for mayor, presided over a ship's chandlery business, where he sold marine paints, cars, nautical instruments, ship's stores, and charts. Neff seldom missed an occasion to identify himself publicly with the Union cause and the Republican party. At his establishment on South Water Street, a flag flew gaily at topmast each Fourth of July, and sadly at half-mast each Memorial Day for the Union dead, commemorations which the Conservatives generally did not observe.[68] But, despite the offices that he accepted from the party, despite his public ceremonial Republicanism, Neff took no active part in campaigns. Furthermore, if he held any political opinions whatsover, apart from his ritualistic identification with the party, those opinions do not seem to have found their way into print.

The most apparent motivation of Neff's political posture seemed to be the requirements of his business, which undoubtedly was heavily dependent upon the patronage of his federal custom house, the revenue cutter, the quarantine station, the lighthouse, and other federal marine installations in the area. Neff's politics appear to have been a matter of business more than a matter of convictions.

There were other candidates for the Wilmington Board of Aldermen whose occupations tended to make them more responsive to the Republican machine in Raleigh and Washington than they were to the Republican voter in Wilmington. Edwin R. Brink, for example, was the local postmaster; Denard Rumley was the federal collector of customs for the port of Wilmington.[69] Like Neff, these men were rarely if ever listed among those "noticed to have been present" by newspaper reporters covering the public meetings of the Republican party. They managed to keep their political opinions as much a private matter as they made their political position a matter of public record.

Two other Republican candidates for the Board of Aldermen were not only strangers to the public political meetings of the city, but also did not even have the distinction of holding important federal jobs. They were William C. Thurston and Robert Henning, both professional bookkeepers. Thurston was employed by a prominent Republican business firm of the city, while Henning was the private secretary of incumbent Conservative mayor John Dawson![70]

Besides George Zadoc French, the most distinguished Republican on the ticket was Silas N. Martin, whose "integrity and

68. Wilmington *Herald*, December 13, 1865; January 16, 1873.
69. Wilmington *Star*, May 14, 1868.
70. Wilmington *Star*, May 14, 1868.

knowledge" had led to his appointment the year before by a Conservative governor to represent North Carolina at the Paris Exposition.[71] Though neither a popular leader nor outspoken in his views, he was in no visible way dependent upon federal patronage, being independently wealthy and retired from business.[72] One can in fact ascribe no motive to Martin's seeking office other than his moderate Republican political opinions.

The Conservatives breathed easier when they realized that, if the genie of Radical democracy was running amuck in the Cape Fear country, at least Wilmington was being spared. They were not in the least disturbed because the original Republican ticket for the Board of Aldermen, except for French and Martin, was an undistinguished list of federal office-holders and political nonentities. The Republican ticket was not "so bad as it might have been," the *Star* sighed with relief. Though some of the candidates were said to be "Radical enough to eat snake-root (and especially the 'copperhead' kind)," most were "disposed to be conservative (observe, please, we don't use a capital C)."[73]

Why did this list include so many conservative nonentities who had no standing with the voters of either party? By the spring of 1868 the Republicans had won the support of certain members of the Wilmington business class and the party's curious choice of candidates for the local administration may have been an effort to make further gains among this small but highly influential group. By the twentieth century the distinction between the two elite classes would become blurred. But during Reconstruction one could still detect in the various patterns of individual association on the lower Cape Fear that it was a matter of concern to well-to-do families whether their wealth originated with an eighteenth-century plantation or a nineteenth-century counting house.

But the business community was scarcely a "middle" class in any ordinary sense. They were at least the equals of the "bloods,"

71. Jonathan Worth to Martin, February 9, 1867, Governor's Papers, Worth, North Carolina State Archives.
72. Martin to Curtis R. Brogden, July 17, 1875, Governor's Papers, Brogden, North Carolina State Archives; Wilmington *Post*, January 26, 1877.
73. Wilmington *Star*, May 14, 1868.

as the gentry was sometimes called,[74] in both wealth and education, lacking in fact only ancestors and perhaps a few aristocratic
vices. Though a small group, the business class was in a politically
strategic position: They dominated Wilmington and Wilmington
dominated the lower Cape Fear. They were courted by both the
Conservatives and the Republicans.

Unlike the gentry, the business class was no homogeneous
group, united by century-old bonds of blood and marriage. On
the contrary they included many first and second generation newcomers in the Cape Fear.[75] In their cultural heritage, furthermore, the families connected with commerce presented a rich
variety; and when they differed politically, the division sometimes
followed the lines of their cultural differences. For example, before Appomattox, the Germans and the Jews had been regarded
as staunch supporters of the old society. In 1853, they had created
the German Volunteers, which provided an outlet for middle class
military ardor in much the same way as the Wilmington Light
Infantry did for the more pugnacious young "bloods." Perhaps
the case of Captain Jacob Wessell indicates some of the pride with
which the Germans and the Jews regarded the Volunteers.
Captain Wessell made a fortune on the lower Cape Fear and in
the late 1850's retired to his native Germany to spend it. With the
outbreak of war, however, he returned to Wilmington on a
blockade-runner and joined his old friends who were fighting
under Lee in the Army of Northern Virginia.[76]

While the Germans and the Jews took pride in the loyalty
they had shown to the Confederacy, such was not the case of the

74. Wilmington *Post*, September 3, 1882.
75. A Wilmington city directory appearing about 1884, listing the birthplaces
of most of the partners of "leading business interests," indicates that sixty-eight
were born in North Carolina, or other Southern states, twenty-three were born in
foreign countries, and fifteen were born in the North, mostly in New England.
However, the family names and business connections suggest that a number of
those giving North Carolina as their place of birth were in fact descended from an
older generation of German, Jewish, and New England settlers on the Cape Fear.
J. S. Reilly (ed.), *Wilmington: Past, Present and Future* (n.p.: n.d. [c. 1884]).
76. Wilmington *Star*, January 7, 1879; Wilmington *Review*, March 30, 1887;
Bryant Whitlock Ruark, "Some Phases of Reconstruction in Wilmington and the
County of New Hanover," *Trinity College Historical Papers* (Durham: Trinity
College, 1889-1924), Ser. 11, 79-112 *passim*.

ante-bellum New Englanders. They were suspected of Union sympathies. One of these, a man who had lived most of his life in the city and was regarded as a model of civic virtue, barely escaped a beating at the hands of an irate Confederate on that account.[77] A possible explanation for the views of the New Englanders is the fact that a number of them were engaged in the lumber industry; and, hence, were not so dependent as the Germans and the Jews upon the "blood" dominated plantation economy. Secondly, the Yankees continued to maintain close ties with their strongly Republican native region.

Whatever the reason, with the coming of peace, at least four prominent New England families joined the Republican ranks,[78] as did most of the postwar immigrants from the same area. Except for the New Englanders, however, the business class was not particularly receptive to Republican ideas. In the spring of 1868 the party was rebuffed in an effort to persuade some Germans to run for office on the Republican ticket.[79] Following the election, furthermore, a Conservative newspaper published a request by a prominent Jewish leader for the editor to scotch rumors that he had voted for the new Constitution, a document which ironically enough, for the first time in North Carolina history, granted the right of Jews to hold public office.[80]

It was probably the contest between the Conservatives and the Republicans for the support of the strategic business class that explains the fact that the Republicans bypassed most of their prominent local leaders in favor of politically obscure men. The popular Republican, using the roof of the market house for his rostrum, might be able to hold entranced the Negro throng in the street below. But the more conservative businessmen, such as the Germans and the Jews, were not so favorably impressed by these performances. To them the popular orator was likely to be a

77. U.S. Congress, Joint Committee on Reconstruction, *Report of the Joint Committee: Part II, Virginia, North Carolina, South Carolina*, Reports of the Committees, Vol. II, 39 Cong., 1 sess., 1866, p. 269.

78. The families of Silas N. Martin, Edward Kidder, George R. French, George Chadbourn, and J. M. Chadbourn.

79. Wilmington Weekly *Journal*, April 3, 1868.

80. Wilmington *Daily Journal*, April 24, 1868.

dangerous demagogue. So, if in selecting a ticket for the Wilmington Board of Aldermen, the Republicans chose only one man with any demonstrated political talent, at the same time they chose men whose economic status proclaimed their conservatism to the cautious business class. The wealth of Martin and French seemed to be insurance that they would not be guilty of the more irresponsible forms of Radicalism, while many of the other candidates were domesticated by their dependence upon patronage.

The Conservatives won the contest for the allegiance of the business class. It is true that the Republicans were able to persuade an obscure German grocer to run for the Board of Aldermen, and withdrew the name of another nonentity from their ticket in order to make room for him; but, except for the New Englanders, the Conservatives would retain the support of the businessmen; and, though for the next thirty years their party would remain a minority in Wilmington, outnumbered two to one, the fact that their ranks would include most of the educated and talented middle class would have unhappy consequences for the Republicans.

By July, 1868, it was apparent that the Republican bid for the support of the business class had failed. At this point the party radically revised its ticket with a view to making it more popular if less respectable. Silas Martin was replaced with Lawson Rice. Unlike Martin, Rice was not rich nor in the eyes of the middle class did he enjoy Martin's prestige of many years standing. But Rice was a more familiar and popular figure in Republican meetings.

A newcomer to the area, until 1863 Rice had been a partner in his family's woodworking business in Lawrence, Massachusetts. After serving in the navy during the latter part of the war, he migrated to the lower Cape Fear, where his family had had connections for more than two generations. There he became associated with General Abbott's Cape Fear Building Company, applying his knowledge of the woodworking industry at the Abbottsburg plant.[81] Like many other New Englanders, he became

81. Wilmington *Post*, December 4, 1881; Wilmington *Daily Journal*, August 10, 1875.

active in the Republican party, receiving so many Negro visitors in his home that the *Journal* once sourly inquired if he were not operating a Negro boarding house.[82]

A change of even greater significance in the Republican ticket for Wilmington was the inclusion of two Negro leaders, William Kellogg, Jr., the proprietor of a small shop for building carriages and wagons, and George M. Price, Jr., a navy veteran who had established a real estate business in Wilmington after the war. Supported politically by his father, a popular Methodist minister, Price had achieved considerable influence in the Negro community.[83] In predominantly Republican Wilmington, once the party had settled upon candidates, their election was almost a foregone conclusion. Yet, though elections had been set for July, 1868, the Republicans were cheated out of a victory at the polls, not by the Conservatives to be sure, but by a limitation of the constitution which they themselves had written, a provision requiring that in order to become a registered voter one must first swear to uphold the constitution. There were no such registered voters. Was Wilmington to remain under Conservative control for months while election officials administered oaths and registered voters? The Republican legislature provided an answer to this problem when it passed an act setting Wilmington city elections for January, 1869, thus providing time for a new registration, but, at the same time, declaring the offices vacant and empowering the Republican governor to fill them by executive appointment.[84] Governor Holden promptly filled the vacancies with the local Republican candidates.

In their eagerness to gain control of North Carolina's chief city, the Republicans had done violence to the formalities of local self-government. Not many years would pass before they would be bitterly denouncing the legislature for overriding the agencies of local self-government. But, for the time being, it was the turn of the Conservatives to conduct their assault from the high

82. Wilmington *Daily Journal*, January 7, 1871.

83. T. M. Haddock (ed.), *Haddock's Wilmington, N.C., Directory and General Advertiser Containing a General and Business Directory of the City, Historical Sketch, State, County, City Government, etc. etc.* [*sic*] (Wilmington: P. Heinsberger, 1871); Wilmington *Daily Journal*, July 20, 1869.

84. North Carolina, *Laws*, Special Sess., 1868, ch. 2.

ground of democracy; and the retiring Conservative Board of Aldermen in Wilmington could now attack the "tyrannical and anti-republican" action of the legislature whereby the "will of the citizens of Wilmington is entirely disregarded;"[85] though, from the point of view of the Conservatives, when the "will of the citizens" was finally consulted, in the January elections of 1869, the verdict was by no means a happier one.

The Conservatives did not surrender control willingly. "Sheriff" Bunting, denying the legality of the deluge of Negro ballots that had buried him in April, ignoring an act of the legislature postponing the election until January, declared the polls in Wilmington open on July 16, 1868; and two sets of Conservative candidates ran against each other, a performance which the Republicans ignored. The next day the Conservatives announced the victors in this "quiet" election; and, not for the last time, Wilmington had two city governments.[86] But Governor Holden, who had broken with President Johnson and was now making common cause with the Radicals, wired for troops and the Conservatives yielded.[87]

It was no ordinary change of administration that took place on July 30, 1868; and the local editor and the Conservative *Star*, in describing the formalities of the transfer, seemed to sense some of the portentousness of the occasion: "At twelve o'clock our worthy Mayor, Honorable John Dawson, slowly ascended the City Hall steps, and with his usual dignified and stately trend, entered his office (his to be no longer), where awaited him, in the full consciousness of his newly and illegally acquired power, the new Mayor, Mr. Joseph H. Neff. . . . The proceedings were carried on in the deathless [*sic*] silence, not even the breathing of the large crowd of negroes, assembled to witness the performance, being audible."[88] Two Negro aldermen had taken their seats in the City Hall. Three blocks from that building, and only three and a half years earlier, Negroes had been bought and sold in Wilmington.

85. Wilmington *Star*, July 30, 1868.
86. *Ibid.*, July 17, 26, 1868.
87. Hamilton, *Reconstruction*, p. 345.
88. Wilmington *Star*, July 31, 1868.

V ⚙ *"Government of Pure Brute Force"*

"AT ONE DASH OF THE PEN," THE *Journal* WROTE CONCERNING the ratification of the new constitution, "we have been remitted from such checks and balances as the accumulated wisdom of the ages had shown to be proper in a free government, to a government of pure brute force; to a government based upon population alone."[1] The Conservatives felt that they were surrendering power, not because their ideas had lost validity, nor because they had lost an argument, nor even because they had lost an election, conducted according to somebody else's rules. They were being overwhelmed by force. This view would influence their attitude toward the laws that a Republican legislature would pretend to pass. It would cause them to take a more tolerant attitude toward certain activities which most societies at most times have regarded as outrageous lawlessness.

Of all the "checks and balances" that the Conservatives had accumulated from the "wisdom of the ages" none had had such a steadying influence upon the half-free presidentially-reconstructed, Black Code regimes of the South as the county militia organizations. It was essentially these same units, reorganized and renamed variously, sometimes known as "county patrols" or "paddyrollers" in ante-bellum days, or as Home Guard companies during the war, that had meant security for the plantation big house as well as terror for the cabin.

1. Wilmington *The Daily Journal*, March 21, 1868, hereinafter cited as Wilmington *Daily Journal* or Wilmington Weekly *Journal*.

In the Cape Fear region New Hanover County had the most important military organizations. Before the war there had been the German Volunteers and the Wilmington Light Infantry, recruited from the middle class and the gentry respectively.[2] With the outbreak of war, furthermore, another company was formed in Wilmington, the Cape Fear Riflemen, drawn largely from the working class.[3] These companies were incorporated into the Eighteenth North Carolina, known as the "Bloody Eighteenth."[4] The members of the Wilmington Light Infantry, however, drawn from families having strong martial traditions, "the very flower of our young chivalry," advanced more rapidly in rank during the course of the war than was true of the other companies, the company serving as a "nursery of officers . . . there was scarcely a single noncommissioned officer or private who went with the command to Fort Caswell in April, 1861, but who obtained some commission from the grade of lieutenant to that of full colonel."[5]

Ostensibly the Eighteenth North Carolina dissolved with the Confederacy, but by December, 1865, another regiment of eight companies had been formed,[6] the New Hanover County Militia, which appears to have been very nearly a reincarnation of the indomitable Bloody Eighteenth. This force, together with Conservative companies that had been formed earlier in Duplin, Bladen,[7] and other counties, soon overshadowed the Union army of occupation, which by 1868 had dwindled to a detachment of fifty-three men stationed in Wilmington.[8]

2. By the last decade of the nineteenth century the Wilmington Light Infantry would have lost some of its aristocratic character. A muster in 1890, for example, listed some German names. Wilmington *Messenger*, May 28, 1890.

3. Wilmington *Daily Journal*, August 25, 1874.

4. Wilmington *Review*, June 19, 1889.

5. Wilmington *The Morning Star*, January 7, 1879. This paper began in 1867 as *The Evening Star*, but after a few months changed to *The Morning Star*, hereinafter cited as Wilmington *Star*.

6. Wilmington *The Daily Herald*, December 15, 1865. This paper first appeared in 1865 as *Herald of the Union*, but shortly thereafter began to appear as *The Wilmington Herald* or *The Daily Herald*, hereinafter cited as Wilmington *Herald*.

7. *The War of the Rebellion: A Compilation of the Official Records of the Union and Confederate Armies*, 128 vols. (Washington: Government Printing Office, 1895), XLVII, Pt. III, Ser. I, 396; Wilmington *Herald*, May 13, 1865; Philadelphia *Inquirer*, August 9, 1865.

8. Joseph Gregoire de Roulhac Hamilton, *Reconstruction in North Carolina*

This seeming revival of Confederate military might on the lower Cape Fear did not result, however, from any lack of vigilance on the part of the Union commander, General George Crook, who had replaced General Ames as officer in charge of the District of Wilmington. On the contrary, General Crook appears to have shared the fear of many Conservatives that the Negroes were planning an Emancipation Day revolt for January 1, 1866, comparable to the one that had momentarily brought down the municipal government of Wilmington the previous August.[9] "It is his wish," the *Dispatch* reported, "that the citizens shall form themselves into companies for volunteer service in case of emergency. He will furnish them with arms and ammunition, and will aid and sustain them with the entire power at his command."[10]

With this reconciliation between the blue and the gray the same paper could predict with confidence that "nothing could be more suicidal than an attempted insurrection on the part of the negroes. The combined strength of the citizens and United States troops would be brought against them; summary vengeance would be visited on all who would be captured; and those who escaped would be hunted and driven like wild beasts, from one point of refuge to another until life would be but little preferable to the death from which they were fleeing."[11] It is possible that the rapid revival of Confederate-Conservative military might during Presidential Reconstruction prevented a Negro insurrection, though apart from the fears expressed by certain Conservatives there does not appear to be any evidence that such a thing was planned. But for all of their military power, the Conservatives seemed incapable of bringing orderly government to the lower Cape Fear.

Within a week of the revival of the New Hanover County regi-

(New York: Columbia University Press, 1914), p. 239, hereinafter cited as Hamilton, *Reconstruction*. By the spring of 1866, the legislature had created, on paper at least, ten regiments for the seven counties of the lower Cape Fear, Bladen, Brunswick, Columbus, Duplin, New Hanover, Robeson, and Sampson. North Carolina, *Public Laws*, 1866, ch. 23.

9. Wilmington *Herald*, January 3, 1866.
10. Wilmington *Dispatch*, November 27, 1865.
11. *Ibid.*

ment, under the command of Confederate officers, it was reported that "every house on the Plank Road, with scarcely an exception, has been visited and pillaged by . . . [armed] bands of refugees, who are encamped around Wilmington, hiding themselves during the day and robbing all night. They represent themselves as soldiers. . . . Several families have been driven off, and others have been trying to get away. . . ."[12] Within another week there had been a gun battle on the Wilmington water front between "police and citizens," on the one hand, and some Negro sailors, on the other. The sailors finally seized a ferryboat and escaped to their ship, leaving behind a wounded sailor and a wounded police officer.[13] In February, 1867, there were reports of the activities of a group of armed men calling themselves the "Regulators." "This band who have been committing such outrages in neighboring counties, and apparently with impunity, are now invading New Hanover, committing all manner of depredations upon the freedmen, stealing their mules, money, &c. [sic], and exciting terror wherever they go. No greater blow could be struck at the labor system than this. . . . This thing *must be stopped, and at once,* or the community, outside of the towns and cities is ruined. . . ."[14]

The Superintendent of the Freedmen's Bureau at Wilmington suggested a possible reason why "the civil authorities are either unable or unwilling to arrest and punish the men belonging to these bands. . . . These Regulators confine their depredations and outrages to the property and persons of the freedmen and the white citizens are either in collusion with them or purchase their own security by a quick acquiescence."[15] With the dignity of law

12. Wilmington *Daily Journal*, December 22, 1865.
13. *Ibid.*, December 28, 1865.
14. Wilmington Weekly *Journal*, February 22, 1867.
15. Allen Rutherford to Jacob F. Chur, February 12, 1867, Governor's Papers, Worth, North Carolina State Archives, hereinafter cited as Worth Papers. Further details concerning the Regulators may be found in Jonathan Worth to James Voty Bomford, February 18, 1867, Worth Papers; United States War Department, Bureau of Refugees, Freedmen and Abandoned Lands (Record Group 105), North Carolina, General Orders . . . Monthly and Annual Reports . . . , Annual Report for 1866 of the Superintendent of the Southern District of North Carolina, Wilmington, October 29, 1866; and United States War Department, Bureau of Refugees, Freedmen and Abandoned Lands, *Report of the Commissioner,* 1867, 40 Cong., 2 sess., p. 667.

thoroughly compromised, it is understandable that the agencies of local government were rarely successful in asserting their authority over the Negroes where there was any prospect of evasion or violent resistance. As late as June, 1868, there was a major riot in Wilmington touched off by the efforts of a Negro mob to set free city prisoners.[16]

The adoption of a new Constitution in 1868, which brought to an end political control by the Conservatives, also removed the legal basis for the county militias that had existed during Presidential Reconstruction. The Republicans begin to consider the type of military organization that they should create for the new regime. They had grown used to looking to the federal government for the force necessary to carry out their Reconstruction policies. It had been federal troops that had stopped the marauding by the Duplin County police in 1865;[17] and federal troops that had broken up the "orphan-raids" conducted by the Sampson County Court in 1866,[18] and it had been for federal troops that Holden had appealed in 1868 when the Conservatives refused to yield control to either the elected or to the appointed Republican officials on the lower Cape Fear.[19]

But could the Republicans continue to count on the federal government? In the first place the Conservatives of the elite classes had been successful diplomats in neutralizing or winning over northern soldiers to their way of thinking. Secondly, now that the South was back in the union, who could say which party would control the federal government five years hence?

The Republicans decided to create a new state militia. They needed a military arm that would be radically different from the militia organizations of the past, one that would strengthen rather than threaten their regime. Yet, it would have been politically difficult for them to have created a militia composed exclusively of the friends of the new regime, and one that consistently ex-

16. Wilmington *Star*, June 23, 1868.

17. Philadelphia *Inquirer*, August 9, 1865.

18. U.S. Congress, Joint Committee on Reconstruction, *Report of the Joint Committee: Part II, Virginia, North Carolina, South Carolina*, Reports of the Committees, Vol. II, 39 Cong., 1 sess., 1866, pp. 270-71.

19. Hamilton, *Reconstruction*, p. 345.

cluded its enemies. Such a policy of disarming one's enemies and arming one's friends would have offended a large number of people who believed that it was possible to have a politically neutral militia.

In theory the militia existed for the purpose of repelling foreign invasion, as well as putting down outbreaks of disorder at home; and, since neither of these functions was supposed to have anything to do with politics; and, since the militia was presumed to be subordinate to the civil authorities, it was considered no business of the state to scrutinize the politics of militia officers. Rather it was the business of the state to concern itself with the military experience of a potential officer, and not with the question as to which cause may have provided him with that experience during the late unpleasantness.

The Republicans almost universally paid lip-service to the ideal of a politically neutral militia; and, with the passage of the Militia Act of 1868, they wrote this ideal into law.[20] This act stipulates that if the militia was "called into service to preserve the peace in any election, the force shall be used to secure a fair and untrammeled vote of all electors without regard to their political opinion," and that, if a militiaman were found guilty of trying "to influence the vote of any citizen" while he was on active duty, he should be fined or imprisoned at the discretion of the court.

There was no political test made of officers other than that they take an oath to the new constitution, a step that most former Confederate officers had already taken by this time. It is true that when Governor Holden began issuing commissions he was not always faithful to the nonpartisan spirit of the Militia Act. Had he considered only military talent rather than politics, he would have entrusted the defense of his regime almost entirely to officers who regarded it, him, his party, and the constitution all as part of a general disaster that they had fought a war to prevent.

In actual practice Holden's militia policy seems to have been an ambivalent one. In some parts of North Carolina he created a politically reliable militia. In other areas he created a militia,

20. North Carolina, *Laws*, Special Sess., 1868, ch. 22.

which may have been competent enough in a military sense, but which lent little or no support to the Republican civil authorities. For their part, the Conservatives were revolted by the extent to which the governor's militia policy seemed to be controlled by political considerations. The *Journal* charged that there were "too many noncombatants filling important offices," a shortcoming which, from the point of view of the Conservatives, must have been inexcusable considering the abundance of splendid but unemployed military talent to be found up and down the Cape Fear. "It tickles Holden's vanity to be Commander-in-Chief of an army, even though . . . Federal Bureau agents and Quarter Masters are promoted to service in the field. These men do not intend to fight, what ever their ignorant and deluded followers may do."[21]

If it was true that too many of the leaders of the new militia were "noncombatants" who had no intention of fighting, the same could scarcely be said of some of the Conservatives. "I have received reliable reports, legally substantiated," a major-general reported to Governor Holden,

that several hundreds of Henry and Spencer rifles (many of them sixteen shooters) with accoutrements, &c. [*sic*], complete, have been received at Wilmington and thence distributed to organizations in this State, styling themselves "Seymour and Blair" Clubs and "K.K.K.'s. . . ." The Constitutional right of all citizens to the possession of arms for proper purposes does not extend to the perfecting of organizations, armed with weapons of a purely military character, such as those reported as having been received in such unusual quantities at Wilmington and other points. . . .[22]

In Piedmont North Carolina, where the Republicans failed to create a politically reliable militia, not many months would pass before such extralegal, quasi-military groups would reduce Republican civil authority to a shadow, the real power resting with the hooded chivalry.

But that was in the Piedmont. The experience of the East, particularly the Cape Fear Valley, was quite otherwise during

21. Wilmington Weekly *Journal*, September 25, 1868.
22. *Ibid.*, October 16, 1868.

these years. Indeed Reconstruction in North Carolina scarcely presents an antithesis more striking than the contrast between the Piedmont, with its political murders and skulduggery, and the lower Cape Fear, during the same years, with its peaceful debates, orderly elections, and normally-functioning courts. Only in the fringe counties of Robeson and Sampson were there outbreaks of Klan and related violence.

The immediate event that brought peace to the lower Cape Fear was the sudden evaporation in the spring of 1868 of the formidable Conservative military establishment in the area. But this was an event that is not easy to explain. Why should Conservative military power first disappear in the area of its greatest strength? During Presidential Reconstruction New Hanover had probably been the only county in the state where they had a force of regimental strength. The old order in the area, moreover, had also been sustained to some degree by the Ku Klux Klan, although there was some duplication of leadership between the Klan and the New Hanover Militia,[23] and the two organizations may have differed more in costume and ritual than in personnel or function.

The Klan seems to have made its first appearance in North Carolina at Wilmington; and Colonel William L. Saunders, a Wilmington historian and at various times editor of the *Journal* and chairman of the North Carolina Democratic Executive Committee, was head of the state organization.[24] Yet in 1868, at the very moment when such organizations were rapidly gaining ground in the Piedmont, not only the New Hanover Militia, but also the Klan vanished from the lower Cape Fear; and there is no further evidence of its activities within fifty miles of Saunders' home town.[25]

23. Colonel Roger Moore was a regimental staff officer in the New Hanover Militia as well as the local head of the Klan. William Lord De Rossett, *Pictorial and Historical New Hanover County and Wilmington, North Carolina, 1723-1938* (Wilmington: published by the author, 1938), p. 30; Wilmington *Herald*, December 15, 1865.

24. Hamilton, *Reconstruction*, p. 461.

25. There would continue to be sporadic Klan activity in Sampson County. As late as 1871 a United States commissioner informed Governor Tod R. Caldwell that in the area around Clinton it would be "useless and dangerous to attempt further

Of course the Conservatives did not suddenly forget their ancient heritage of arms. But, unlike their confederates in central North Carolina during Congressional Reconstruction, they were scrupulous to confine their military interests to activities that in no way could be construed as a challenge to the local administration. For example, they founded a rifle club, which established a firing range on Eagle Island near Wilmington and awarded prizes to the best marksmen.[26]

In a similar vein was the Cape Fear Academy, a boys' school, which General R. E. Colston founded at Wilmington in 1868. General Colston was assisted in this enterprise by Frank H. Alfriend, a biographer of Jefferson Davis; as well as Richard K. Meade, "of Virginia," it goes without saying, who was further qualified for his post by the fact that he was "a gentleman well known for his literary attainments, and services in the 'lost cause.' "[27] The association of the Academy with the lost cause was further strengthened, on the occasion of a visit of General Robert E. Lee to Wilmington, when "each member of the corps enjoyed the honor of an introduction and a cordial shake of the hand of the old general."[28]

The appearance of the cadets on the streets filled some aging Confederate veterans with a nostalgia for the intoxicating days of 1861: "General Colston's band of little 'rebs' were out yesterday on parade, in all of the glory of the gallant grey, brass buttons and bright muskets. They served to remind us strongly of the time when . . . [we] first donned the grey and bore the musket behind a soul-stirring fife and drum to the glorious tune of 'Dixie.' "[29]

"We have never seen better drilling since the bloody Eighteenth," the same paper later remarked.[30]

The skirmish drills and target practice of the cadets in the

---

arrest without the assistance of the military." Edwin W. Quigg to Caldwell, October 5, 1871, Governor's Papers, Caldwell, North Carolina State Archives, hereinafter cited as Caldwell Papers.

26. Wilmington *Daily Journal*, July 17, 1875; Wilmington *Star*, March 27, 1877.
27. Wilmington *Daily Journal*, September 10, 1869.
28. *Ibid.*, April 30, 1870.
29. *Ibid.*, April 16, 1869.
30. *Ibid.*, January 17, 1871.

suburbs of Wilmington seemed to have prompted no expressions
of hostility from the Republicans, though one of their military
maneuvers in the downtown area caused a flurry of excitement.
The drove of tame deer that grazed on the lawn before the City
Hall had witnessed indifferently many tempestuous demonstrations by Wilmington's boisterous Negro throng. Yet these same
animals, who owed their positions at the City Hall to a Republican administration, when they sighted a relentless band of
"double quicking" young men in rebel gray approaching the
grounds, were suddenly seized by panic. They stampeded wildly,
two of them bounding over the iron grillwork, making good their
escape.[31]

Why was it that the Conservatives of the Piedmont could
make a judge flee in terror while those of the lower Cape Fear,
with their splendid martial traditions, could only scare deer? The
answer appears to be twofold. In the first place the Republican
authorities on the lower Cape Fear enjoyed the confidence of the
Negro multitude, an important force in the area particularly at
Wilmington. The Conservatives had previously demonstrated
how difficult it was to govern without that confidence. Despite
the size of their county militia, despite General Robert Ransom's
police force of Confederate veterans, consisting at one time of one
hundred men, the Conservative regime had not always been able
to maintain order. The Republicans, on the other hand, were
able to maintain better order in Wilmington with a police force
of only seventeen whites and fifteen Negroes.[32]

The Republican administration on the lower Cape Fear seems
to have drawn political strength from the new system of popularly
elected magistrates that the new Constitution had introduced. It
could hardly be said that these justices, so many of them common
laborers with limited education, brought legal wisdom to the
bench. One of them, in fact, a Negro house painter, even tried to
determine the guilt or innocence of a man accused of murder by
means of the medieval ordeal of blood, the suspect being required

31. *Ibid.*, December 8, 1869.
32. Wilmington *Star*, August 12, 1868.

to place his hands on the victim's body on the supposition that if he were guilty fresh blood would flow from the murdered man's wounds.[33]

The democratically elected magistrates sometimes held primitive ideas, and rarely brought any legal learning to the bench. But they helped bring peace to Wilmington.[34] The ordinary people usually accepted the verdicts of these unlettered judges drawn from their own ranks; and there was no riot in Wilmington during the nine years of Republican administration, 1868-77.

Besides the strong political support that the Republicans enjoyed on the lower Cape Fear, a second reason for the relative stability of their regime in the area is the fact that they established there a formidable military force of their own, the lower Cape Fear being one of the few regions of the state in which Governor Holden authorized the formation of militia companies which were Republican in fact if not in name. A former Union officer, Colonel J. W. Schenck, who remained in the area several years after the war and had been elected New Hanover County sheriff, undertook the training of the new militia. The results could scarcely have reminded the Conservatives of the aristocratic Wilmington Light Infantry, which now no longer had a legal existence.

"We tell Colonel Schenck that his is engaged in an illegal and dangerous business," the *Journal* roared. Though Schenck was undoubtedly acting under the Militia Act of August 17, 1868, from the point of view of the *Journal* scarcely any law in North Carolina had been "legal" since the new constitution had been ratified. The colonel "may be a brave man," the paper continued in the same threatening tone, and he "may have won undying laurels in the late war, but when he undertakes to organize militia companies of negroes, and from his residence compliment their

33. Wilmington *Daily Journal*, January 20, 1876.
34. One of the earliest moves to reduce the importance of the popularly elected justices, however, came not from the Conservatives, but from the Whiggish group within the Republican party, who wanted to see a special criminal court created for Wilmington "to rid us of the insupportable taxation arising from the malpractice of the justices of the peace. . . ." M. London to Caldwell, November 21, 1873, Caldwell Papers.

midnight drills and offer rewards for their proficiency, he is step-
ping on dangerous ground."[35]

The force that Schenck began training in the fall of 1868 in
time emerged as the Twenty Second Regiment of North Carolina
Militia, consisting of companies "A" and "B" of the Wilmington
Rifle Guards; the Charles Sumner Light Infantry; the Brooklyn
Zouaves, named for a Negro neighborhood of Wilmington; and
the Wilmington Dragoons. Governor Holden placed in joint
command of this regiment two native-born Civil War veterans,
Colonel George L. Mabson and Colonel William Parker Canaday,[36] both of whom were staunch Republicans. The fact that
these two men had served on opposite sides during the war was
only one of several contrasting features of their respective careers.

George L. Mabson, "tall and slender [,] straight and thin,
presenting the ghostly appearance of a sage philosopher and states-
man,"[37] was the mulatto son of George W. Mabson[38] a white
"gentleman who stood high in Wilmington society."[39] The elder
Mabson had provided for the education of both of his mulatto
sons, George becoming a lawyer and William a schoolmaster.
Both in time would serve in the legislature.[40]

Paternal concern for their welfare, however, did not serve to
reconcile the two brothers either to the South's Peculiar Institution or to the tattered relics of that institution that would survive
for a century after Appomattox. With the outbreak of war,
George, who was then residing in Massachusetts, volunteered for
the Fifth Massachusetts Cavalry and took part in the capture of
Petersburg and Richmond.[41] Upon his discharge from the army,
he returned home to the Cape Fear, and in 1870 was elected to the

35. Wilmington Weekly *Journal*, September 18, 1868.
36. Wilmington *Daily Journal*, September 3, 1875.
37. Wilmington Weekly *Journal*, August 6, 1869.
38. Wilmington *Star*, July 31, 1868.
39. Wilmington *Post*, March 31, 1876.
40. Elaine Joan Nowaczyk, "The North Carolina Negro in Politics, 1865-1876"
(Master's thesis, The University of North Carolina, 1957), p. 180; Randolph Abbott
Shotwell and Nat Atkinson, *Legislative Record Giving the Acts Past, Session Ending
March, 1877: Together with Sketches of the Lives and Public Acts of the Members
of the Houses* (Raleigh: Edwards and Broughton, 1877), p. 9; W. H. Quick, *Negro
Stars in All Ages of the World* (Richmond: S. B. Adkins & Co., 1898), pp. 257-60.
41. Wilmington *Post*, March 31, 1876.

North Carolina House. The following year he became the first
Negro attorney admitted to the charmed circle of the New Hanover County Bar.[42]

William Parker Canaday had little in common with Colonel
Mabson except political opinions. A white native of Carteret
County, his humble origins and limited education are inadver-
tently announced in much of his writing. Yet he was a man of
considerable gifts, with a personal integrity to which even his
enemies would attest.[43]

With the outbreak of war in 1861, the seventeen-year-old
Canaday enlisted as a private in the Confederate army, and remained in the army until its final defeat in 1865, rising in rank
from private to lieutenant. During his youth he had developed
a bitter distaste for what appeared to him to be the snobbishness
and arrogance of the "bloods," an attitude which, coupled with
his sympathy for the plain people of the South, converted him at
the age of twenty-three, only two years after he had doffed the
Confederate gray, into a charter member of the North Carolina
Republican party. Unlike many white Republicans, his democratic beliefs were fairly consistent, making him a vigorous
champion of Negro rights. In 1872, he began a ten-year association with North Carolina's most important Republican newspaper, the Wilmington *Post*, a paper to which he brought a
militant democratic spirit, if not high literary standards.[44]

The development of the Republican militia probably reached
its highest point about 1875, at which time the *Journal* charged
that "there are now nearly, or quite as many negro companies in
this city, as there are white companies throughout the limits of
North Carolina."[45] It is interesting that though the *Journal* and
the *Post* debated the militia question for a month, a debate in
which the state Adjutant General participated, no exact information emerged concerning the correctness of the original charge as

42. Wilmington *Daily Journal*, June 20, 1871.
43. *Ibid.*, January 18, 1869, quoting the New Bern *Journal of Commerce*, no
date; Wilmington *Star*, June 2, 1877.
44. Wilmington *Post*, October 6, 1876, and *passim*.
45. Wilmington *Post*, January 6, 1876, quoting Wilmington *Journal*, December
19, 1875.

to whether there were more Negro or white companies. Probably this curious lack of factual knowledge was due to the unstable character of militia companies during Reconstruction.

During Reconstruction many militia organizations tended to become inactive, though one might remain a long while on the official militia rolls as a paper company before it finally legally ceased to exist. At the same time private bands would have been organized which had *de facto* if not *de jure* existence. The fate of a private *de facto* armed band largely depended upon the relative strength, in the courts and in the legislature, of its political friends and enemies. Its friends in the legislature might be able to put enough pressure on the governor, even though he be of the opposite party, to force him to incorporate the band as a company in the state militia and issue arms for it.

On the other hand, as in the case of an unofficial Negro company within the jurisdiction of a Conservative judge, it was possible for the enemies of a private band to obtain a court injunction against it declaring it to be "illegal and calculated to cause mischief."[46] After 1870, when the Conservatives gained control of the legislature and slowly began to extend their control to other branches of the state government, Conservative companies gradually became more numerous as Republican ones disappeared.[47] Because of the reluctance of the Republicans of the lower Cape Fear to allow their official companies to become inactive, in this region the Conservative campaign to disarm the Negroes took a long time indeed. As late as 1877 there were still two Negro companies in the area, as compared to four white, Conservative-led ones.[48] But by 1890 the last Negro company had been abolished on the Cape Fear.

As early as 1875, however, a Conservative legislature was able to persuade a Republican governor to authorize the revival of

46. Wilmington *Star*, January 2, 1873.

47. Curtis R. Brogden, the last Republican governor of Reconstruction, attempted unsuccessfully to arrest this development. He ordered the adjutant general to issue no further arms to volunteer companies on the grounds that he doubted if his authority allowed "the indiscriminate arming of such companies, as choose to organize throughout the State, . . ." Special Notice of John C. Gorman, Adjutant General, August 2, 1875, Governor's Papers, Brogden, North Carolina Archives.

48. Wilmington *Star*, September 9, 1877.

the Wilmington Light Infantry, which had been "the very flower of our young chivalry."[49] The company reappeared on the streets of Wilmington at the very height of Republican and Negro military activity. This made a difference, because things had changed since the ante-bellum days when the members of this company had been the pride of the gentry. The military titles that adorned their already splendid names were no longer so distinctive. This is indicated by the experience that a certain "gentleman" had one August afternoon in 1876 when he happened to be down on the Wilmington water front, where the sweating gangs of Negro longshoremen loaded and unloaded the ships. Seeing an acquaintance of his at some distance away, he shouted to him, "Colonel!" At this moment "six men halted, wheeled in their tracks and looked in the direction of the voice, each thinking he was the individual addressed."[50]

When the Republicans introduced universal manhood suffrage into the South they initiated a political revolution that brought people into the political equation whose opinions had never before counted, and, in so doing, radically transformed the social composition of the power structure. The effort to achieve political democracy failed and the twentieth century would find the official South attempting to return to the Conservatives' halfway house between slavery and freedom. Yet in certain areas of the South, such as the lower Cape Fear, for a number of years after 1868 the democratic experiment was working. This is not to say that it was a success undiluted by failure. On the contrary, even the chief beneficiary of the experiment, the Negro, had reasons not to be completely satisfied with the results. Nevertheless, the new regime made more friends than enemies on the lower Cape Fear. It was firmly consolidated there. It did not fall of its own weight. Rather its demise came about as a result of the intervention of a Conservative legislature and of a series of events taking place elsewhere.

Republican control of the state government was shattered by a series of blows that the Conservatives delivered between 1870 and

49. Wilmington *Star*, January 7, 1879.
50. *Ibid.*, August 19, 1876.

1876. Yet the success of this offensive resulted from events occurring as early as 1868, at the very inception of the Republican administration. There were some curious occurrences in Raleigh in 1868. Not the least of these was the appearance in town of George Swepson, a Conservative banker and railroad president, who immediately began giving away a quarter of a million dollars.[51]

If Swepson's generosity was remarkable, his talent as a peacemaker was hardly less so. Even though dissension-torn Raleigh might not appear to be a likely place for the fulfillment of Isaiah's prophecy that the "lion shall lie down with the lamb," it certainly seemed as if Swepson and his Republican lobbyist, Milton Littleworth, were achieving some comparable results. Due to their efforts, in fact, native-born and stranger, Negro and white, Radical and Conservative, men who had been almost at knife points, discovered that as far as Swepson's railroad projects were concerned, at least, they could reach some cordial agreements.[52]

Lest these deliberations raise the suspicion of scandal, Swepson took the precaution of making a loan to the most influential Conservative newspaper, Josiah Turner's *Sentinel*; and the resulting mortgage proved to be a veritable ring in the most scandal-sensitive journalistic nose in the state. Turner's captive nose lost much of its facility for detecting anything unsavory about the activities of railroad lobbies and was chiefly employed afterward

51. North Carolina, *Report of the Commission to Investigate Fraud and Corruption Under Act of Assembly Session 1871-1872* (Raleigh: James H. Moore, State Printer and Binder, 1872), pp. 316-19, and *passim*, hereinafter cited as *Shipp Report*. Most of this money was distributed ostensibly as "loans," but neither Swepson nor his beneficiaries were able to demonstrate to the Shipp Committee in 1871 that these were ordinary loans. They failed to produce the legally binding documents that formalize normal business loans, nor were they able to demonstrate that security was offered to insure repayment or indeed that any part of the money had been repaid.

52. Railroad appropriations did indeed become a party issue late in 1868 and in 1869, though never a clear-cut one. Most Republicans continued to support appropriations. Most Conservatives began to oppose them, most of the time. Perhaps the example of Plato Durham may illustrate the high degree of flexibility many legislators showed on this issue. In general he was a leader of the anti-lobby Conservatives. Yet he supported aid to the most corrupt railroad of all, the Western North Carolina, which was to run through his district. Charles Lewis Price, "Railroads and Reconstruction in North Carolina, 1865-1871" (Doctoral dissertation, The University of North Carolina, 1959), pp. 372-75.

in sniffing out the pettier forms of graft, such as the tendency of certain legislators to present the state with inflated accounts of their travel expenses.[53]

The quarter million dollars that Swepson gave away in Raleigh came back to him several times over when the state appropriated about seventeen million dollars in aid to railroads, of which Swepson's own line, the Western Division of the North Carolina Railroad, received more than one-third. Unfortunately, however, though this outlay almost doubled the indebtedness of North Carolina, very few miles were added to the state's railroad system. Rather most of the money was applied to speculation, to attorney's fees, to profits for bogus contractors, and to other devices that railroad lobbies on both sides of the Mason-Dixon line had worked out for transferring public funds into private pockets without the time and expense of constructing railroads.[54]

By election time in 1870 many of the details of the railroad scandals were still not public knowledge, but the main outlines of the affairs were. People knew that a great deal of money had been spent, that few lines had been built, and that the Republican party was in control. Many voters were not aware that when Swepson set out to corrupt legislators, he had shown a commendable freedom from party prejudice. Nor would these voters stop to ask if Democratic legislatures had been any more successful in combating the almost irresistible persuasion of the railroad lobbies. Rather the reaction of many people in 1870 was simply one of "rascals are in control. Throw the rascals out." The election promised to be a close one.

When the Republican candidate now went before the people he carried with him a suspicion of corruption that hung from his

53. Jonathan Daniels, *Prince of Carpetbaggers* (Philadelphia: Lippincott, [1958]), p. 190.

54. Hamilton, *Reconstruction*, pp. 437-40, 444, 448-49; Charles L. Price, "The Railroad Schemes of George W. Swepson," *East Carolina College Publications in History: Essays in American History*, ed. Hubert A. Coleman *et al.* (Greenville, N.C.: Dept. of History, East Carolina College, 1964), I, 45-46 and *passim*. However, the latter study concludes that it "was never the intention of Swepson to steal the money outright. He did, however, plan to use the funds of the Western Division [of the Western North Carolina Railroad] for speculation in North Carolina bonds. In this way he hoped to build up the capital he needed to carry out his various railroad projects and also perhaps enhance his personal fortune."

neck like a decaying albatross. Yet, so popular had been the democratic revolution in government that the Republicans had carried out, they probably could have won an election conducted under normal conditions, an election in which the candidates of both sides would be free to present their views and the voters could cast their ballots without fear of reprisal. But in 1870 these conditions did not exist in Piedmont North Carolina, the most populous section of the state.

If one takes the period of roughly twelve months before the election, that is, for the year ending in August, 1870, one finds the Klan credited with five murders in Orange County; five in Alamance County, including their hanging the County Chairman of the Union League; three in Caswell County, including their cutting Senator John Stephen's throat; three in Jones County; and some scattered ones elsewhere. During the same general period one finds twenty-two recorded Klan floggings in Catawba; seventy-six in Alamance; nine in Chatham; eight in Caswell; six in Moore; and scattered ones elsewhere. People who displeased the Klan suffered a variety of other bodily injuries. Also, homes and barns were burned and other property destroyed.[55]

What had happened to law enforcement in this part of the state? A possible explanation for this is that for the first two years of his administration Governor Holden had never completely given up the fiction of a politically neutral militia. In a belt across the middle of North Carolina, this had meant a Conservative militia, led by former Confederate officers. Furthermore, he shrank from the political consequences of using Negro companies[56] from the East to restore order in the Piedmont where the population was about 70 to 80 per cent white. Lacking force, the civil authority had degenerated into empty pronouncements and bluster. The result was a weird reversal of the relationship between the men who guarded the law and those who broke it.

55. Hamilton, *Reconstruction*, p. 277 and *passim*; Otto Olsen, "The Ku Klux Klan: A Study in Reconstruction Politics and Propaganda,"*The North Carolina Historical Review*, XXXIX (1962), 340-62, hereinafter cited as Olsen, "Klan."

56. William Woods Holden to Ulysses Samuel Grant, March 10, 1870, Holden Papers, Department of Manuscripts, Duke Unviersity, hereinafter cited as Holden Papers, Duke.

While hooded terrorists boldly paraded the streets, Judge Albion W. Tourgée changed his abode every night for fear of his life.[57] The time had come in Piedmont North Carolina for the judge to flee and the murderer to pursue.

Two months before the election of 1870 Holden began taking measures toward the suppression of extralegal violence by the creation of a politically reliable militia, a move which two years before had helped bring peace and law to the lower Cape Fear. He revived the Second North Carolina Volunteers, an old wartime Union regiment recruited largely from the western part of the state.

Holden had turned to the right place for recruiting a regiment against the Klan, as the Republican party was nowhere so strongly based as in the southern Appalachians. So lofty and rugged was this land that it seemed to be able to resist the erosion of time itself. It had not been engulfed by the successive waves of change that had rolled over America, neither by the westward sweep of plantation slavery to the south nor of modern industrialism to the north, each creating distinct new classes with sharply divergent modes of life. The nineteenth century had surrounded and almost deluged the uplands that sloped away from the cloud-shrouded peaks of the Great Smokies. But on those heights the backwoods eighteenth century still endured, a land of independent yeoman farmers, a relic of what America had once been.

A Union stronghold during the war, the Appalachians had been like a federal blade thrust southward, almost cutting the Confederacy in two; and it was to the Union traditions of this region that the Republicans now appealed in a handbill that appeared in the mountain hamlets:

RALLY UNION MEN IN DEFENCE OF YOUR STATE! RALLY SOLDIERS OF THE OLD N. CAROLINA 2D AND 3D FEDERAL TROOPS! RALLY TO THE STANDARD OF YOUR OLD COMMANDER!

Your old commander has been commissioned to raise at once a regiment of State troops, to aid in enforcing the laws, and in putting down disloyal midnight assassins.

57. Hamilton, *Reconstruction*, p. 484.

The blood of your murdered countrymen, inhumanly butchered for opinion's sake, cries from the ground for vengeance.[58]

Six hundred and seventy mountaineers answered the call, almost two-thirds of whom were youths below the legal military age.[59]

How effective was Holden's use of the militia? Niccolò Machiavelli once wrote that "men must either be caressed or else annihilated; they will revenge themselves for small injuries, but cannot do so for great ones; the injury therefore that we do to a man must be such that we need not fear his vengeance."[60]

But Governor Holden had little in common with Machiavelli. The injuries he inflicted upon his enemies did much to arouse their desire for revenge, but did little to impair their means for achieving it.

Though Klan intimidation had continued for two years, Holden did not actually bring troops into action until twenty days before the election, and then in only two of the dozen or more terrorized counties. Furthermore, the reputed numerical strength of the Klan in Alamance County alone was about equal to that of the regiment, made up largely of untrained youngsters, that Holden divided between Alamance and Caswell counties.[61] It seems doubtful whether such obviously temporary and inadequate measures, even in the occupied counties, could have done much to restore the confidence of the Republicans or to revive the party activities that had been frozen by the murder of prominent leaders.

If military occupation and martial law did little to help the Republicans in Alamance and Caswell counties, it did even less for them in the rest of the Klan-dominated Piedmont. In fact, it provided the Conservatives with an issue which they could use all over the state: They could now campaign from the high ground of civil liberty and opposition to military rule. Thus, the governor's small-scale and belated military measures provided his

58. Hamilton, *Reconstruction*, p. 500.
59. *Ibid.*, p. 504.
60. Niccolò Machiavelli, *The Prince* (New York: The New American Library, 1952), p. 37.
61. Holden to Grant, July 20, 1870, Holden Papers, Duke; Hamilton, *Reconstruction*, p. 464.

enemies with a political issue without significantly impairing their physical intimidation.[62]

Ku Klux terror, as well as the railroad scandals and other Republican political liabilities, resulted in Conservative majorities in both houses of the legislature in the election of 1870. Furthermore, by refusing to seat certain Republican legislators on technical grounds, the Conservative legislators converted their simple majority into a two-thirds majority, making it possible for them to impeach Governor Holden for the "illegal" arrest of alleged Klan members and other similar charges.[63]

Congress, still Republican, reacted belatedly to events in the South by passing the Ku Klux Act and the Federal Election Law of 1871. So far as North Carolina was concerned, however, these measures were largely a case of locking the barn door after the horses had been stolen. Having seized control of the decisive branch of the state government, the legislature, the Conservatives were now in a position to employ legal rather than extralegal methods to extend their power; so, following some convictions under the Ku Klux Act, they allowed their shady auxiliary to fall into disuse.[64] Colonel Saunders could now give his undivided attention to editing the Wilmington *Journal*.

But, in the meanwhile, taking advantage of their control of the legislature, the Conservatives had so gerrymandered the election districts that they were able to maintain that control without receiving half of the votes cast. Thus, in 1872, following a decline in the use of terror, the Republicans were able to recover their popular majority and elect a governor; but the time had passed when they could gain control of the legislature, the decisive branch of the government, by means of a small majority at the

62. Governor Holden's hesitant use of the militia has parallels throughout the South. A monograph dealing with the relationship between the militia and politics concludes that "social revolutions are not accomplished by force unless that force is overwhelming, merciless and continued over a long period." Otis ᐧ A. Singletary, *Negro Militia and Reconstruction* (Austin: University of Texas Press, 1957), p. 147.

63. North Carolina, *Trial of William W. Holden, Governor of North Carolina. . .* , 3 vols. (Raleigh: "Sentinel" Printing Office, 1871), I, 9-18.

64. Olsen, "Klan," p. 361 and *passim*; Douglas C. Dailey, "The Election of 1872 in North Carolina," *The North Carolina Historical Review*, XL (1963), 340 and *passim*, hereinafter cited as Dailey, "Election of 1872."

polls.[65] Reconstruction democracy, though spoiled in infancy by the ways that George Swepson had found for spending a quarter of a million dollars, had nevertheless managed to survive the ferocity of the Klan. But only long enough to be strangled completely by the craft of legislative lawyers.

In the history of Reconstruction there is much to demonstrate the extent that government is founded on force, stable government on overwhelming force. It is true that after a government has endured for generations it becomes easy to lose sight of this principle. With the passage of time the violent foundations of government become overgrown with tradition and justifying ideas; so that, like a house the foundations of which have become overgrown with moss and ivy, it becomes possible for one to imagine that it is the covering overgrowth rather than the foundation that supports the structure. The experiences that southerners had during Reconstruction do not foster such an illusion. On the contrary, at such times in history when a constitutional system is being challenged, it becomes possible to distinguish between those elements in its apparent foundations which actually sustain the structure and those elements which merely appear to do so. It then becomes clear that, without the sustaining force of a company of militia, a judge's dictum is a futile noise and his writ a meaningless scrap of paper.

65. S. P. Williams, "The Problem of Redistricting in North Carolina" (Master's thesis, Duke University, 1935), p. 78 and *passim*; Dailey, "Election of 1872," XL, 355-56.

VI ❧ Return to the Rule of "Property, Virtue, and Intelligence"

THE SUMMER OF 1869 WAS A TIME OF DROUGHT. THE WATERS OF the Cape Fear fell lower than they had ever been in the memory of any living person. River transportation came almost to a standstill. Steamboats were grounded helplessly at various points between Wilmington and Fayetteville. As the slight flow of fresh water failed to neutralize the action of the flood tides, the river before Wilmington gradually became brackish, and strange changes began to take place in the ecology of its waters. Salt water crabs made their appearance on the water front, to the delight of small boys who caught them in large numbers.[1]

As the river grew still and brackish, a curiously analogous stagnation was taking place in the political life of the people who lived along its murky waters. In January the Conservatives had boycotted the Wilmington city elections, allowing two sets of Republican candidates to run against each other.[2] In fact, the Conservatives appeared to be only mildly interested in anything that the dominant Republicans did or said. "Politics are beyond all question more quiet in the city now than known since the war," the *Journal* wrote.[3]

In view of the outraged clamor that the Conservatives would later raise over "negro domination," the political quietness of

1. Wilmington *The Daily Journal*, July 29, September 24, 29, 1869, hereinafter cited as Wilmington *Daily Journal* or Wilmington Weekly *Journal*.
2. *Ibid.*, January 5, 1869.
3. *Ibid.*, September 25, 1869.

Wilmington seems odd; because, as these words were written, the mayor's desk, which had so long been dignified by the presence of John Dawson, was occupied by a Negro.[4] Since Mayor Neff had been called out of town on a business trip, the Reverend Henry N. Jones, a Negro alderman, had been chosen by the Board of Aldermen to serve in his absence. Yet the prospect of having a Negro presiding over North Carolina's principal city for three weeks does not appear to have even caused a ripple of indignation in Conservative circles. "Laying aside caste," the *Journal* commented broadmindedly, "we confess to a decided preference to Jones" as compared to his white Republican predecessor.[5]

In all probability the apparently casual attitude of the Conservatives toward politics was due to their momentary acquiescence to Republican rule. However, the seeming indifference that they showed in 1869 to politics served the objectives of their party more effectively than had their political pugnacity of the previous year. Paradoxical as it may seem, the Republican party was so internally unstable that it needed an outside challenge to keep it from coming apart at the seams and disintegrating into a series of feuding factions.

The political situation in 1869 may have looked quiet from where the editor of the *Journal* sat, but it must have appeared quite otherwise wherever large groups of Republicans gathered. In contrast to the polite and orderly meetings of the Conservatives, wherever the Republicans gathered there was excitement and lusty debate. The Republican representative in the North Carolina House, General Llewellyn Garrish Estes, a native of Maine, had resigned his seat in July; and the problem of choosing a replacement for him had brought into the open some factional rancor within the party.

4. Joshua G. Wright to Julius Walker Wright, September 23, 1869, Murdock-Wright Papers, Southern Historical Collection, The University of North Carolina, hereinafter cited as Murdock-Wright Papers.

5. Wilmington *Daily Journal*, September 7, 1869. In this connection, a member of an old landed family wrote that the "Negroes are in the ascendency, and I have no doubt will occupy all the offices. I don't know if I would as leave have them as the scalawags." A. E. Wright to Julius Walker, June 3, 1870, Murdock-Wright Papers.

Estes was typical of the group of men who had dominated the Republican organization on the lower Cape Fear since its inception. Most of them were men who, while associated with the Union army in the area, had become interested in various local business schemes; and, as a result of these, they had made their homes on the Cape Fear following their discharge from the army. In view of the fact that a number of them, as administrative officers in the army of occupation, already had gained experience in managing the public affairs of the region, it is understandable how easily these men were drawn into politics, taking over the leadership of the Republican party.

Republicans who were natives or long-term residents of the region, on the other hand, did not push themselves forward during the first two years of the party's existence. Most of the Negroes still had very little political experience. But also the native white Republicans, probably no more than 10 per cent of the whites on the lower Cape Fear,[6] generally were not eager to take a conspicuous part in politics. They undoubtedly feared Conservative economic reprisals and ostracism with its attending rupture of family ties and banishment from churches. Because of these considerations, until 1869, a clique that had been associated with the Union army was able to manage the party with little opposition.

The leaders of the party were confronted with a revolt, however, when a rumor circulated that they planned to replace General Estes with General Allen Rutherford, also a Union veteran though from a prominent family long connected with North Carolina. But, perhaps because the name of General Rutherford aroused too much opposition from the native Republicans, they withdrew it and chose John S. W. Eagles, a Negro. Though a native of the Cape Fear, this former Union army first sergeant[7] was a loyal member of the Grand Army of the Republic,[8] a veterans' organization, but virtually a party within a party, by

6. In May, 1868, the *Journal* estimated that in Wilmington there were some 3,500 potential voters: 2,000 Negroes, and 1,500 whites, of whom 100-150 were Republicans. Wilmington Weekly *Journal*, May 29, 1868.

7. *Ibid.*, July 30, 1869.

8. Hereinafter abbreviated as GAR.

means of which the army clique controlled the Republican organization in the area.

In view of the number of competent Negro veterans that the party leaders might have chosen, it is interesting that they picked Eagles. Though Eagles seems to have been a magnetic politician on the neighborhood level,[9] his public statements give the impression that he might have been out of his element in the legislature.[10] Perhaps, however, the choice of such a candidate was deliberate: If the clique of newcomers could no longer elect one of their own circle, at least they could elect a candidate who would be unusually dependent upon his backers.

Since it appeared that the northern clique would be able to control Eagles, a group of neighborhood leaders and weakly-established Negro businessmen began a revolt against the northern domination of the local party organization. In the same way in which the coterie of veterans, mostly white, had advanced the name of a Negro, the native faction, mostly Negro, advanced the name of a native white, Solon V. Larkins. Moreover, since veterans were the order of the day, young Larkins had the distinction of being a veteran of both armies, having deserted the Confederacy for the Union. Though not a person of wealth or prominence, he was an enthusiastic campaigner, whose lingering regional prejudices seemed directed more against northern whites than against southern Negroes.[11]

The two factions then began campaigning for their respective candidates in much the fashion of two separate parties. At the New Hanover County Republican Convention two sets of delegates appeared from almost every precinct.[12] As a result, it seemed for a time that the gathering might be more likely to end in a riot than in a convention. The first round in the contest was the struggle for the control of the chairmanship; and the northerners won it when they succeeded in electing George W. Mabson, an aristocratic mulatto. Though Colonel Mabson was a native of the lower Cape Fear, as a veteran of the Fifth Massachusetts

9. Wilmington Weekly *Journal*, August 31, 1869.
10. Wilmington *Daily Journal*, August 1, 1869.
11. *Ibid.*, July 20, 1869; Wilmington Weekly *Journal*, May 15, 1869.
12. Wilmington *Daily Journal*, July 13, 1869.

Cavalry, he was fiercely loyal to the northern generals who dominated the GAR in the area.

The next problem was to decide which of the rival sets of "delegates" were the true delegates, properly elected. If this problem had any solution at all, it certainly had no easy one, because each set of delegates had been elected by gatherings that had all the paraphernalia of bona fide precinct conventions. The northern and GAR faction suggested that this matter could be expedited by having Chairman Mabson, their man, appoint a credentials committee. But the native faction stubbornly insisted upon settling the matter on the floor. The meeting dragged on in a noisy impasse. As the localists seemed to be gaining control of the hall, their opponents began shouting for an adjournment. Following a confused voice vote, the chairman declared the motion carried. Ignoring cries for an actual count, Mabson came down from the rostrum and marched from the hall, followed by the northerners and the GAR.[13]

The men who walked out of, or adjourned, the convention later organized an orderly meeting and nominated Eagles as the Republican candidate for the House. Those remaining behind, in an equally orderly meeting, nominated Larkins as the Republican candidate; and, as the Republicans quarreled, the Conservatives looked on with detached amusement.

General Abbott, now a United States Senator, speaking at a rally for Eagles, angrily denounced the tactics of the nativists, and threatened to "mete out political death and political damnation after death, to any man who will hereafter attack a Northern man as such." But some men at the same gathering did not show Abbott's disdain for sectional malice, provided of course that it was directed against their opponents; and transparencies mimicked the Dixieland speech of the leading Larkins supporters: one depicted the Negro, Edgar Miller, as saying, "Mr. President, I rise to a Pint of Order." Another spelled the name of R. P. Barry, a native white, as "Captain Ah! Pea Barry."[14]

Such was the tone of the campaign. "Last night the sound of

13. Wilmington Weekly *Journal*, July 23, 1869.
14. Wilmington *Daily Journal*, July 24, 1869.

the drum was almost continually heard through our streets," the *Journal* reported. "Torchlight processions marched and counter-marched through the city until long past the hour of mid-night; and the air resounded with yells and mingled cries for Larkins and Eagles and the night was made hideous. . . . About daylight the two parties rested on their arms and drew a few breaths before commencing the actual conflict."[15] Eagles won the election by a narrow margin.[16]

The question arises as to what was the real meaning behind all the heat and noise of Republican factional conflict. If we confine our attention only to the year 1869, it appears to be a struggle between northern and southern leaders for control of the local organization. The following year, however, the party divided into two equally hostile factions, a split so severe that it allowed a Conservative, Samuel A. Ashe, to recover his family's ancestral seat in the lower North Carolina house.[17] But in the case of the 1870 split the North-South division is by no means clear. More-over, as some northerners moved out of the region and those who remained became more assimilated, the regional origin of the various leaders of the party became less important. Yet, if this development removed one excuse for contention, it certainly did not diminish the inclination of the Republicans to quarrel.

Can Republican factionalism be attributed to the political in-experience of the Negro? It is true that the Negro was inexperi-enced for the first years after the war. But factionalism became a permanent feature of the Republican party, conspicuous during its entire thirty years of life on the lower Cape Fear. During these years the Negroes gained considerable political experience, many of them becoming astute parliamentarians, pursuing their intra-party quarrels with a certain expertness.

The underlying causes appear to have been more basic, having to do with the economic relationships prevailing in the area, with what the Negro expected of politics, and with the limitations of nineteenth-century concepts of democracy. The coming of demo-

15. *Ibid.*, August 5, 1869.
16. *Ibid.*
17. Donald MacRae to "Brother," August 6, 1870, Hugh MacRae Papers, Depart-ment of Manuscripts, Duke University.

cracy to the Cape Fear country had not brought to earth the intoxicating visions that swam before the eyes of the Negro in the spring of 1865. It is true that every year or so he could help choose a justice of the peace or a legislator. But what did he do during the other 364 days of that year? He did most of the same things that he had done as a slave. He was still tied to the most arduous and poorly paid jobs with little hope of advancement. As under slavery his standard of living was little above that which was physically required to insure a continuing labor supply.

But if politics did not account for a large part of the total activity of the Negro, it was nevertheless a part that he particularly cherished. Perhaps he regarded politics as the one area of his experience in which his opinions counted, a corner of life in which one might find the means for redeeming the rest. He poured his energy and enthusiasm into the railroad-ridden politics of the Gilded Age, but his people seemed to make no further progress after the year 1868.

An important part of the problem was that, as a national organization, the Republican party had nothing further to offer the Negro. In 1868, they had won for him a certain political and legal equality; and the Negro, for his part, had made possible the election of a Republican president.[18] But once in control, the Republican party was finding new sources of power; and the problems of the Negro were becoming a smaller concern of party leaders. Like most nineteenth-century Americans, Republican leaders believed that the purpose of government was to administer the common business of people living in a society that was essentially just and hence permanent. They would have regarded as quite improper a notion that has gained credence in the twentieth century, that the government has a duty to change the character of society with a view of making it more just. According to the most respectable concepts of their day, the Republicans had done about all they could for the Negro.

But if the political theory of the Gilded Age offered no means whereby a group of people such as the Negroes might improve

18. Charles H. Coleman, *The Election of 1868* (New York: Columbia University Press, 1933), p. 370.

their lot, the political practices of that day offered the means whereby certain individuals might do so. If a Negro politician was not able to do anything for his people, he might, like certain of his white colleagues, be able to do something for himself and a few friends.

Yet in at least one respect the problems of the Negro politician were different from those of his white contemporary: If the standards of political conduct became so low that one became afraid of being compromised, a white politician was ordinarily free to retire to private life and wait for public ethics to improve. But for a Negro this was not so easy. Retiring to private life, more often than not, meant that a Negro had to go to a political adversary and ask for a job. Once a Negro acquired the reputation of being a politician, for better or for worse, he became dependent upon political jobs for a livelihood. The Negroes placed their highest hopes in the shady political institutions of the Gilded Age, and those institutions tarnished some of their most promising leaders.

To understand the political dynamics that transformed hope and idealism into cynicism and self-aggrandizement, it may be helpful to consider the career of William H. Moore, a "long-legged," black-skinned house painter. Though the Conservatives were not likely to be pleased in 1868 with any Negro who participated in politics, there were differences in degree; and Moore, a Republican registrar, became the special object of the *Journal*'s displeasure. Five hundred prominent people in Wilmington were still disfranchised for their Confederate activities,[19] and one of Moore's duties, as a registrar, was to see that none of these was allowed to register to vote.

"By his insolence and impertinent questions, he rendered himself particularly obnoxious," the *Journal* wrote. "This negro has done all in his power to deprive white men of the right to vote under the Reconstruction Acts, and yet he seeks to gain his living in this community, where he endeavors to materially to injure the citizens. He is by occupation a painter. Let his conduct mark him, and let us see that in our own defense we support no such

19. Wilmington Weekly *Journal*, May 29, 1868.

viper either employing him to work for us, or employing those who give him work."[20]

This was no small threat to Moore's livelihood. The same paper estimated that, in round numbers, property ownership in Wilmington amounted to $3,200,000; and was distributed politically as follows:

Conservatives	$2,978,000
"white Radicals"	150,000
Negroes	72,000

The editors further claimed that, of the city's potential 3,500 voters, two thousand were Negroes employed by Conservatives, adding that by "concerted action before the time when it will be necessary for our citizens again to elect municipal officers, the election can be controlled in the interests of the property and business of the city, by employees who will sympathize with their employers."[21] If it is true that the Conservatives planned to make use of their economic power and that more than 90 per cent of property that might require the services of a painter belonged to Conservatives, the family of the house painter, William Moore, was likely to face some lean days.

There are a number of indications, furthermore, that the Conservatives, in their efforts to soften the political posture of their opponents, intended to make full use of their control over the corn crib and the smokehouse. The Republican *Post* asked its readers to report all political firings to General Allen Rutherford.[22] A Republican governor received a complaint that Robeson County landlords had threatened Negroes with eviction if they voted for his party,[23] while a popular Negro leader from Wilmington wrote him that, if the governor would appoint him to some job that "will pay anything," he in turn would resign his seat in the North Carolina House, because "I have a large family,

20. Wilmington *Daily Journal*, April 12, 1867.
21. Wilmington Weekly *Journal*, May 29, 1868.
22. Wilmington *Post*, April 23, 1868.
23. Edward Ancrum to Tod R. Caldwell, September 15, 1872, Governor's Papers, Caldwell, North Carolina State Archives, hereinafter cited as Caldwell Papers.

and [am] not able even to obtain one day's work in this city from a democrat. . . ."[24]

But when a Conservative called for applying economic pressure on a Republican, he did not always admit that it was being done for specifically political reasons. Rather it was because he took exception to the bad manners of some militant Negro. Thus the *Star* demanded that Democratic money lenders withhold credit from a certain Republican challenger who "behaved in an extremely objectionable manner at the polls of the second ward, on Thursday last. . . ."[25]

The same paper later added that the "black flag should be raised, and resolutions adopted by the Democratic club of this city [be] carried out to the letter. Let no Radical be employed where a Democrat can be obtained. . . ."[26]

The press discussed how this campaign could be carried out in respect to different occupations, the *Star* suggesting that white musicians should be trained so that "we will no longer be dependent upon a Radical band for our musical enjoyment."[27] But a similar effort in another trade apparently came to grief judging from references to some "intensely Democratic white barbers who have recently shaved our people in more senses than one. . . . We had better let the white barbers alone if we can not find some who are better known to our people than the light-fingered gentlemen who lately exhibited their keen-edged razors and snow-white towels in the basement of the First National Bank."[28]

Before the year was out, however, the *Journal* could report progress on the water front, where seventeen Negro Radicals had been replaced by Irish Democrats. "They receive precisely the same pay as was given the colored stevedores," the paper wrote, and they were "stout, active fellows who . . . know how to stow away a cargo. We welcome them as the pioneers of a new labor-

24. William McLaurin to Caldwell, March 27, 1873, Caldwell Papers.
25. Wilmington *The Morning Star*, July 18, 1868. (This paper began in 1867 as *The Evening Star*, but after several months changed to *The Morning Star*. Hereinafter cited as Wilmington *Star*.)
26. *Ibid.*, August 9, 1868.
27. *Ibid.*, August 20, 1868.
28. *Ibid.*, September 22, 1868.

ing population, who must follow and build up our ruined system on a new basis."[29]

For many years to come there would be indications that the Conservatives were making political use of their economic power. But it is difficult to say to what extent these tactics were effective against individual Republicans of local prominence. Certainly William H. Moore was no longer listed as a painter after 1868. The jobs he began to follow, in fact, appear to have been an effort to get beyond the economic reach of the Conservatives. For a time he operated a barbershop, and, in the summer of 1869, the Republican Board of Aldermen issued him a license to sell liquor. Later he tried farming, then selling "Key Stone Linament" and "Indian Powders," then job printing, and still later he worked as the local agent of a Negro newspaper.[30]

But for all of his versatility, if we may judge by the length of time he held these various occupations, Moore's livelihood remained precarious. He came to look longingly toward jobs which the Republican party used to reward faithful party workers. On April 2, 1869, a Republican mass rally passed a resolution calling for the appointment of Moore to a position in the Treasury Department in Washington. While this resolution seems to have been ignored by the men who operated the Wilmington-to-Washington patronage pipeline, during the same year the Republican mayor of Wilmington engaged Moore as a city detective. In 1874, furthermore, he was elected to a term in the North Carolina House.[31]

Yet Moore continued to suffer from the very commonplaceness of his problem. On the Cape Fear there were too many Negroes whose already precarious existence had been made more insecure by political discrimination. The Republican legislature created a few jobs for such people by expanding the functions and expenses of the state government to what was then an unprecedented scope. So shocked were the Conservative newspapers by this evidence of corruption that, even in the midst of the cam-

29. Wilmington *Daily Journal*, December 3, 1868.

30. *Ibid.*, June 7, 1870; Wilmington *Star*, July 18, 1878; Wilmington *Messenger*, January 12, 1890.

31. Wilmington *Daily Journal*, April 3, 1869; January 4, 1870; August 12, 1874.

paign to exclude active Republicans from gainful employment, they found time to give full vent to their righteous wrath.[32]

But the problem that the Republican party faced was beyond the talents of the legislators: Political jobs remained few, the William Moores a legion. If a man had one of the coveted political jobs, there was always at least one other man without one, but who deserved a job as much as he. If one wanted to keep his job, then he must seek to discredit those who were standing in line waiting for that job. If he were too scrupulous to resort to such tactics, he would find himself with a bad reputation and no job. As a result, local Republican leaders were constantly engaging in petty quarrels with their rivals, men who were as vigorous in their defense of Negro rights as themselves.[33] Such was the real basis for the factional disease that afflicted the Republican party of the lower Cape Fear.

Since there were never more than half enough jobs, periodically one half of the neighborhood leaders had to band together and attempt to politically annihilate the other half. The ostensible justification for such battles is not always easy to detect. In 1869, one side had created the campaign image of an indigenous Republican leadership, leaders whose roots sank deep into the soil of the Cape Fear country. The other side linked itself to the

32. Joseph Gregoire de Roulhac Hamilton, *Reconstruction in North Carolina* (New York: Columbia University Press, 1914), pp. 275 ff., hereinafter cited as Hamilton, *Reconstruction*.

33. By all odds the most cantankerous Republican on the lower Cape Fear was James Heaton, who as a youth had accompanied his carpetbagger father into the area at the close of the war. As a street-corner speaker the younger Heaton became popular among both white and Negro Republicans, and he managed to retain a few loyal friends through all the brawls of his violent career. Some of the worst aspects of Republican factionalism are reflected in his activities during July, 1878. At a party rally in Pender County he became involved in an affray with another northern Republican, Flaviel W. Foster. A shot from Foster's pistol missed Heaton, who, using a hickory walking stick, gave Foster a beating that left him "for some time in nearly an unconscious state. . . ." (Wilmington *Star*, July 3, 1878.) Four days later he was involved in a fight with a Negro Republican leader in Wilmington. The throng on the street seized both men, disarmed them, and dragged them before a Republican magistrate. (*Ibid.*, July 7, 1878.) Nine days after this, Heaton was addressing a rally when a rival, a Republican sheriff, began heckling him. Whereupon Heaton made a "flying leap from the stand from which he was speaking, and alighted in the crowd in close proximity to the sheriff, when both belligerents made for each other, amid the shouts and yells of the bystanders. The police arrested both. . . ." (*Ibid.*, July 17, 1878.)

image of a victorious army that had set free the slaves. But with the passing of the years both images began to fade. Local leaders no longer attempted to drape such refining visions over the ugly quest for office, with its endless cycle of reconciliation and betrayal. "Mr. Cheerman," an unfriendly reporter once quoted Moore as saying at a meeting, perhaps exaggerating his Negro accent, "Judas Iscariot betrayed our Savior for thirty pieces of silver, but dar is men right here on dis floor who can be bought for less dan dat."[34]

Bought by whom? Men like Moore did not generally have the means to buy anyone. But at the head of the party on the lower Cape Fear stood two distinct sorts of men: There was the popular idol, generally a Negro; but there was also the wealthy patron, almost always a white. The existence of this distinction probably intensified the party's factional disease. If the popular leaders had been in real control of the party, it appears likely that the organization would have shown more internal stability. The more capable of the street-corner spellbinders would have won positions of leadership and, once in that position, would have enjoyed a measure of security against their less talented rivals.

But it was clearly a fact that the fall of a man from a position of leadership could result not only from his loss of popular favor but also from the whim of a patron. Thus the insecurity, and hence mutual jealousy, of such men as Moore was intensified by the fact that, besides having to compete publicly for popular favor, they also had to compete privately in behind-the-scenes negotiations for the favor of some wealthy patron. It appears likely, in fact, that the high degree of control exercised over the party by a small circle of patrons, a group known on the lower Cape Fear as the "Ring," was made possible by a deliberate policy of fostering competition between the apparent leaders of the party, the popular idols.

Who were the men so darkly referred to in the Conservative press as the "Ring"? The Republican party of Wilmington, which dominated the lower Cape Fear, appears to have consisted of some two thousand Negroes plus from one hundred to one

34. Wilmington *Daily Journal*, April 14, 1872.

hundred fifty whites, white support varying more than that of the more steadfast Negro. The party in the city included fifteen or twenty prosperous businessmen who maintained residences in Wilmington, though some of them also had residences as well as business interests elsewhere.[35] In a party of the penniless multitude, these fifteen or twenty men could exercise influence far out of proportion to their actual numbers. They were the Ring.

The Ring consisted of perhaps a half-dozen first and second generation New Englanders from families that had settled on the Cape Fear in ante-bellum days.[36] After the war, furthermore, these men were joined by another group, also mostly from New England, who had been connected with the Union army and the military government of the region.[37] The Ring was still further reinforced by certain defections from the ante-bellum governing class, generally men with an old Whiggish background such as Edward Cantwell and the two Daniel Lindsay Russells, father and son. There were also certain well-to-do Negro, or partially Negro, families, such as the Sampsons and the Howes, who were perhaps sufficiently influential to be considered part of the Ring, though these families also produced popular leaders.

The interrelations between the Ring and the neighborhood leaders explains much of the curious behavior of the Republican party. In 1869, certain members of the Ring, namely those associated with the Union army, backed a native-born Negro candidate in preference to one of their own number. In so doing they were by no means surrendering their influence over the party. Rather they were simply adopting a tactic that certain other members, those who were native-born or long residents, were already observing, the tactic of allowing the popular leaders of the party to occupy the offices, except for a few choice ones, and of permitting the same men to conduct the boisterous public meetings of

35. Wilmington Weekly *Journal*, May 29, 1868.

36. In particular Silas N. Martin; Edward Kidder; George R. French, and his sons; and several members of the Chadbourn family.

37. Especially George Z. French, and his brothers; James Wilson; David Heaton and his son, James C. Heaton; Colonel Flaviel W. Foster; and the three Union generals, Joseph C. Abbott, Allen Rutherford, and S. H. Manning.

the party, while the gentlemen of the Ring decided questions of policy from the dignified seclusion of their offices.

How can one group of men control a party if another group leads it? This was done by two means: by patronage and by money. We have seen that the question of political jobs was one of capital importance to local Negro politicans; and the wealthy Republicans of the Cape Fear had the necessary connections in Raleigh and Washington to influence decisions as to which man would be appointed to a particular job. Furthermore, even as early as the third quarter of the nineteenth century, it had already become difficult for a candidate without means to win over one with solid financial backing.

Occasionally it happened. A particularly popular candidate could sometimes win over the choice of the Ring. But even on these rare occasions, the victorious candidate would not necessarily be permitted to assume the office to which he had been elected. This was because the law required that men occupying certain offices be bonded. Consequently, unless the winner could persuade some members of the Ring or other rich men to sign his bond, he could not actually serve in the capacity to which he had been elected.

In this connection a white Republican on the lower Cape Fear, following an election defeat, wrote that while a few eastern counties had been "saved at the polls," even these were about to be "lost by our poverty, officers elect failing to give bonds. . . ."[38] And it was with satisfaction that a Conservative editor could observe that "the efficient and accommodating Clerk of the Superior Court for Pender County, is still filling that position. It will be remembered that a Republican was elected as Clerk but he failed to file an acceptable bond and the Board of County Commissioners declared the office vacant. Mr. Bannerman [the Conservative incumbent] was thereupon appointed by [Conservative] Judge McKoy."[39] In actual practice, therefore, a person was elected to public office by a favorable combination of ballots and

38. Daniel Lindsay Russell to Thomas Settle, September 16, 1874, Thomas Settle Papers, Southern Historical Collection, The University of North Carolina.
39. Wilmington *Review*, January 6, 1883.

dollars. In almost all cases of conflict, however, dollars proved stronger than ballots. Thus, in the final analysis, the popular neighborhood orators, like William Moore, led the party in much the same sense that a wagon is "led" by a team of horses. They led, indeed, but just where they led was determined by the hands that grasped the two reins, one of which was patronage, the other money.

As the years passed, the political influence of money increased; as the Negroes failed to make any new gains, the sunburst of their idealism faded and gradually turned into despondency and cynicism. Back in 1867 some Negroes in New Hanover County had walked thirty-seven miles in order to register for voting, and "their faces radiant with smiles" reminded one white Republican of the song, "There's a good time coming."[40]

On the last voting day in the election to ratify the Constitution of 1868, moreover, there is even a report of a Negro being brought to the polling place in an ambulance, his leg having been amputated only a half-hour before.[41] But in 1875 we find a local party worker writing a member of the Ring that, in order to carry Blue Springs Township,[42] he would need two hundred pounds of bacon and a barrel of flour, to "draw the colored people to the election who have not been there some elections past."[43] It no longer seemed worthwhile to walk thirty-seven miles to vote for the party of freedom.

The Republican organization on the lower Cape Fear, already moribund in its infancy, led by mutually jealous, quarrelling men of the people, guided by "bosses," tarnished by Gilded Age railroad politics, was, nevertheless, destined to suffer a life span of thirty-one years. If the local organizations could be credited with a certain innocence of secret faults, this was due to the efficiency with which its local dignitaries transformed the private sins of rival leaders and patrons into public scandals; and, if the party was not at last cleansed by its custom of conspicuously washing its

40. Wilmington *Post*, September 3, 1867.
41. Wilmington *Star*, April 24, 1868.
42. Later this township became the nucleus of Hoke County.
43. David Purcell to Daniel Lindsay Russell, July 1, 1875, in Daniel L. Russell Papers, Southern Historical Collection, The University of North Carolina.

dirty linen up and down the Cape Fear, at least the spectacle provided the Conservatives with almost perpetual entertainment.

Yet for all its weaknesses, there was still much to recommend the local administration of the Republican party. "The Radicals are making so many improvements in town, you would hardly imagine that this city was dear old Wilmington," wrote the Conservative owner of a failing plantation, which he found "sad indeed to see . . . so altered. . . . Every one is uneasy about the taxes [in Wilmington], which will be enormous, and we have no way of preventing them from wasting the money of our poor people."[44] Perhaps some uneasiness was justified. As the guiding elite of the Republican party was unusually small and its party workers especially needy, the administration was probably more inclined toward favoritism than had been the case of the Conservative squirearchy.

But the Republicans maintained better order, and yet employed less cruelty and violence, than their predecessors. Except for Robeson and Sampson counties, both near the disorderly Piedmont, the courts operated normally and the men of either party could meet or demonstrate without intimidation. On the lower Cape Fear the Republican administration was overturned, not as a result of its internal weaknesses, which though numerous were insufficient, but as a result of intervention by a Conservative legislature.

Though in 1870 Republican power was broken in the decisive Piedmont area, the party remained strong in the mountains and in the tidewater section. Of the local bases remaining to the Republicans, perhaps the most important was the lower Cape Fear, dominated by Wilmington. From the vantage point of our twentieth-century urban society, one could easily overlook the significance during Reconstruction of this town of hardly twenty thousand. About double the size of the next largest town, it was the North Carolina community with the best claim to being a city. It was important to the Conservatives as the home of some of their more important leaders and newspapers. But it was even

44. Joshua G. Wright to Julius Walker Wright, March 26, 1869, Murdock-Wright Papers.

more important to the Republicans: Despite the fact that their strength lay in the more remote rural areas, the Conservatives controlling almost all towns, at least Wilmington was a Republican stronghold.

Some of the more able Republicans lived in Wilmington. Though overwhelmingly a party of the poor and unlettered, the organization in the city included about a dozen men of wealth and prominence. Furthermore, the raucous street meetings and open-air debates had produced some politicians who, though not educated, were none the less able. Wilmington orators helped in Republican campaigns in other parts of the state. The city was also important in the newspaper battle. Though this was a highly unequal contest, there being in 1870 twenty-six Conservative newspapers in the state as opposed to seven Republican,[45] Wilmington was one of the few centers in which the Republicans had an effective press, the *Post* claiming to be the largest paper in the state.[46]

It is not surprising that once the Conservatives established themselves in the Piedmont they would then give some attention to Wilmington. The first step in this direction, however, was not aimed toward capturing the city but rather toward reducing its influence. Since Wilmington dominated the large and populous county of New Hanover, the Conservative legislature took the northern two-thirds of the county, including almost all of its agricultural population, and formed it into a new county, Pender, named for a Confederate general. Even though the Republicans were in a slight majority in the new county, the Conservative planters had hoped that they would be able to control it once the Negroes, mostly sharecroppers, were cut "loose from the Radical ring of Wilmington."[47]

In the meanwhile, this move had reduced New Hanover County, now more strongly Republican than ever, to an area comprising little more than the city of Wilmington plus an almost uninhabited peninsula. At the same time the representation of

45. Hamilton, *Reconstruction*, p. 425.
46. Wilmington *Post, passim.*
47. Wilmington *Daily Journal,* January 29, 1875.

New Hanover County in the North Carolina House was reduced from three to two seats.

Initially, however, the new county, Pender, did not live up to the expectations of its founders. In the first county election the Republicans won all offices, a development which the *Journal* charged had come about because "some two or three hundred voters had disappeared from Wilmington recently and come over into Pender. This importation and colonization of voters in the new county, in conjunction with lamentable disaffection and neglect of duty in our own ranks, bearing upon the county offices and county [administrative] site, has doubtlessly enabled the Radical party to succeed. . . ."[48]

Before the campaign to create Pender County had reached fruition, however, the Conservative leaders in Raleigh had already devised some legal magic that would enable a Conservative minority to defeat a Republican majority in Wilmington's municipal elections. The city was divided into three wards which were held to be equal in property value if not in population. Each of these wards would elect three aldermen, who in turn would elect one of their own number as mayor.[49]

The predominantly white, middle class, Conservative center of the city, an area sometimes referred to as the "Gallows Hill" section, containing about 21 per cent of the population, was designated as wards one and two, which together elected two-thirds of the aldermen. The northern and southern suburbs of the city, where most of the Negroes as well as the white working class lived, were connected by a fantastic corridor that skirted through the fields and bushes around the eastern end of the city, and were designated as ward three, which contained about 79 per cent of the population, and had the right to elect one-third of the aldermen.[50]

In accordance with the provisions of the new charter an election was held; and, despite a Republican boycott, a new Board

48. *Ibid.*, April 16, 1875.
49. North Carolina, *Private Laws*, 1874-75, ch. 43.
50. Wilmington *Post*, September 22, 1876.

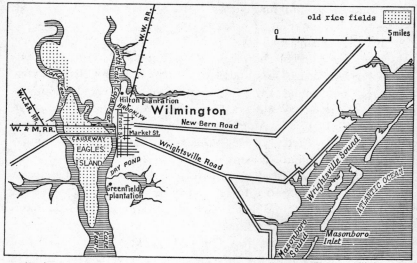

Wilmington Area

of Aldermen was elected. The Board in turn elected Adrian H. Van Bokkelen as mayor. Though a native of New York, before the war Van Bokkelen had moved to Wilmington where, on the city water front, he had established the largest turpentine distillery in the United States.[51]

"Earnestly devoted to the Southern cause,"[52] he had also become associated in some minds at least with the harshness of the slave system. The *Post* remarked that "many of our old citizens remember" the circumstances that surrounded the death of a certain slave, Hampton Brown. Van Bokkelen had flogged Brown so savagely that the slave, crazed by pain, had thrown himself into the Cape Fear and drowned.[53] In predominantly Negro and

51. Wilmington *Review*, August 13, 1883.
52. *Ibid.*
53. Wilmington *Post*, April 15, 1883.

Republican Wilmington, Mayor Van Bokkelen would not have done well in a popular race for mayor.

In the meanwhile, the Republican Board of Aldermen declared that the new charter for Wilmington, passed by the Conservative legislature, was unconstitutional; that the election that had been held under it was illegal and void; and that the administration of the city would not be turned over to the Conservative mayor and Board of Aldermen.[54] But unlike such pronouncements made by Piedmont Republicans in 1870, this was no empty bluster. The Republicans of the lower Cape Fear still held the local, official power mechanism firmly in their hands: They had a politically reliable police force; and both the Republican mayor, Canaday, and the Republican senator, Mabson, were also colonels in a politically reliable county militia regiment. For seven years this official power mechanism had had no extralegal competition.

It was now rather the turn of the Conservatives to fume in helpless rage: "The talk of the usurpers has . . . the smell of Canby gun powder and the clang of Canby bayonets," the *Journal* thundered, referring to the Union general who had been in command of North Carolina in 1868. But "neither Canby nor Canby's people now rule in North Carolina." And, as for the constitutionality of the Wilmington charter, not even a federal court would dare "interfere with the execution of the laws of our state."[55] But there was nothing for the Conservatives to do except to leave the Republicans in possession of the city while they sued for possession through the courts.

Meanwhile, the Conservative legislature passed a law that "if any Alderman of the City of Wilmington shall refuse to surrender his office upon the expiration of the same by due course of law [,] he shall be guilty of a misdemeanor, and upon conviction thereof, shall be fined not less than two-thousand dollars and imprisoned not less than two years."[56] The *Journal*, without exaggerated sadness, prophesied the day when the Republican mayor

54. Wilmington *Daily Journal*, March 9, 1875.
55. *Ibid.*, March 16, 1875.
56. *Ibid.*, March 14, 1875.

and Board of Aldermen would "have their heads shaved and wear striped clothes."[57]

But the "usurpers" continued to administer the city court, the Conservative mayor and Board of Aldermen being careful not to run afoul of "usurper" law enforcement; and they continued to perform all the functions of a *de facto* government. After some four months the Conservative suit reached the North Carolina Supreme Court, which still included a majority of Republican judges; and the Conservative gerrymander for Wilmington was declared unconstitutional.[58] In the areas of the state in which legal details needed to be respected, the "Canby" Constitution and Republican judges stood between the Conservatives and one-party control.

The local victories of southern Republicans could be of only momentary significance because large events in the nation were favoring their enemies. The Democratic party had gained control of Congress. In North Carolina the election of 1876 swept the Conservatives to a popular majority in a close but fairly honest election. For the first time since Negro suffrage they elected a governor. Even more important was the ratification of some Conservative amendments to the "Canby" Constitution. One of these abolished the popular election of county officials and instead made these positions subject to appointment by a legislature now firmly controlled by Conservatives. Another amendment reduced the number of state judges, a measure that made it possible for them to purge Republicans from the bench more rapidly.[59]

The Conservatives had dealt the Republican party of North Carolina a series of blows from which it never completely recovered. They had, in fact, reduced it to a party of futility: The Republicans could no longer compete on an equal basis for legislative or congressional seats because of the gerrymander. For local offices they could no longer compete at all, as these jobs were no longer elective; but rather they had been added to the store of loaves and fishes that the Conservatives in the legislature used

57. *Ibid.*
58. Van Bokkelen *v.* Canaday, 73 N.C. 198 (1875).
59. North Carolina, *Ordinances, Passed by the N. C. [sic] Constitutional Convention of 1875* ([Raleigh: Josiah Turner, State Printer and Binder, 1875]), pp. 8-9, 17.

to reward their multitude of local party workers, thus creating the basis for a vast, state-wide machine. Also, now that the Conservatives had possession of all three branches of state government, they could proceed much more rapidly in their campaign to abolish Negro and Republican militia companies, and replace them with Conservative ones, thus gaining control of the power mechanism in the predominantly Republican area.

In 1877, the Conservatives again attempted to gain control of the local governments of the lower Cape Fear using some of the same methods that the Republicans had successfully resisted two years before. First the legislature wrote a charter for Wilmington substantially the same as the one that the Supreme Court had previously declared unconstitutional. The voters in Wilmington were to be permitted to perform all the motions of citizens electing a representative government, but the election was to be conducted in such a way as to allow the opinions of the minority to prevail over those of the majority.

This feat was accomplished by the creation of five wards which, though highly unequal in population, were each equally represented by two aldermen. The strongly Republican Brooklyn and Dry Pond sections, which contained a total of about 2,300 Negro and white working-class voters, and which in 1875 the legislature had attempted to join by a corridor into one gigantic ward, were now designated as two wards, represented by a total of four aldermen.

The Conservative Gallows Hill section, on the other hand, in which there was a total of about 1,150 predominantly white, middle-class voters, was designated as three wards, represented by a total of six aldermen. Elections would continue to be held in Wilmington, but they would be quiet affairs containing few surprises: It had now become difficult for the six men who had received the nod from the Conservative leaders to fail to be elected as the majority aldermen, while the four men approved by the Ring were likely to be elected as members of the Republican minority.[60]

60. North Carolina, *Laws and Resolutions*, 1876-77, Ch. 192; Wilmington *Post*, January 8, 1877.

In respect to the county administrations, it was no longer necessary for the Conservatives to risk defeat at the polls such as they had suffered in Pender in 1875. Rather, ⸻der the amendment that they had made to the Constitution, when the term of office of county officials expired in 1877, no new elections were held. Instead, the governor began filling these positions with men that a Conservative editor said would " 'represent the property, virtue, and intelligence of the people.' "[61]

Two years before such measures had provoked vigorous Republican resistance on the lower Cape Fear. But, in the meanwhile, defeats on the state and national level, changes in the Constitution, in the courts, and in the militia, had underscored the futility of any further efforts by the Republicans to defend their local regime.

Defeat is a bitter experience. Yet to the vanquished there is perhaps nothing so utterly galling as the spectacle of betrayal that so often accompanies defeat, seeing men from one's own ranks accommodate themselves to the conqueror at the expense of former friends. After the election disaster of 1876, the timeless face of Judas Iscariot appeared more than once in Republican ranks.

For a long time the Republicans of the lower Cape Fear were not aware of the kind of arrangements that Rutherford B. Hayes had made in order to make himself the President of the United States. For months they were not aware that he had become president by agreeing to abandon the southern Republicans to their worst enemies.[62] On the contrary, in March, 1877, when the news reached Wilmington that Hayes had been inaugurated as president, Cape Fear Republicans thought that his victory was also their own. Colonel Mabson even ordered one of the militia companies still remaining to him to fire a hundred rifle salute on the city water front.[63]

But little by little the truth began to seep down from Wash-

61. Wilmington *Star*, June 22, 1877, quoting Raleigh *Observer* reaction to New Hanover County appointments, no date.
62. Comer Vann Woodward, *Reunion and Reaction* (Garden City, N.Y.: Doubleday, 1956).
63. Wilmington *Star*, March 4, 1877.

ington. "Our statement that the President's policy is a practical surrender of the rights of a large body of citizens at the South receives additional confirmation every day," a white Republican editor wrote. While Hayes might feel that he was acting in the large national interest of the party, "we do believe that he is listening to the advice of those who are seeking to oppress and practically disfranchise the colored Republicans of the South, and that his policy is giving these oppressors the power and the opportunity long sought."[64]

The President's policy must have appeared hateful indeed to the southerners who had voted for him. Because so long as the Republicans had been men of power and influence, in the give and take of politics, even their enemies had found it expedient to treat them with a certain deference. But now, in the process of making appointments, by choosing southern Conservatives in preference to Republicans, Hayes was dramatizing the fact that the southern Republicans were without friends or political influence anywhere. They were now ready victims.

Whatever possibilities the man in the White House may have seen in these maneuvers, they must have appeared quite differently to a man such as the Reverend Isaac W. King, a popular white Republican leader on the lower Cape Fear, and a circuit preacher for a group of Free Will Baptist churches. One of the Reverend King's churches was in the Dry Pond area of Wilmington. The others, however, were in rural areas in which the Conservatives had found a particularly cogent weapon in their demand for white solidarity under Conservative leadership.

In a letter to a relative living in a rural district in which the Reverend King preached, a Wilmington Conservative wrote that King

has several churches up there or large congregations to preach to, and I know he still goes up there with his satchell [sic] in his hand dressed like a gentleman. . . . I met him on Tuesday morning, and inquired if he were the man who had presided at last night's Radical meeting, and he said he was . . . , and I started the boys upon him, and you never saw a man so abused in your life, and he could only set [sic] and

64. Wilmington *Post*, December 13, 1877.

take it. . . . Heretofore he has had a respectable standing for one of his style, but now even his brothers hate him, in [sic] a conversation with one of them a few days since he requested me to do Isaac all the damage I could with his Cuntry [sic] congregations, and . . . I want all who have been friends to him to turn the cold shoulder hereafter and let him associate with his Nigger Equals, he does not belong to the white people any longer, but to the Nigger Scallowags and Carpet Baggers.[65]

Perhaps the success of this campaign to drive the Reverend King out of his churches can best be summarized by an item which a fellow white Radical wrote several months later in a struggling Republican newspaper, not as an advertisement, but as an editorial. Significantly the title, "the Reverend," no longer dignifies King's name: "Isaac King's meat shop . . . is the place to get nice stall fed beef, pork, sausage, etc. Friend King keeps the very best meats sold in this market."[66] In the Redeemed South, certain Republicans would have to make some painful adjustments.

65. D. J. Gilbert to Dr. W. J. Gilbert, September 30, 1876, appearing in Wilmington *Post*, January 19, 1877.
66. *Ibid.*, November 30, 1877.

VII ❧ Economic Life of the Lower Cape Fear

PERHAPS ONE COULD SEE IN THE EXPERIENCE OF A CERTAIN whale an evil omen for the prospects of the Cape Fear estuary as a seaport. In the spring of 1866, this fifty-six foot creature, swimming along with the flood tide, found his way into Smithville Bay, at the mouth of the Cape Fear. But when the monster, after exploring the bay for a time, decided to return to the sea, he found that with the falling of the tide his outward passage was blocked: There was simply not enough water over the New Inlet bar, a fact that was beginning to sadden the lives of Wilmington commission merchants. So, quite unappreciative of the distinction of being about the only freshwater whale in captivity, he swam impatiently up and down the muddy waters of the Cape Fear estuary while awaiting, like many another mariner before him, a flood tide to help him negotiate the passage to the bluewater freedom beyond the bar.[1]

During Reconstruction, Cape Fear pilots believed that, at least for the first two-thirds of the nineteenth century and perhaps even longer, the harbor had been undergoing a gradual but certain deterioration. There was a tradition in the area that the earliest navigators had found a clear channel, thirty feet deep,[2] leading

1. Wilmington *Daily Herald*, March 22, 1866. (This paper first appeared in 1865 as *The Herald of the Union*, but shortly thereafter began appearing as *The Daily Herald* or *The Wilmington Herald*. Hereinafter cited as Wilmington *Herald*.)

2. In discussions of channel depths, more often than not, writers fail to indicate the phase of the tide to which their figures refer, tidal fluctuation averaging about

into the bay,[3] a passage which would have made the harbor available to any merchant ship existing during the eighteenth and early nineteenth centuries. While this tradition is not verified by any surviving records of early surveys, it is not impossible that the channel may have had such a depth in early historical times. It appears likely that the rapid settlement and clearing of land in the Cape Fear valley in the early eighteenth century may have resulted in soil erosion which added considerably to the silt burden of the river, turning its black waters into amber. Some of this silt may have been deposited along the bars at the river's mouth. In any event, the oldest surviving survey, one made in 1733, disclosed only fourteen feet of water over the bar.[4]

In addition to the silt from upcountry soil erosion, the harbor seems to have suffered considerable damage as a result of a storm; in the fall of 1761, "a violent and long continued North East storm" struck the low-lying peninsula shielding the estuary from the sea.[5] Twelve miles north of the cape, at a point on the peninsula particularly barren of protective vegetation, the furious wind drove the light beach sand before it, cutting down a segment of

four and a half feet at the bars. Wilmington *The Daily Journal*, March 31, 1871, hereinafter cited as Wilmington *Daily Journal* and Wilmington Weekly *Journal*. However, despite the fact marine charts give depths at "mean water," newspaper discussions, unless otherwise stated, apparently refer to "high water," the phase of the tide during which heavily laden ships could clear the bars with the greatest safety.

3. John Brickell, *The Natural History of North Carolina* (Dublin, Ireland: James Carson, 1737), p. 4, hereinafter cited as Brickell, *History*; Wilmington *Daily Journal*, March 22, 1870; Report of the Harbor Committee of the Wilmington Chamber of Commerce, 1868, contained in Henry Nutt Scrapbook, p. 1, Southern Historical Collection, The University of North Carolina, hereinafter cited as Nutt Scrapbook. Though involved in various business enterprises, Henry Nutt had a consuming interest in the problems of the Cape Fear harbor. His Scrapbook is a collection of letters, documents, reports by himself and others, all concerning Cape Fear navigation.

4. Henry Nutt, "Report to General Joseph G. Totten, Chief Army Engineer, March 30, 1853," p. 15, contained in Henry Nutt Scrapbook, Southern Historical Collection, The University of North Carolina, hereinafter cited as Nutt, "Report, 1853."

5. *Ibid.*, p. 16; J. S. Reilly, *Wilmington: Past, Present and Future* (n.p.: n.p., [c. 1884]), p. 45, hereinafter cited as Reilly, *Wilmington*. People on the lower Cape Fear were uncertain as to exactly when this storm occurred, several different years being suggested. One writer, however, presented a convincing argument for September 20, 1761. Wilmington *Daily Journal*, June 21, 1871.

the land to below the level of the flood tide, so that a raging sea found its way across the narrow neck of land to the Cape Fear river,[6] creating "New" Inlet and Smith's Island.

Several generations passed, however, before the harbor suffered the full impact of the New Inlet breach. For years Smith's "Island" was only an island at high tide; and the more leisurely citizens of Wilmington continued to drive their carriages down the strand to the cape and the palmetto groves at Bald Head, fording the swash at low water. But each rush of the flood tide cut the swash deeper, adding to the silt burden of the river until by the end of the eighteenth century, New Inlet was six feet deep.[7]

The outcome of harbor surveys, conducted during the first half of the nineteenth century, varied considerably as channels shifted and as new bars and islands came into being and old ones passed away. But the general direction of the harbor's development was unmistakable: As New Inlet gained in breadth and depth, the main channel near Bald Head was growing more shallow, until at last at mid-century, the two channels were equalized at about thirteen feet.[8] A common explanation for this development was that the power of the river current, "while ample to scour out and keep open one good outlet, was insufficient for two."[9]

As early as 1827, North Carolina congressmen were able to obtain federal aid in an effort to maintain the state's principal port. Congress appropriated enough money for some dredging of the channel. But the sand borne by the sea wind, the tides, and the river's current was more than a match for a dredge boat; and it could do little more than slow down the process of deterioration. At the same time, some funds were used for the construction of jetties, log fences built across some of the more shallow entrances to the harbor, in an effort to force the current to deepen the main ship channels. The results of these efforts are an example of an inexpensive, small-scale venture ending in failure and almost pure waste, whereas a more costly operation might

6. Wilmington *Daily Journal*, December 12, 1869.
7. Nutt, "Report, 1853," p. 15.
8. *Ibid.*
9. *Ibid.*, p. 16; Wilmington *Daily Journal*, December 12, 1869.

have achieved permanent results. A series of storms, beginning in 1857, made a clean sweep of the flimsy jetties and restored the harbor to at least as poor a condition as that of thirty years before, despite a total expenditure, since 1827, of more than $350,000.[10]

Paradoxical as it may seem, the Civil War years, which found the harbor in about the worst condition that it had ever been in during its entire history, were precisely the years of its greatest importance and commercial prosperity. The main reason for this was that the treacherous shoal waters off Cape Fear presented considerably greater difficulties to the federal fleet than they did to swift, shallow-draught blockade-runners, which could utilize the skill of local bar pilots. The shallow channels leading into the estuary were no obstacle to these ships, and for the last half of the war most Confederate foreign trade passed through Wilmington.[11]

But the obstacles to navigation by deep-draught ships, such a boon to exporters during the war years, had a considerably different significance with the coming of peace. Even as the harbor was filling up, the draughts of ships were growing deeper. By the beginning of the eighties, a harbor would need a fourteen and a half foot channel to attract even a few transatlantic steamers.[12] Yet in 1869 the harbor could not accommodate ships drawing more than ten or twelve feet, and these could enter and leave only at flood tide.[13] The prospect that Wilmington might soon be restricted to only coastal shipping had implications that one pessimist found sinister indeed: "Because the Cape Fear seems to be gradually filling up, and vessels of a large class cannot now enter our port, and because the produce of the State is seeking ports in other states, while the trade and commerce *of our own* languishes,

10. William P. Craighill to A. A. Humphreys, January 23, 1871, Nutt Scrapbook, pp. 5-6; Wilmington *Morning Star*, February 13, 1886. (This paper began in 1867 as *The Evening Star*, changing shortly thereafter to *The Morning Star*. Hereinafter cited as Wilmington *Star*.)

11. James Sprunt, *Tales of the Cape Fear Blockade*, ed. Cornelius M. D. Thomas, (Winnabow, N.C.: Charles Towne Preservation Trust, 1960), *passim*.

12. James Sprunt, *Information and Statistics Respecting Wilmington, North Carolina, Being a Report by the President of the Produce Exchange Presented to its Members, April 1883* (Wilmington: Jackson & Bell, Water-Power Presses, 1883), p. 97, hereinafter cited as Sprunt, *Information*.

13. Wilmington *Daily Journal*, December 12, 1869.

many people suppose that North Carolina is doomed and may sooner or later yield to the law of circumstance [and] merge her territory into Virginia and South Carolina. . . ."[14]

To save the port, North Carolina congressmen appealed for federal aid. During Reconstruction, Congress, to be sure, had shown a certain generosity toward schemes designed to improve transportation facilities. The lobbyists, who scurried around Capitol Hill, were each, like some anxious midwife, trying to bring to birth a cherished project; and if, in the days of the Credit Mobilier, these infant projects did not always mature in such a way as to fulfill the altruistic hopes expressed by the lobbyist, at the same time, one can hardly deny that these undertakings contributed to the general welfare of a number of individuals.

Yet, although Congress was generally partial to projects for improving transportation and Republicans were in control both in Washington and on the lower Cape Fear, North Carolina congressmen, like other southerners, experienced some difficulty in getting federal aid. It appears likely, actually, that the failure of the Republican party to consolidate its position in the South may have been due, at least in part, to the fact that party leaders too long bypassed the South in the distribution of patronage, and held too long to the belief that they had a captive Negro vote that could keep the South Republican. Indeed, it was not until 1870, the year the Conservatives gained control of the North Carolina legislature, that a Republican Congress got around to voting money to improve the Cape Fear harbor.[15]

Once Congress began to appropriate money for improving the port of Wilmington, however, the sums were generous and made on a regular basis. The Wilmington Chamber of Commerce appointed a committee to go to Washington and serve as a harbor lobby, and thus maintain this happy state of affairs. For the harbor committee, the Chamber of Commerce was careful to pick representatives from both political parties, the whole question of port improvement being remarkably free from partisan rancor.

14. *Ibid.* Emphasis in the original.
15. *Ibid.*; Reilly, *Wilmington*, p. 47.

The ability of the two parties to subordinate their differences to their common interest in the port later bore fruit: When the Democrats gained control of Congress, there was no interruption in the appropriations to the Cape Fear project, and the work on the harbor could continue without delays.[16]

The outcome of this co-operation must have been gratifying indeed to the people of the lower Cape Fear. Congress made twelve appropriations between 1870 and 1882 that totaled $1,502,-500, about four times the amount that the federal government had allotted to the Cape Fear over a thirty-year period before the war.[17] With such funds available, the army engineers in charge of the project could attempt much more fundamental solutions to the problem of the harbor than had been possible before.

It was none too soon; because the land that protected the estuary from the sea was wasting away, as the high easterly winds drove the light beach sand into the harbor. As the height of the shielding land was cut down nearer and nearer to that of high tide, the land was becoming increasingly vulnerable to the ravages of the sea. Each storm left its mark. New Inlet was now about three-quarters of a mile wide; and, just to the south of it, the sea had cut another swash; and the intervening land, known as Zeke's Island, was being rapidly devoured by the waves. It was through these inlets that easterly winds drove the flood tide; and with it came light, floating sand, drawn with the tide like drifting snow. The tide ebbed out to sea through the Old Ship Channel, twelve miles to the south; but only after much of its sand burden had been deposited in the harbor.[18] If the work of the winds and the tides were allowed to continue unchecked, it appeared that, where there had once been a harbor protected by beaches, there would soon be only a continuous, useless salt marsh.

The first problem was to arrest, if possible, the process of erosion that was destroying the land shield. To do this the army engineers had built across the path of the northeasterly winds parallel lines of rail fences, a few feet apart, between which were

16. Wilmington *Daily Journal*, January 17, 1874; Reilly, *Wilmington*, p. 47.
17. Reilly, *Wilmington*, p. 47.
18. Wilmington *Daily Journal*, March 22, 1870; January 20, 1871.

placed brush. These brush and rail fences trapped wind-driven sand, raising protective dikes to the height of the fences. In order to secure more permanently these shielding dunes, the harbor engineers had them planted in "Carolina Beach grass" and other plants that were tough enough to resist the abrasion of blowing sand, and that could survive in sterile, salty, and almost waterless soil. Such plants do not grow luxuriantly; but they afforded some protection to the harbor and, in so doing, gradually transformed the chemistry of the soil.[19]

The second problem the engineers faced was to close all the entrances to the harbor except one, forcing the river current to sweep out one deep channel. But which inlet should be left open? New Inlet was the most convenient channel to shippers. Because Frying Pan Shoals extended twenty miles out to sea south of Cape Fear, as a kind of submerged extension of the cape, Wilmington was about thirty-two miles closer to the open sea by way on New Inlet. Furthermore, for the fleet of small coastal schooners, called "corn crackers," that operated between Wilmington and Albemarle Sound, the distance was sixty-four miles longer by way of Old Ship Channel, not to mention the fact that the longer route would force them to navigate the dangerous waters south of Cape Fear.[20]

Unfortunately, the engineers had to subordinate the problems posed by commerce to those posed by nature. A survey revealed that the floor of New Inlet contained rock,[21] so that it would be difficult for either the river current or a dredge boat to deepen the channel. It was also through this inlet that the wind-driven tides floated a vast quantity of sand into the harbor. After some discussion of these problems, Colonel James H. Simpson, chief officer in charge of the project, decided to try to turn the harbor clock back to 1761, closing up New Inlet. By so doing he believed

19. *Ibid.*, March 20, 1872; U.S. Department of Agriculture, *Soil: The Yearbook of Agriculture, 1957* (Washington: Government Printing Office, 1957), pp. 321-26; Henry Nutt to W. W. Harriss, July 13, 1871, and Nutt to William L. De Rosset, November 9, 1871, Nutt Scrapbook, pp. 11, 13.

20. Wilmington *Daily Journal*, May 28, 1876; Wilmington *Review*, January 21, 1882.

21. Wilmington *Daily Journal*, February 8, 1871.

that the "bar can be restored to its original depth, and that the largest ships can be floated over it safely."[22]

In order to close the inlet, instead of using jetties, the log fences that had proven so vulnerable to storms, Colonel Simpson made use of cribs, heavy log frames filled with rock. The lines of cribs, with which he obstructed the inlet, served much the same purpose as had the rail-and-brush fences on land. They trapped the sand borne through the inlet by the tides, until the beach was built to above the level of high tide. After ten years of work, 1871-81, Smith's Island was connected to the mainland by a long thin isthmus.[23]

On the lower Cape Fear in the 1870's and 1880's, it was a person with little local pride indeed who was not pleased to learn that the pilots were finding more and more water over the bar; and, in 1890, a short time after the Galveston *News* had bragged that the H.M.S. "Bentala" had cleared the Galveston bar with a cargo of 4,094,027 pounds of cotton, the Wilmington *Messenger* could proudly reply that the same ship would clear the Rip with 4,358,819 pounds of cargo. "The Bentala . . . will go out of our port," the paper added, "drawing seventeen feet of water."[24] But there were a few other problems that might prevent Wilmington from rivaling Galveston as a seaport.

During the latter half of the nineteenth century, the lower Cape Fear could scarcely be said to suffer from the backwardness of its transportation system. Not only was there a revival of the importance of the harbor, during this time, as a port of call for transatlantic shipping, but also the region had well-developed inland and coastwise connections by both rail and water. Coastal and river craft, though declining in importance, continued to move a considerable amount of freight. As a result of the war and the federal blockade, the regular steamship service that connected Wilmington with Charleston and Savannah, in ante-bellum days, had been premanently superseded by railroad communication. With the coming of peace, however, three steamship companies

22. *Ibid.*, January 20, 1871.
23. Nutt to W. W. Harriss, April 7, 1871, Nutt Scrapbook, p. 9; Wilmington *Star*, February 13, 1886.
24. Wilmington *Messenger*, January 1, 1890.

were re-established, each of which connected Wilmington with a different northern city: The Baltimore and Wilmington Company operated three ships; the Southern Steamship Company kept two ships plying between Wilmington and Philadelphia; and the New York and Wilmington Company maintained three ships.[25]

There was also centered about Wilmington considerable water-borne traffic of a more local character. The Wilmington Produce Exchange reported in 1886 that, besides seven tugboats used on the lower river and harbor, there were four steamers connecting the city with Fayetteville, 112 miles above Wilmington on the Northwest Cape Fear, the main branch of the river. There were also four other steamers connecting Wilmington with the various points along the Black River, a Cape Fear tributary. Besides the steamers there were ten flat-boats, used to haul naval stores to the city, craft which ranged in capacity from two hundred to four hundred barrels. In addition there were sixteen coastal sailing schooners. Most of these were the so-called "corn crackers" that hauled corn from the Albermarle Sound area to Wilmington, though some operated between the city and points along the coast of South Carolina.[26]

Local, water-borne commerce was a cheap form of transportation, but one that was beset with a number of dangers and uncertainties. The cape called "Fear" did not bear that name because of maritime superstition. Even the skipper of a "corn cracker," with all of his knowledge of the waters around the cape, could sometimes pile up his craft on top of a phantom island or some shoal that was playing hide-and-go-seek with the chartmakers.[27] Furthermore, even river shipping was not without its hazards. Though considerable cargo moved by steamer, during the "nine flush water months," between Wilmington and Fayetteville, the upper seventy-five miles of the route was "badly obstructed by sunken logs, snags, overhanging trees and shoals. . . ."[28]

25. Charles Lewis Price, "Railroads and Reconstruction in North Carolina, 1865-1871" (Doctoral dissertation, The University of North Carolina, 1957), p. 18, hereinafter cited as Price, "Railroads"; Wilmington *Review*, April 9, 1884; Wilmington *Daily Journal*, June 29, 1873; Reilly, *Wilmington*, p. 94.

26. Wilmington *Star*, August 7, 1886.

27. Wilmington *Review*, April 15, 1885.

28. Wilmington *Star*, February 13, 1886.

Normally, by carrying less cargo, the steamers could reach Fayetteville during the low water months of the late summer and fall, but in particularly dry years they became grounded, and so remained for weeks at a time. Moreover, these craft had flat bottoms that presented a very great area at slight depth. As effective as a ship constructed in this fashion might be for navigating the shallow waters of the upper river, it was not nearly so successful when a crust of ice formed on the Cape Fear. Even during the flush water season, steamers could be paralyzed by a freeze.

Perhaps the experience of some shivering travelers illustrates the plight of the steamboat in its competition with the railroads. In January, 1886, two steamers, the "Bladen" and the "Hurt," loaded at Fayetteville and headed down a frozen river toward Wilmington. After several days, more characterized by difficulties than by progress, the two skippers, admitting defeat, tied up their ships at Tarheel. Whereupon, the passengers disembarked and walked twenty miles overland to Lumberton, where they were able to take a train for Wilmington.[29]

During Reconstruction there was no more important railroad center in North Carolina than Wilmington, which was the home of three railway companies. The oldest of these, the Wilmington and Weldon, in its early days the longest railroad in the world,[30] ran north out of Wilmington for 162 miles through a good agricultural region to Weldon, where it made connection with another line leading to Petersburg and Richmond. The fact that the railroad terminated at Weldon, in the rich Roanoke valley, made it possible for Wilmington commission merchants to attract cotton and wheat to their market that had previously gone to a closer and better port, Norfolk.[31]

It was probably the prosperity of the Wilmington and Weldon,[32] as well as the stimulating effect that it had on the city's commerce, that provided the inspiration for many subsequent railroad schemes, such as the Wilmington, Columbia, and Augusta Railroad, originally called the Wilmington and Man-

29. *Ibid.*, January 17, 1886.
30. Price, "Railroads," p. 11.
31. *Ibid.*, pp. 11, 29.
32. *Ibid.*, p. 30.

chester. Like the Wilmington and Weldon, this road was designed to tap the hinterland of a rival port, in the latter instance, Charleston. Yet, in this respect, the road, unlike its predecessor, must be counted largely a failure. Except for the war years, the W C & A probably moved very little cotton from Piedmont South Carolina and Georgia to Wilmington. Charleston had a well-developed railway system of its own, and during Reconstruction, at least, its port offered more bottoms bound directly for Europe. Wilmington, on the other hand, even as late as 1884, after its port improvement program was well underway, still had to transship some cotton to Europe by way of larger ports, thus adding to the expenses of the Wilmington buyer and depressing the price that he could offer a planter.[33]

Although the W C & A failed to make grass grow in the streets of Charleston, it nevertheless achieved some results that must have been almost as gratifying to its owners. It brought considerable quantities of lumber and naval stores to Wilmington,[34] the city being closer to the Piney Woods counties of northeastern South Carolina than it was to the cotton-growing Piedmont region of that state. Also, for many years Wilmington presented a far larger and better established market for naval stores than Charleston.[35] Even more important, the line became a link in a major, north-south railway. Furthermore, since regular steamer service between Wilmington and Charleston was not revived after the war, the W C & A railroad became the sole link between eastern North Carolina and South Carolina.

Having attempted, with varying success, to tap the economic hinterland of rival ports, railway investors on the lower Cape Fear next undertook to penetrate the Piedmont region of North Carolina, an area in which Wilmington shippers could expect less competition. In 1855, the legislature had chartered the Wilming-

33. Reilly, *Wilmington*, p. 64.
34. Price, "Railroads," p. 18.
35. Thomas Gamble, "Pages from Wilmington's Story as America's First Great Naval Stores," and "Charleston's Story as a Naval Stores Emporium," both contained in *Naval Stores: History, Production, Distribution and Consumption*, ed. Thomas Gamble; this volume contains articles by various authors including several by Gamble himself (Savannah, Ga.: Review Publishing and Printing Co., 1921), pp. 31-34, 35-36, hereinafter cited as *Naval Stores*, Gamble, (ed.).

ton, Charlotte, and Rutherfordton Railroad to build a 268 mile
line from the port to Rutherfordton at the foot of the great Blue
Ridge. Unlike the earlier roads the W C & R would form the connecting link with no through routes, nor would it connect Wilmington with important cities. The most important town on the
line, in fact, would be Charlotte, which in 1860 had slightly over
two thousand people.[36] If the W C & R was going to make money
it would have to be by hauling local freight.

Fortunately, the prospects for this were good. For the first
sixty miles the road would run through the Piney Woods, where
naval stores would provide a brisk traffic during the warm
months.[37] But if a railway had to depend upon naval stores during the winter months, it was likely that its business would
become about as sluggish as the flow of cold pine gum itself. West
of the Piney Woods, however, lay cotton country, and it was
during the cool months that cotton found its way to market.
Thus the W C & R was not likely to enjoy much prosperity until
it had been completed from Wilmington to the richest cotton
counties of the Piedmont.

In 1861, the venture appeared to be on the brink of success.
A hundred miles of track had been laid west of Wilmington. The
line was out of the Piney Woods. It had opened up the first of the
cotton counties, though it had not yet reached the lands with the
most abundant harvests. But then General Beauregard's artillery
had opened fire on Fort Sumter, and the bright prospects that the
W C & R people entertained were not the only visions of the
future that were shattered in the general disaster that followed.[38]

With mountains of bales piling up on the water front of
blockaded Wilmington, opening up new cotton country was not
one of the major preoccupations of the Confederacy. On the contrary, the government needed iron rails for the lines that were

36. United States, Office of the Census, *Eighth Census of the United States: 1860.
Population.* (Washington: Government Printing Office, 1864), p. 359.

37. But naval stores which came to market by water were collected over the
summer in the areas of production and shipped down stream during the "flush
water" months, October to March. Percival Perry, "The Naval Stores Industry in
the Ante-Bellum South" (Doctoral dissertation, Duke University, 1947), p. 86,
hereinafter cited as Perry, "Naval Stores."

38. Price, "Railroads," pp. 15-16.

militarily strategic far more than it needed the W C & R. As a result, Richmond undertook measures for dismantling the line and transferring its rails elsewhere. After some ten miles of track had been taken up, however, Governor Vance, who was covering his retreat from Unionism with the slogan, "fight the Yankees and fuss with the Confederacy," interposed the power of the state government and stopped any further dismantling of the road.[39]

But, though the line was permitted to keep most of its track, it was permitted to keep little else. It retained, in fact, only one of its seven prewar locomotives plus a few worn-out cars.[40] The company was thus able to limp along until the end of the war, when it was put out of operation completely by military damage, the desire to wipe out the W C & R being one of the rare areas of agreement between the Confederate and Union commanders in the region.[41]

After Appomattox, the military government of the Cape Fear region restored the line to operation on a minimum basis. But, due to the legacy of war and because the road still could not tap the main sources of Piedmont cotton, the specter of bankruptcy still hovered over its activities. While the affairs of almost any private business can affect the interests of the community at large, perhaps none can become a matter of public concern more readily than those of a railroad. The future development of Wilmington as a cotton market depended upon the completion of the W C & R, while such prosperity as the port presently enjoyed from the naval stores trade was jeopardized by the shaky financial condition of the same line. The link between the fate of this road and the general fortunes of the Cape Fear community would have some bearing on what would pass for political morality in the region during Reconstruction.

Rabelais created a literary character, Panurge, who might have felt quite at home in the railway politics of Reconstruction. This

39. *Ibid.*, pp. 53-54; Glenn Tucker, *Zeb Vance: Champion of Personal Freedom* (Indianapolis: The Bobbs-Merrill Co., 1965), p. 362; Hugh Talmage Lefler and Albert Ray Newsome, *North Carolina: The History of a Southern State* (Chapel Hill: The University of North Carolina Press, 1963), p. 448.

40. Price, "Railroads," pp. 37, 102.

41. *Ibid.*, p. 99.

individual was said to have had "sixty three ways of solving his problems, the most honorable of which, and the one most commonly used, being highway robbery."[42] Certainly, George Swepson must have had that many ways of enticing support for his railroad bills, and a number of these can be more admired for their ingenuity than for their propriety. He spent, in fact, a quarter of a million dollars removing legislative roadblocks to his program, a grandiose undertaking that in two years almost doubled the public debt of war-prostrate North Carolina.[43]

George Z. French, the Reverend James Sinclair, General Joseph C. Abbott, and other political figures of the Cape Fear country received sizable sums of this money.[44] This, plus the fact that these men were carpetbaggers, the pedigreed villains of so much of southern historical writing, has led some observers to conclude that these legislators "sold" their votes to the railroad lobby.[45]

Indeed, they accepted the money and worked and voted for the railway appropriations. But, with or without Swepson's money, what position could they be reasonably expected to take in regard to these bills? Even if we assume that they were motivated by no other instinct than self-aggrandizement, it appears likely that they would have favored the legislation with or without lobby funds. They all stood to gain politically as railroad appropriations were popular with their constituents. Some of them stood to gain economically as well. The in-laws of the Reverend Sinclair owned a great deal of land near the W C & R; and for one to say that a wealthy man, such as General Abbott, who owned three thousand acres on the same line,[46] "sold" his vote when he

42. *Gargantua et Pantagruel*, Book II, Ch. 16.

43. North Carolina, *Report of the Commission to Investigate Fraud and Corruption Under Act of Assembly Session 1871-1872* (Raleigh: James H. Moore, State Printer and Binder, 1872), pp. 316-19, hereinafter cited as *Shipp Report*; Joseph Gregoire de Roulhac Hamilton, *Reconstruction in North Carolina* (New York: Columbia University Press, 1914), pp. 427-28, 448, hereinafter cited as Hamilton, *Reconstruction*.

44. *Shipp Report*, pp. 316-18.

45. Horace Wilson Raper, "The Political Career of William Woods Holden with Special Reference to his Provisional Governorship" (Master's thesis, The University of North Carolina, 1947), p. 267.

46. Wilmington Weekly *Journal*, November 16, 1867; Wilmington *Post*, October 9, 1881.

voted for measures that would further enrich him, is to show a certain inability to distinguish between the corrupted and the corrupters, to say the least.

It appears to be nearer the mark to say that Swepson, who was a member of the minority party, the Conservatives, and not a member of the legislature, distributed railroad lobby funds with a view to strengthening the influence of Republican legislators who had strong railway interests in their constituencies and who were vigorous advocates of railroad appropriations.

In any event, by fair means or foul, particularly the latter, the legislature was induced to issue bonds; and the thirteen million dollars raised in this way were appropriated to needy railroads, of which the W C & R received three million. Only two roads, in fact, received more: the Western Division of the North Carolina Railroad, of which Swepson was president, and the Chatham Railroad, in which he was probably heavily interested.[47]

Thus, since the owners of the W C & R realized roughly twelve times as much money from the transaction as did all the corrupt legislators in both parties, it might be worthwhile to note the political affiliations of these men. About two-thirds of the stock belonged to Conservatives. About one-fourth belonged to the city of Wilmington, which in 1868 had passed under Republican control. The remaining shares belonged to Silas Martin and perhaps to other Republicans such as Edward Kidder.[48] The president of the line, 1863-69, was Colonel Robert H. Cowan, who had been a member of the Secession Convention, a Confederate officer, and a Conservative member of the lower house.[49] The bipartisan character of this company, plus the general interest the Cape Fear region had in its prosperity, may help explain the curious attitude the people of that section would assume toward the scandalous revelations that legislative investigations would make during the next two years.

47. Hamilton, *Reconstruction*, p. 448; Charles L. Price, "The Railroad Schemes of George W. Swepson," *East Carolina College Publications in History: Essays in American History*, ed. Hubert A. Coleman *et al.* (Greenville, N.C.: Department of History, East Carolina College, 1964), I, 42.

48. Wilmington Weekly *Journal*, October 30, 1868; Wilmington *Star*, October 18, 1872, February 12, 1879.

49. Wilmington *Star*, November 12, 1872.

In most parts of North Carolina, 1870-71, newspaper readers were captivated by the evidence of railroad frauds that was being uncovered by legislative committees. The first of the investigations, though chaired by former governor Thomas Bragg, a Conservative, was bipartisan in inspiration and did not degenerate into a quest for political ammunition.[50] Following their capture in 1870 of a firm majority in the legislature, however, the Conservatives created the Shipp Committee, which reopened the investigations giving them a strongly partisan character. Though the committee did not appear to be calling the witnesses or asking the questions that would be embarrassing to the Conservative party,[51] the Republicans had now lost all control over the investigating process and there was little they could do except heckle and fume in helpless rage.

But in Wilmington the reaction of both parties was different. Neither seemed interested in the shocking exposé being unfolded at Raleigh. Wilmington Conservatives did not find in the revelations many new items to add to their already long list of Republican misdeeds. In fact, news of the hearing got into the press of both parties most frequently in the form of a reprint from a Raleigh paper placed at the bottom of a column as a filler.

At an annual meeting of the Board of Directors of the W C & R in 1871, perhaps as a measure of the degree to which they were impressed by this public demonstration of Republican perfidy, the Conservative majority elected a Republican director, Silas Martin, who was also mayor of Wilmington, as the new president of the company; and re-elected him in 1872, after the record of his party's depravity had finally been completed by the Shipp Committee.[52]

As sad as it is to relate, the wages of sin are not always death; they are sometimes prosperity. The unhappy events of Reconstruction seemed to have been the turning point in the history of the W C & R. It launched a vigorous construction program, changed its name to the Carolina Central Railroad, and rode out

50. North Carolina, *Report of the Railroad Investigation Commission* (Raleigh: James H. Moore, 1871), *passim*. This report is generally known as the *Bragg Report*.
51. *Shipp Report, passim*.
52. Wilmington *Star*, October 18, 1872.

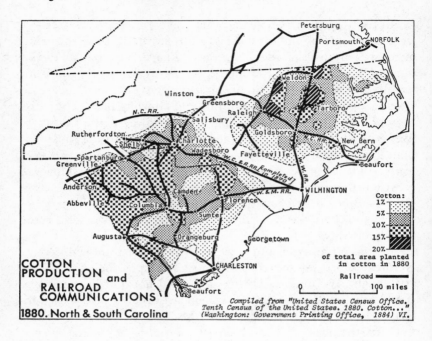

COTTON
PRODUCTION and
RAILROAD
COMMUNICATIONS
1880. North & South Carolina

Cotton:
1%
5%
10%
15%
20%
of total area planted
in cotton in 1880

Railroad ━━━
0   100 miles

Compiled from "United States Census Office.
Tenth Census of the United States. 1880. Cotton..."
(Washington: Government Printing Office, 1884) VI.

the Panic of 1873 magnificently. "Work on the C C Railroad was never for one day interrupted," the Republican *Post* proudly reported; and by 1875 it had been completed through to Charlotte and Shelby, opening up the richest cotton counties of the Piedmont. And the bales began to roll. "In four or five years," the *Post* dreamed, "Wilmington should export 400,000-500,000 bales."[53]

The *Post* was too optimistic. But, nevertheless, the twin accomplishments, the opening up of Piedmont North Carolina cotton to the Wilmington market after 1875 and the completion of the harbor improvements in 1881, were to have important con-

53. Wilmington *Post*, January 8, 1875.

sequences for the lower Cape Fear. The fact that, beginning in the 1880's, the master of a merchant ship could find considerably more water available over the Cape Fear bar, and considerably more cotton available on the Wilmington water front, made the harbor a more popular port of call for vessels in the cotton trade.

Then, in turn, because more ships tied up in the Cape Fear that were seeking to haul cotton cargoes to Europe, Wilmington cotton buyers, who were no longer burdened with the expense of having to transship cotton to Europe by way of larger ports, could now offer prices that put Wilmington in a more favorable position in respect to rival cotton markets. Not only could the port now attract the cotton of Piedmont North Carolina, but also it could compete with Norfolk for the cotton of the Roanoke valley, in northeastern North Carolina, and with Charleston for the cotton of Piedmont South Carolina.

But when one compares the increase in cotton exports from Wilmington with the total tonnage of ships clearing the port, it is clear that something was wrong. There was no increase in total tonnage corresponding to the rise in cotton exports. It is apparent that harbor improvements, by accommodating the channel to the fact that ships now had deeper draughts, and, thereby, perhaps saving the port at the same time, had not increased its total importance. Actually the rise of Wilmington's cotton exports did no more than compensate for the stagnation and decline in other aspects of its economy, particularly in the naval stores trade.

Though more than a century old, Wilmington remained a city in the wilderness. From the banks of the Cape Fear estuary, the great Piney Woods stretched away to the west for fifty miles. Yet, from colonial days, this lonely expanse of country, with its lean white soil, had been the basis for much of Wilmington's prosperity, and had made it the world's largest market for naval stores.

Certainly during the months following Appomattox, the naval stores industry did not appear to be in a state of decay. On the contrary, it was the aspect of the economy that seemed to be enjoying the most vigorous revival. But one of the reasons for the sudden rebound of naval stores after the war was the primitive

COTTON EXPORTS, IN THOUSANDS OF BALES, FOR SELECTED PORTS

(Figures have been rounded off to the nearest thousand; and in each case, are for the year ending June 30)

Total Tonnage, in Thousands of Tons, of American and Foreign Ships Cleared

	1875	1880	1885	1890	1895	1900	1905	1910
Norfolk (thousands of cotton bales)	67	254	296	266	192	46	21	7
total shipping tonnage	49	119	111	99	157	392	450	811
Wilmington (thousands of cotton bales)	15	37	66	112	202	275	345	299
total shipping tonnage	72	95	82	88	88	81	81	68
Charleston (thousands of cotton bales)	265	314	340	240	341	*	78	116
total shipping tonnage	119	148	149	121	117	53	19	60
Savannah (thousands of cotton bales)	426	425	390	535	537	726	1,194	1,283
total shipping tonnage	167	170	181	255	300	344	433	385
New Orleans (thousands of cotton bales)	995	1,398	1,336	1,825	2,088	1,706	2,366	1,233
total shipping tonnage	523	859	675	1,015	998	1,721	1,986	2,103
Galveston (thousands of cotton bales)	225	294	230	456	1,349	1,569	2,269	2,114
total shipping tonnage	128	99	90	170	400	817	1,082	908

*data not available
Source: United States Department of the Treasury, Bureau of Statistics, Commerce and Navigation, Vols. 875-910.

character of the industry. It had seen few changes in production techniques since the dawn of history.

Prehistoric man had learned that the sticky gum that oozes from wounds in the bark of pine and fir trees, not being soluble in water, can be used to seal the cracks in the bottoms of boats. Furthermore, he had learned that by cooking it, this gum could be concentrated into a thick black mass, or pitch, which was even better for caulking a vessel or the roof of a house or protecting other objects against water. With the great discoveries and the Commercial Revolution, there was an enormous increase in demand for naval stores, the production of which was then concentrated in Scandinavia.

Since, during the days of wooden navies, naval stores were a highly strategic commodity, the English government began, in the seventeenth century, to subsidize experiments in their production in various American colonies, with a view of obtaining a source for the Royal Navy that would be independent of the diplomatic web of Europe. These experiments were most successful in the Cape Fear valley, where the longleaf pine yielded gum in unusual abundance. As late as the decade before the Civil War, North Carolina accounted for about two-thirds of the production of naval stores in the United States, and much of the remaining third was produced in adjacent areas of South Carolina and was sold on the Wilmington market.[54] In 1850, the two Carolinas produced more than 95 per cent of the naval stores manufactured in the United States.[55]

Enormous quantities of cheap tar were produced in the Cape Fear valley by a technique known as "tar burning." So rich is longleaf pine in resinous gum, that its wood is highly resistant to

54. Charleston, the chief market in South Carolina, had one naval stores inspector in 1859, while Wilmington had twelve. Perry, "Naval Stores," p. 161; Peter Duncan Randall, "Geographic Factors in the Growth and Economy of Wilmington, North Carolina" (Doctoral dissertation, The University of North Carolina, 1965), p. 40, hereinafter cited as Randall, "Geographic Factors in the Growth and Economy of Wilmington."

55. Jay Ward, "Naval Stores: The Industry," in *Trees: The Yearbook of Agriculture, 1949*, U.S., Department of Agriculture (Washington: The Government Printing Office, 1949), pp. 286-87, hereinafter cited as Ward, "Naval Stores"; Thomas Gamble, "The Production of Naval Stores in the United States: How the Industry Has Moved from Carolina to Texas. . . ," *Naval Stores*, Gamble, (ed.), p. 77.

decay. As a result, the heart of a fallen pine may lie for more than a century on the forest floor, preserved by the gum it produced while living; and the first Europeans arriving in the Piney Woods found a vast, original accumulation of fallen, dead pine, known as "fat lightwood.' Tar burners would gather lightwood and stack it compactly on a low mound of hard earth, which they had previously scored with trenches that radiated out from the center. They would then cover the wood with dirt and light it. The heat from the smothered fire reduced the wood, melting the crystallized gum into tar, which by means of the trenches, would flow, mixed with sand and trash, out from under the kiln. Sometimes tar was marketed in its crude state. In other instances, by boiling it in a pot, impurities could be removed and it could be further concentrated so that it could be sold as pitch. Tar and pitch were collected in barrels made by Piney Woods coopers.[56]

There was also in the Cape Fear region an extensive "gum naval stores" industry, that is to say, production that is based on tapping living trees. During the winter months, the Piney Woods people would spend much of their time cutting new "boxes," which, in reality, were cavities chopped into the trunk of the tree. The floor of the "box" was scooped out sufficiently to hold about a quart of sap. With the coming of warm weather, the gum would begin to flow; and about mid-March "dipping" would begin. The sap, or crude turpentine, would be ladled from the boxes and collected in barrels. In the meanwhile, clotting would take place in the cavity, so that congealed gum had stopped the fresh flow. Whereupon, "chipping" would begin. A V-shaped gash would be cut in the bark just above the box, so that fresh gum would flow into it. But after a week or ten days, this, in turn, would become clogged; and a new gash would be cut above it. Chipping was

56. For further details of the ante-bellum tar-making technique in the Piney Woods see Perry, "Naval Stores," pp. 64-75; and Frederick Law Olmsted, *A Journey in the Seaboard Slave States in the Years 1853-1854 With Remarks on Their Economy*, 2 vols. (New York: G. P. Putnam's Sons, 1904), I, 387, hereinafter cited as Olmsted, *Journey*. The remarkable stability of the production methods in the industry may be seen in the close correspondence between those described by Olmsted and the observations made, 1802-6, by the French botanist, François André Michaux, *The North American Sylva*, 2 vols. (Paris: C. d'Hautel, 1819), II, 275 ff.; and those made, 1730-31, by Brickell, *History*, pp. 265-66.

repeated three or four times a month throughout the warm months. A crop of boxes would continue to be profitable for an average of ten or twelve years.[57]

Crude turpentine was distilled in order to recover spirits of turpentine, used in medicine and paint, and rosin, used in varnish and soap. A turpentine still, much like a whisky still, was often located in a ravine, where a stream of running water could be used to cool the "worm," a coil of pipe used to condense the turpentine vapors. The worm was one of the few improvements that the industry had seen during the span of recorded history, primitive man having used the woolly side of a sheepskin to capture the turpentine vapors escaping from the boiling pot. After the spirits of turpentine had been driven off, condensed, and put in kegs, the residue in the still would be drawn off, put in barrels, and sold as rosin.[58]

The eventual collapse of tar production from fat lightwood, of course, was inevitable: The original accumulation of lightwood, though vast, was none the less limited. But the rapidity with which the supply was exhausted may have had something to do with the system of slave labor that was employed. Frederick Law Olmsted, visiting the Cape Fear country in the 1850's, compared the primitive, wasteful "tar burning" process that he observed there with the more economical destructive distillation oven then being used in northern Europe, and noted that the European process produced such clean tar that it could compete with American tar even in our own ports.[59]

But there was nothing inevitable, on the other hand, about the demise of the gum naval stores industry, based as it was on living, reproducing trees. Although the Piney Woods slaves impressed Olmsted as being "unusually intelligent and cheerful,"[60] at the same time, he did not find these men to be devoted conservation-

57. James Battle Avirett, *The Old Plantation: How We Lived in the Great House and Cabin Before the War* (New York: F. Tennyson Neely Co., 1901), pp. 66-69; Olmsted, *Journey*, I, 379-80, 386.

58. Ward, "Naval Stores," p. 268; Olmsted, *Journey*, I, 384.

59. Olmsted, *Journey*, I, 387.

60. *Ibid.*, I, 388.

ists. He found many boxes cut too deep, endangering the life of the tree.[61] Chipping also was carelessly done so that

in ninety-nine "orchards" out of a hundred, you will see that the chip has always been much broader and deeper than, with the slightest care to restrict it, it needs to have been. . . .

In some orchards, you will see that many trees have been killed by fire. The wire-grass, which grew among the trees the previous year, is frequently set on fire, either accidentally or purposely, when dead and dry, in the spring. It burns slowly, and with little flame, and the living trees, the bark of which is not very inflammable, are seldom injured. But where a tree has been boxed, and the chips lie about it, these take fire, and burn with more flame; so that frequently the turpentine in the box, and on the scarified wood above it, also takes fire, and burns with such intensity as to kill the tree. The danger might be avoided by raking away the chips and leaves, for a foot or two about the roots; but I nowhere saw this precaution taken. I mention these things, by the way, as further illustration of the general inefficient direction of slave-labor; or indicating, as might be rather claimed by the owners, that the high cost of the labor prevents its direction to these minor points of economy.[62]

American Negro slavery was an historical anachronism, and appeared to be wedded to the most primitive productive techniques. The system seemed incapable of harvesting the bounty of human intelligence, calculated stupidity being the slave's formula for survival. It was always a long way between master's brain and eye and the blind hands of each slave; and fear and the desire for brute survival were not motives that could unlock the creative magic in those dumb hands.

Whether or not slave labor was to blame, the consequences of the destructive exploitation of naval stores overtook the people of the Cape Fear country during the latter half of the nineteenth century. The brisk trade in naval stores during Reconstruction appears to have drawn the last drops of vitality from the Piney Woods; and, in 1872, we find a traveler, who had visited the area lying between the Cape Fear and the Pee Dee River, in South Carolina, exclaiming that "there are no sound trees in that region.

61. *Ibid.*, I, 379.
62. *Ibid.*, I, 381-82.

They have been boxed and reboxed till they are 'done for.' "[63] But there were other longleaf pines. The Piney Woods is actually a belt, varying in width, but stretching along the coast from North Carolina to Texas.

The industry began migrating from the Cape Fear. "About five-hundred colored turpentine workers from the forest of South Carolina and Georgia, arrived in the city yesterday," the *Review* noted. They were "on their way to spend Christmas holidays at their homes in Duplin, Wayne and Sampson counties. They had plenty of money and as they stopped over during the day some of our dealers made their presence profitable."[64] The naval stores industry relocated in the Piney Woods counties of the Deep South. There, utilizing relatively free labor, the operators were able to incorporate certain minimum principles of scientific forestry, a number of which had been practiced in Europe for generations.[65] As a result, a 1949 study, conducted by the United States Department of Agriculture, concluded that, in its present base, "the production of gum naval stores can continue indefinitely."[66]

Like naval stores, lumber was a Piney Woods industry that recovered quickly after the war. By 1872, in addition to the Cape Fear Building Company's Abbottsburg complex, there were five lumber mills operating on the Wilmington water front.[67] The connection between the coterie of Republican leaders, or "Ring," and the lumber business is evident when one considers that, of these six major lumber mills in the Cape Fear country, three belonged to Republican leaders.

Besides producing lumber, the Abbottsburg complex manufactured wooden railroad rolling stock, prefabricated houses, which were marketed at points as distant as Cuba, as well as a variety of other wood products.[68] Abbottsburg, however, would entail disappointment and perhaps even tragedy for General Abbott. In the

63. Wilmington *Star*, November 5, 1872, quoting the Charleston *News*, n.d.

64. Wilmington *Review*, December 20, 1883.

65. Carl E. Ostrom and John W. Squires, "Naval Stores: The Forest," in *Trees: The Yearbook of Agriculture, 1949*, United States, Department of Agriculture (Washington: Government Printing Office, 1949), p. 292.

66. Ward, "Naval Stores," p. 287.

67. Wilmington *Daily Journal*, March 21, 1872.

68. *Ibid.*, April 11, 1873.

first place, the Negroes of the community did not always remember to show their gratitude to the party of Lincoln and of the Cape Fear Building Company. In one rare instance of class solidarity, some Negro sawmill workers bolted the Republican party and elected a white fellow worker, a Piney Woods Democrat, as magistrate of Abbottsburg Township.[69]

But primarily General Abbott's troubles were economic. Besides suffering from the ordinary fluctuations of business conditions, his enterprise also had the special problems characteristic of an extractive industry, the tendency to exhaust resources within easy reach of an established plant. With the onset of the Panic of 1873-78, the Cape Fear Building Company was forced to close its doors completely; and Abbottsburg, which had been proclaimed by Radical and Conservative alike as the symbol of bold enterprise and progress, fell into ruin, slowly throttled by the relentless encroachment of a second growth, scrub forest, while General Abbott, in his last years bankrupt and abandoned by many of his political allies on the Potomac and on the Cape Fear, sat brooding in his Wilmington home.[70]

The Wilmington mill of the Chadbourn clan, a family that included a number of prominent Republican leaders, survived the panic; and, with the return of prosperity in the eighties, two generations of Chadbourn brothers and cousins founded the lumber town of Chadbourn in Columbus County, located on the Wilmington, Columbia, and Augusta Railroad in a magnificent expanse of virgin pines. The thriving town would soon recall Abbottsburg in its days of prosperity.[71] Thus, the lumber industry might wax and wane with the fortunes of the business cycle, a fluctuation that resulted in a frenzied cutting over of certain local areas at times when market conditions were good; but, in the long run, the possible extent of the industry was limited by the rate of annual growth of the Piney Woods. Lumbering, therefore, did not add much breadth and stability to the economy of the Cape Fear country.

69. Wilmington *Post*, August 20, 1875.
70. Wilmington *Review*, October 10, 1881.
71. *Ibid.*, March 5, 1887.

Closely related to lumbering was the wood preservation industry. With the near-exhaustion of heart pine, railroads were forced increasingly to rely upon ordinary timber for crossties and for the construction of trestles. So vulnerable was this common timber to the ravages of insects and decay that, wherever it was used for crossties, the annual replacement rate reached 450 ties to the mile.[72] Thus from the demands of railroads, as well as the growing requirement for poles to support various types of electric wire, a considerable need had arisen for a cheap method to protect wood that was exposed to earth and water.

A solution to this problem was begun in 1875 when the Louisville and Nashville Railroad built a plant in Pascagoula, Mississippi, for the preservation of common timber by impregnating it with creosote, which, like tar, may be derived from fat lightwood or coal. By 1880, two more such plants had been built;[73] and, in 1886, Ludwig Hansen and Andrew Smith, owners of the patent rights on a creosote preservation process, appeared in Wilmington and with a group of other investors founded the Carolina Oil and Creosote Company. The company, like a number of forest enterprises in the area, seemed to have been largely Republican in its political persuasion. In 1888, for example, the Board of Directors elected as president, William Parker Canaday, former Republican mayor of Wilmington; and as secretary and treasurer, General William Mahone, who currently dominated the Republican machine in Virginia.[74] The following year the directors, who now included a former Republican senator from Nevada, elected as president, Warren Miller, who had just been defeated as Republican candidate for the governor of New York.[75]

The Carolina Creosote Company planned to manufacture its

72. Thomas R. Truax, "Preservative Treatment of Wood," in *Trees: The Yearbook of Agriculture, 1949*, United States, Department of Agriculture, (Washington: Government Printing Office, 1949), p. 623.

73. Stanley Fitzgerald Horn, *This Fascinating Lumber Business* (Indianapolis: Bobbs-Merrill Co., 1951), p. 242, hereinafter cited as Horn, *Lumber*.

74. Wilmington *Review*, October 24, 1888; Comer Vann Woodward, *Origins of the New South*, Vol. IX of *A History of the South*, eds. Wendell Holmes Stephenson and E. Merton Coulter (10 vols.; Baton Rouge: Louisiana State University Press, 1951), pp. 99-101.

75. Wilmington *Review*, May 14, 15, 1889.

own creosote from fat lightwood. Though the original accumulation of this resource was nearing exhaustion, small quantities would be available in the Cape Fear country for some time to come. Furthermore, by building modern destructive distillation retorts, the company planned to make more efficient use of remaining stocks than was customary in the Piney Woods. The directors were also aware of the possibilities for making creosote from coal, which was now being mined on Deep River, one of the tributaries of the Cape Fear.[76]

In addition to retorts for making creosote, the company also built gigantic cylinders for pressure-cooking ordinary timber in a solution of creosote until it became thoroughly saturated with the substance. The process was so new that no one could say with certainty how much life it would add to structural timber. However, a twentieth-century study of a railroad bridge across Lake Pontchartrain, in Louisiana, indicated that the creosote-treated timber was in good condition after sixty years of service.[77]

The introduction of the creosote process into the Cape Fear country created a market for types of timber which previously had had little economic value. "We saw today a gentleman from near the banks of the Northeast River in Duplin County," the *Review* remarked, "who since last October has been employed in getting timber for the Carolina Oil and Creosote works. He now has four rafts on the way here which will arrive in a day or two unless accident befalls them. These rafts are made of poles of old field spruce pines (hitherto the most useless timber in the state) . . . . He has a large quantity of this sort of timber . . . and what has been an eyesore has now become the most profitable property in his possession."[78]

The Carolina Oil and Creosote Company appears to have prospered. At the thriving lumber port of Fernandina, Florida, it constructed a second plant, the management of which, incidentally, provided a job for an unemployed, professional Republican officeholder from Wilmington.[79] Later they built a third plant at

76. *Ibid.*, June 10, 1887; Wilmington *Daily Journal*, June 1, 1872.
77. Wilmington *Review*, June 10, 1887; Horn, *Lumber*, p. 243.
78. Wilmington *Review*, June 6, 1887.
79. Wilmington *Star*, November 11, 1886.

Seattle, Washington, which was organized as a subsidiary company, the Puget Sound Creosote Company.[80]

Curious as it may seem, fertilizer production on the lower Cape Fear, like the timber preservation business, owes its beginnings to an established lumber industry. Since colonial days the region had shipped lumber to the West Indies. But the lack of a profitable cargo for the return voyage to Wilmington had long been a problem. Shippers were frequently forced to the costly expedient of returning the lumber ships in ballast.

Following the Civil War, however, it occurred to a group of investors that if the lumber ships were returned to the Cape Fear with cargoes of West Indian guano instead of worthless ballast a fertilizer industry might be established in the area. This prospect was made even more inviting by the excellent rail connections that Wilmington had with the cotton growing regions of the Carolinas. In 1867, these men founded the Cape Fear Guano Company. It is noteworthy that a number of the founders had other business connections that would tend to sharpen their interest in the project: Two railroad presidents, R. R. Bridges of the Wilmington and Weldon and W. J. Hawkins of the Raleigh and Gaston, could look forward to increased traffic on their roads if the venture succeeded, while Edward Kidder, Republican leader and large exporter of lumber, could anticipate that a profitable return cargo from the islands would reduce his shipping cost.[81]

Unfortunately, in 1867, the Carolina cotton growers were in no position to pay for fertilizer and the Cape Fear Guano Company failed. Two years later, however, with the gradual recovery of the cotton industry, a number of the same investors made a second attempt with the formation of the Navassa Guano Company, named for the Caribbean island between Haiti and Jamaica from which they obtained their guano. In this effort they were joined by several members of the wealthy and talented MacRae family, one of whom was already engaged in the small-scale production of "Land Plaster," a fertilizer made from crude gypsum that he imported from Nova Scotia.[82]

80. Wilmington *Review*, October 27, 1888.
81. Wilmington Weekly *Journal*, July 19, 1867.
82. *Ibid.*, July 30, 1869; Wilmington *Daily Journal*, March 23, 1872.

Furthermore, the French brothers and others soon demonstrated the value of utilizing the local deposits of marl found along the Cape Fear in manufacturing fertilizer. The industry enjoyed success and was expanded by new companies entering the field, including the Powers and Gibbs Company, the Sans Souci Fertilizer Works, and the Acme Fertilizer Company. By the end of the century Navassa Guano and the three newcomers were producing a total of seventy thousand tons of fertilizer a year, which was being marketed in five states.[83]

By far the most important event of postwar, nineteenth-century North Carolina was the coming of the Industrial Revolution, particularly the rise of the textile, tobacco, and furniture industries. As a result of this event, the twentieth century would see the lower Cape Fear bypassed and all but eclipsed by the burgeoning industrial towns of the Piedmont. Why did the Industrial Revolution develop so unevenly in North Carolina?

It is clear that it was not from any particular lack of foresight on the part of local entrepreneurs that these industries failed to transform the lower Cape Fear. On the contrary, there were a number of individuals in the area who were conscious of the momentous import that the textile industry held for the future. The MacRae family, for example, though Conservative in their politics, were generally forward-looking in their business views and were, hence, precocious in their efforts to bring new industry to the Cape Fear. As early as 1874, Donald MacRae and a half-dozen other local businessmen, four of whom were Republicans, founded the Wilmington Cotton Mill.[84]

Despite this early beginning and despite the continued, enthusiastic support that the venture received from the local press, the industry survived but scarcely thrived on the lower Cape Fear. The Wilmington Cotton Mill would remain a project that has been much admired in the region, but little imitated. What went wrong? For one thing all of eastern North Carolina lacked water power, an important consideration in locating cotton mills in the nineteenth century. Secondly, unlike the Piedmont as well as

83. Wilmington *Star*, January 10, 1897.
84. Wilmington *Daily Journal*, April 11, 1874.

certain parts of the coastal plain, the Cape Fear country lacked a large, stable labor force. The lonely Piney Woods counties, with their shifting forest industries, did not have the comparatively dense and rooted population, subsisting on a well developed agriculture that characterized some parts of North Carolina.

Of the older industries on the Cape Fear, the one that recovered from the war least successfully was rice production. This seems to have resulted from the unusual extent to which rice-growing had become linked with slavery. Rice was one of some half-dozen industries which in the colonial period had brought about a revival of slavery, an ancient social institution that had all but disappeared from the Old World. Besides being centered in warm countries, a common feature of these industries was that in each a profitable commodity could be turned out as the result of techniques so primitive as to make few demands on the brain and initiative of the primary producer.

These profitable, yet backward, industries put chains on the Negro. But a chain has two ends; and, as surely as one end bound the Negro to bondage, the other bound his master to the productive techniques of a bygone era, while the nineteenth-century world rushed on past him.

The rice planters, for example, were even reluctant to adopt the use of draft animals, and well into the nintenth century land was broken by gangs of slaves using hoes. It was only with the opening up of virgin cotton lands in the Southwest, and the consequent increase in the price of slaves, that ox-drawn plows were adopted, an innovation that had been in general use in Europe for a thousand years. Furthermore, in 1812, Dr. Robert Nesbit of Charleston had developed a seed drill that would plant eight to twelve acres of rice a day. Yet the machine "was considered too complicated for Negroes," and, in the age of the Bessemer process, rice continued to be sown by hand, just as it had been in Neolithic times.

Though rice was planted in orderly rows, this was not done so that it could be worked with horse-drawn cultivators. Rather the rows provided footpaths for slaves who cultivated the plants with hoes; and, after the fields had been flooded, removed the weeds by hand. The harvesting technique was also backward. In other small grain crops, free labor had replaced the sickle with the scythe which had been further improved with the cradle. Beginning in the 1850's, moreover, horse-drawn reapers were being introduced. But in the day of Darwin, as before the dawn of history, rice continued to be cut with the sickle.[85]

That people knew how to grow rice using little equipment other than a spade, a hoe, and a strong back, however, was not a total liability to the industry during the period of social chaos and dislocation following the Civil War. Indeed some Negroes did grow rice for their own use during this time.[86] Also, as the forest industries demonstrate, the fact that a commodity could be produced with primitive equipment could prove an important factor in its rapid revival.

But the rice planters faced serious problems. "It is a well-known fact," an editor asserted, "that of the old planters on the Cape Fear River, who had the temerity to undertake the planting of rice with free labor as it existed in 1865, 1866, 1867 and 1868 not one succeeded."[87] A planter could no longer count his cost in terms of how much corn meal and fatback a prime field hand would eat in a year. Rather, he now had to count his cost in terms of how many working days it would take to clean out a canal during a cold December or how many days to weed a crop by hand. The monstrous amount of work that was absorbed by rice production was no longer concealed by slavery, nor was the intensity of that work. It was work that had to be paid for at wages that would make his malaria, snake, and alligator-infested quagmires competitive with work on the railroads and in the forest industries.

Yet, though the adjustment of the American rice industry to free labor and modern technology would take a long time, it nevertheless by the turn of the century achieved dramatic success. Indeed the twentieth century would see American rice, produced by well-paid operatives in the Southwest being sold in the Far

85. Lewis Cecil Gray, *History of Agriculture in the Southern United States to 1860* (2 vols.; Washington: Carnegie Institute of Washington, 1933), II, 727-29.
86. Wilmington *Review*, August 23, 1882.
87. *Ibid.*

East at prices competitive with that produced locally.[88] Though the Cape Fear country did not share in the ultimate benefits of this revolution, one can nevertheless observe in that region some of the early phases of the quest for new methods of producing this ancient crop.

The real revival of the commercial production of rice was largely inspired by certain policies of the federal government, particularly its tariff policy. It is ironical that the hard-pressed rice planter, who had been flattened by one Republican policy, emancipation, which had doubled his labor cost,[89] could by the 1880's see a possible road to salvation in another Republican policy, one that transformed the posture of the federal government in its relations with private business. For the Democratic tradition of *laissez faire*, the Republicans had substituted a principle of their own, which might be described as *laissez se faire millionnaire*. By the eighties the tariff had reached such a level that some rice could be grown profitably even with emancipated labor and backward technology.[90]

Emancipation having created a sensitive relationship between labor productivity and profits, experiments were now begun for improving techniques. One such effort was characterized as "unheard of" on the Cape Fear, though the technique in question had in fact been utilized in other branches of agriculture for a century and a half. A planter was described as "cultivating about twelve acres of lowlands or rice fields by plows, instead of in the old way by hoes. . . . The cost of cultivation by plows is fully one-third less than by hoes. . . . If his experiment turns out as happily as he expects it will, the cultivation of the Cape Fear rice fields will be much easier and at less cost."[91]

Yet, though there were efforts to improve methods, nothing occurred on the Cape Fear that could be justly called a "revolution," as every new idea had to run a gauntlet of old habits and

88. Joseph Cannon Bailey, *Seaman A. Knapp: Schoolmaster of American Agriculture* (New York: Columbia University Press, 1945), p. 143, hereinafter cited as Bailey, *Knapp*.
89. Wilmington *Review*, August 24, 1882.
90. *Ibid.*, August 23, 1882.
91. *Ibid.*, August 4, 1881.

patterns of thinking that had been molded by slave society for generations. One planter complained, for example, that

since the emancipation of the slaves, the cost of agricultural labor in the South has increased more than one-hundred percent. In the rice districts of the Carolinas and Georgia, females obtain from fifty to seventy-five cents [a day]. Males from sixty cents to a dollar-twenty-five per diem—this without the efficiency to be expected from free labor. These laborers in some localities openly refuse to undertake tasks, [considered] easy under a sterner system, and essential to rice cultivation.[92]

The writer, it will be noted, is still thinking in terms of getting better results from the old methods, now that the planters were using more expensive free labor. The Negro, it would appear, did not share this conclusion.

Nevertheless, slowly, painfully, and above all, subsidized by the tariff, a revival of commercial rice production was underway by the late seventies. The highest estimated harvest for the Cape Fear district was that for 1881, 124,000 bushels or not quite two-thirds the ante-bellum level.[93] In the years that followed lower yields were estimated. Yet, as incomplete as it was, the revival of the seventies and eighties was the Indian Summer of the Cape Fear industry. Commercial production in the area was to be totally eclipsed by a revolution that was then taking place in Louisiana.

In 1883, a group of land speculators, known as the Watkins Syndicate, bought a tract of state and federal land in southern Louisiana that was about the size of the state of Delaware. To promote their land sales, the syndicate shrewdly employed Seaman A. Knapp, President of Iowa Agricultural College and who already had behind him a distinguished career as an agricultural scientist. They gave Knapp a free hand in setting up experimental farms, scattered throughout the area, that would demonstrate to prospective buyers the agricultural potentialities of the syndicate's lands.[94] Knapp carefully selected the farmers for the demonstration farms, most of them coming from the Midwest. In

92. *Ibid.*, August 24, 1882.
93. *Ibid.*, August 3, 1881; Wilmington *Daily Journal*, December 1, 1875.
94. Bailey, *Knapp*, pp. 109, 119.

exchange for liberal concessions in land, seeds, and livestock, the selected farmers agreed to accept a measure of direction from Knapp in the scientific management of their farms.[95]

Rice was a strange crop for the men from the Midwest who settled on demonstration farms in southern Louisiana in the eighties. But these men had been schooled in the most highly mechanized agriculture on earth. Nothing came more naturally to them than to begin experimenting with rice-growing using the small-grain techniques with which they were familiar. And, during the next two decades, these Midwesterners, under the leadership of Knapp, brought about more changes in the production of rice than the industry had seen since the days of Confucius.

By 1903, Knapp could announce that one binder, two men, and four horses could do as much work as two hundred harvest hands.[96] Perched with dignity upon their high seed drills and harvesters, the Midwesterners had ridden proudly out of the Middle Ages; and, in so doing, they had eclipsed commercial rice production in its historic American homeland, the Carolina rice belt, extending from the Cape Fear along the tidewater to Georgia.

Why did Knapp and his followers succeed in revitalizing the industry while the efforts of the Cape Fear planters failed? There were some important geographical reasons for this. The Midwesterners achieved their dramatic success, not upon swamp lands such as those that line the lower Cape Fear, but upon lands that could not only be irrigated but also thoroughly drained. It is also a geographical fact that the Gulf region is suited to the growth of Kiushu rice which produces 25 per cent heavier yields than Carolina rice.[97]

But a psychological factor may also be involved. Knapp and his followers began their experiments with essentially the same type of land and the same strains of rice as were used by the planters along the lower Cape Fear, and initially at least they knew less about the crop. It was by trial and error that they discovered which lands could be drained well enough to support the weight of their machines.[98] But the starting point of their thinking was a machine and not an ancestral estate. Even the success of Kiushu rice, though made possible by Gulf-state geography, owed something to a lust for innovation and discovery that was not always conspicuous in the stately mansions that lined the lower Cape Fear. Verging on the age of seventy, sometimes traveling by muleback, Seaman Knapp scoured Asia from Ceylon to Japan, searching for a strain of rice that would suit his purposes; and Kiushu was the prize that he brought home.[99]

It would be a mistake, however, to deal with rice production in the Cape Fear country in purely economic terms. The failure of rice to resume its prewar importance had far-reaching social consequences. Before the war it had sustained aristocratic culture; and the failure of the industry to recover meant that even though the Negro was not yet entirely free—his continuing status bearing some of the earmarks of his former condition—at the same time it would be impossible for anyone to reconstruct an approximation of the old society. The gentry was thus fated to be absorbed into the business class. The proud names would remain, but they would adorn some of the same types of business enterprise as did the German, Jewish, and New England names.

Thus the two major supports of the ante-bellum economy, rice and naval stores, collapsed at about the turn of the century. Fortunately, however, the economy of the Cape Fear country did not collapse thanks to other economic developments in the region. Due in part to the creosote process, lumbering continued to be important. As a result of improvements in the port and the completion of the Wilmington, Charlotte, and Rutherfordton Railroad, Wilmington emerged as a significant cotton market. Fertilizer and truck farming, furthermore, were becoming increasingly important in the area. Therefore, the over-all effect of the collapse of the major ante-bellum industries and the compensating developments in other areas was to slow down the total economic growth of the region at the very time when the industrialization of Piedmont North Carolina had been sharply accelerated.

98. *Ibid.*, pp. 120-21.
99. *Ibid.*, p. 135.

VIII ∾ *Preoccupations of the People*

"BUT LITTLE BUSINESS WILL BE DONE ON THE 6TH," THE *Dispatch* predicted. Because it was on April 6, 1866, that the Grand Tournament had been set; and the attraction of such an event, the editor thought, "will prove too strong for cotton and tar and we think our merchants can very well dispense with the services of their employees that day."[1]

The *Dispatch* was right. During recent years there had been little news so likely to cheer fashionable society on the lower Cape Fear as was this announcement. During the war the news had been bad and had grown steadily worse. For the gentle folk, even the coming of peace had not brought the ecstatic joy that it had brought to the Negroes. Peace was defeat. It was occupation by enemy soldiers. It was Negroes running riot. It was the smallpox epidemic of the past winter; and now, with the return of warm weather, the community was threatened by death in a new guise, cholera. The local administration, certainly, by means of a sanitation campaign carried out by Negro convicts, was working feverishly to prevent such an outbreak; but the appearance in the streets of Wilmington of freedmen wearing chains was in itself a dread reminder of the terrible pestilence that threatened.[2]

Life had become drab and grim. Largess and hospitality, like the heroic gray, had fled from the Cape Fear. Now one counted himself fortunate if he could find a job as a clerk in a commission house, and if he could spend his days there, like some Yankee

1. Wilmington *Dispatch*, March 30, 1866.
2. *Ibid.*, February 21, 1866.

or Jew, sitting on a high stool recording the receipts of cotton and tar.[3] But a tournament was designed to set free, for a day at least, the heroic spirit that is sometimes found imprisoned in the external shell of a commission house clerk.

Thought of cotton, tar, smallpox, and cholera could be left far behind by the crowds that gathered on the tournament grounds to watch a display of chivalry, described as "the most splendid that has ever been witnessed in the Cape Fear country. . . . Each bold horseman was a practiced . . . lancer, and each noble steed was worthy of his rider; the trial of skill was long . . . and closely contested but finally terminated" with prizes being awarded to the "Knight of the Highlands," the "Knight of the White Plume," and the "Knight of the Cape Fear." Another rider, however, who with unconscious irony had been dubbed "Knight of La Mancha," fared no better in the contest than did his illustrious predecessor in a celebrated bout with a windmill.

The Knight of the Highlands, having been awarded the first prize, had thus also won the right to name the "Queen of Love," and his choice proved to be "a lady of most royal mien." "The prizes having been awarded, the lists were reopened for the challenges of any unsuccessful knights who might desire to contest one another, for the privilege of competing with the champion knight. Following a long and interesting trial, the Knight of Wilmington was proclaimed the victor, who straightaway threw down the gauntlet to the Knight of the Highlands, who readily accepted the banner, and re-entered the lists. . . ."[4] The jousting on the field was followed by a ball: "The assemblage of quiet, well-bred, richly attired people at the City Hall last evening, was decidedly the largest that we have ever seen in North Carolina. . . . About nine o'clock, the royal party headed by the Queen of Beauty and the successful knight, entered the hall and moved majestically to

3. "No one now owns a Sound [beach] residence for pleasure, every one has gone in for making money," sighed the proprietor of a failing plantation who only recently had "offered my services to four of the largest commission houses, to work for no pay, only to learn the business, but I have been unable to secure a position." Letters from Joshua G. Wright to Julius Walker Wright, March 25 and February 14, 1869, Murdock-Wright Papers, Southern Historical Collection, The University of North Carolina, hereinafter cited as Murdock-Wright Papers.

4. Wilmington *Dispatch*, 1866.

the other end of the room . . ."[5] where local dignitaries made speeches that provided a fitting climax to the invigorating experiences on the tournament field and in the ballroom. And thus, with uplifted spirits, fair virtue could return to her parlor, to her volume of Sir Walter Scott. Brave chivalry could return to his stool at the commission house, to his ledgerbook of tar and turpentine receipts.

There would be other tournaments on the lower Cape Fear, but they would attract less attention. The cult of medieval nobility was fading. A contributing factor in its demise may have been the formation in 1871, by a group of Negroes, of the Wilmington Tournament Association which sponsored at least one bout and planned others.[6] The sight of Negro Sir Galahads jousting with each other may have helped members of the elite classes to have seen the quixotic character of their own performances. Perhaps a more fundamental cause for the waning interest in tournaments, however, was the decline of the aristocratic mentality, as the rice-planting gentry disappeared as a group distinct from the business class. As one observer sourly remarked, "I think the entire batch had better drop the 'lance' and 'take up the shovel and the hoe. . . .' "[7]

But men have never been able to subsist long without cults, through which they can glorify their experiences and place them in some kind of historical perspective. An experience that many whites had shared had been the Confederate war effort, particularly participation in the "Bloody Eighteenth." As years passed, memories of the war became less painful, and thus it became more pleasurable to recall the Confederacy's moments of glory, and the Old South's special points of pride.

One can detect the gradual emergence of an Old South and Confederacy cult. The Conservatives nurtured its growth with tender care, since its devotees were likely to include most whites, but no Negroes. It therefore tended to forward one of their im-

5. *Ibid.*, April 10, 1866.

6. Wilmington *The Daily Journal*, May 2, 1871, hereinafter cited as Wilmington *Daily Journal* or Wilmington Weekly *Journal*.

7. Alexander MacRae to Donald MacRae, April 3, 1866, Hugh MacRae Papers, Department of Manuscripts, Duke University.

portant political objectives, that of establishing political cleavages along the lines of race rather than of ideas, of allowing skin color to decide one's vote and the courthouse ring to decide the rest. They gave expression to the cult through observances of General Robert E. Lee's birthday,[8] and even more dramatically by annual memorial services for the Confederate war dead.

Ostensibly, Confederate Memorial Day ceremonies were non-political commemorations devoted to the veneration of fallen valor. Sometimes the sponsors went so far as to invite leading Republicans, who were Confederate veterans, to deliver orations for these occasions. Though such invitations were sometimes accepted,[9] this fact does not quite prove the contention of the sponsors that the proceedings were politically neutral.

A Republican who accepted invariably put himself in an awkward position. In the cemetery, in the presence of his comrades-in-arms living and dead, no matter what he said in his speech, he could hardly escape the fact that as a Republican he had alienated himself from the Confederate tradition, that he had allied himself with Negroes and with his former enemies. The Republican party could be represented as true blue, but not as true gray.

There was also a Union tradition on the lower Cape Fear, a number of men in the area, particularly Negroes, having served in the Union army and navy. These veterans had formed a local chapter of the Grand Army of the Republic, which was not only chiefly responsible for keeping alive the Union tradition in the region, but also was an important faction within the Republican party.

Both the Union and the Confederate commemorations took place in May of each year. So solemn were these occasions that no one would have admitted the propriety of such a mundane consideration as politics at such a time. Yet as a practical matter it was difficult to pay homage to fallen valor and, at the same time, to ignore the continuing ideas for which that valor was expended.

8. Wilmington *Morning Star*, January 19, 1885; January 20, 1895. This paper began in 1867 as *The Evening Star*, but changed shortly afterwards to *The Morning Star*, hereinafter cited as Wilmington *Star*.

9. *Ibid.*, May 15, 1878.

The North-South reconciliation theme, to some extent, provided an escape from this dilemma.

Nevertheless a certain political rivalry between the two observances was never far from the forefront. The Radical, William P. Canaday, for example, despite his four years service as a Confederate soldier, had no use for the cult of the Confederacy and the Old South. In 1882, he wrote that the

> businessmen seem to think they should keep the 10th., the Confederate Memorial Day, . . . but on [sic] the day set apart to do honor to the brave men who died for the American Union, they believe in treating with the greatest contempt. [sic] The masses or laboring classes are in favor of the Union, and believe in keeping this day holy, and to attend services at the cemetery. We well remember the time when not ten white men attended the services at the cemetery on the 30th., but now hundreds do themselves the honor to be present. . . . On account of the number of laborers who stopped work it looked very much like a holiday on our streets.[10]

Canaday may have exaggerated the extent of white participation in the Union commemoration. Certainly, in another such service held two years later, we find a Conservative conceding that the Union "procession was a very large one," but adding that it was composed "almost exclusively of colored people."[11] Yet an elaborate affair it was indeed. The procession, including five fire companies, the Draymen's Association, the local chapter of the Grand Army of the Republic, a band, a choir, "citizens in carriages," "men on horseback," "schools in charge of teachers," and "citizens on foot," marched to the cemetery where dignitaries made speeches, climaxed by the ritualistic decoration of the graves with flowers, while from the river the revenue cutter, "Colfax," thundered salutes.[12]

Despite apparent efforts to keep both cults politically neutral, it is perhaps significant that the main addresses were often delivered by persons aspiring to some legislative seat, who somehow managed to combine beating swords into plowshares in

10. Wilmington *Post*, June 4, 1882. This paper appears at various times as *The Wilmington Post, Tri-weekly Post* and *Daily Post*.
11. Wilmington *Review*, May 31, 1884.
12. *Ibid.*, May 29, 30, 31, 1884.

Memorial Day speeches with beating the bushes in the Piney Woods for votes. But the tendency to play politics with the war dead was a failing that one could generally detect more readily in the pretensions of the rival commemoration than in the more refined sentiments of his own cult. "Heretofore there has been too evident an attempt to mingle Radical politics with these Federal memorial celebrations," the *Journal* admonished, "but we trust that hereafter they will be made occasions solely for tribute to the heroism of the dead."[13] Yet when a cult ceases to serve some continuing purpose of the living, it ceases to exist.

In the molding of cults, and, in fact, in the molding of ideas generally, newspapers probably played the most important role. The first paper to appear in the area following the federal occupation in 1865 was the *Herald*, published daily by Thomas M. Cook, a war correspondent who arrived with the Union army. For some eight months following the war the *Herald* was the only newspaper published in the region, and this fact, in turn, was about the only journalistic asset that Cook had.

Cook's political position was hardly calculated to win friends for his paper. Though himself a very conservative New York Democrat, he had important differences with the Conservatives of the lower Cape Fear. They were "Rebels." Cook was even more isolated from the people in the area who would later become Republicans. He did not like Negroes. But, besides having a political position that could rally no important group, Cook published a bad paper. His news coverage was spotty, and his awkward style of writing fell below the standards to which newspaper readers in the area were accustomed. The *Herald* survived the coming of competition by little more than six months.[14]

In the fall of 1865, two additional daily papers appeared in Wilmington. The *Journal*, a prewar paper that had been suspended at the time of the federal capture of the city, was reopened by James Fulton, a native of Ireland, and Alfred Lanier

13. Wilmington *Daily Journal*, May 31, 1872.
14. Wilmington *Daily Herald, passim.* This paper first appeared in 1865 as *The Herald of the Union,* but shortly afterward began to appear as *The Daily Herald* or *The Wilmington Herald,* hereinafter cited as Wilmington *Herald.*

Price.[15] A month later the *Dispatch* began publication for the first time, edited by William H. Bernard and John D. Barry. Both papers were Conservative, and both were more ably written than the *Herald*. But the years immediately following the war were difficult ones for newspapers, and, in 1867, the *Dispatch* failed, as had seven of the fourteen daily newspapers that had been started in the South since Appomattox.[16]

Bernard, however, undaunted by his experience with the *Dispatch*, launched another Conservative daily the same year, the *Star*. Urbane, lively, having good news coverage, the venture was an immediate success. At first he published it as an evening paper, but quickly he began to issue it in the mornings, in competition with the *Journal*; and gradually edged the older publication to the brink of bankruptcy. "I hope, dear General, you can do something for us," the hard-pressed editor of the *Journal* wrote to a friend. "You are thrown with wealthy [Conservative] party men, or may have friends who could lend or give security."[17] But the final blow came in the form of a strike of the Typographical Workers' Union: "The conspiracy against the *Journal* has taken a wider range and now embraces among its members not only the printing fraternity of the city, but our old enemy the Radical party as well, many of whose members have contributed money to buy off our [strike-breaking] printers. Twenty dollars apiece, and transportation back to their homes in Georgia did the work for them and for us. . . ."[18]

After twenty-six years of publication the *Journal* was forced to close. Whereupon, Joshua T. James and Charles A. Price, both of whom had been connected with the *Journal*, founded the *Review*, which eventually bought the "press, type, and good will" of the older paper.[19] James and Price published the *Review* as a daily, but retained the name, "*Journal*," for the weekly edition.

15. Wilmington *Daily Journal*, December 15, 1865; February 27, 1872.
16. Wilmington Weekly *Journal*, April 1, 1867.
17. Joseph Adolphus Engelhard to Matt Whitaker Ransom, July 21, 1874, Matt W. Ransom Papers, Southern Historical Collection, The University of North Carolina.
18. Wilmington *Daily Journal*, August 18, 1875.
19. Wilmington Weekly *Journal*, December 6, 1877.

Like the *Journal*, the *Review* was declared to be Conservative, though it would handle politics, in actuality, quite differently from the manner followed by its predecessor. The senior editor, James, had worked for the Republican *Post* for three years before becoming city editor of the *Journal*, and he had remained on good terms with the Republicans.[20] He may have continued contributing articles to the *Post* even after beginning work for the Ku Klux Klan-oriented *Journal*.[21] He had friends in both camps, so, as senior editor of the *Review*, he published a paper that was technically Conservative, but largely nonpolitical.

In order to reduce the competition with the *Star*, which had proved to be so disastrous to the *Journal*, James and Price published the *Review* as an evening paper. Probably for the same reason, the writing style of the *Review* was slanted toward slightly less sophisticated, less educated readers than those to whom the *Star* appealed.[22]

The *Review* writers knew how to entertain their readers with local gossip. The objective that such journalists often pursue is to titillate gently the sexuality of their readers without really shocking them. Since in the twentieth century we are accustomed to news writers who achieve this goal by the use of gross suggestion and pictures, it is easy for us to overlook the fact that the nineteenth-century journalist sometimes had the same objectives. But in his day custom dictated that he use more subtle means. Even then, however, he sometimes felt that he had to cover his tracks with some thumping assertions of Victorian morality. For example: "The beautiful grove at Hilton is put to rather debased use on Sunday afternoons; so we have been told by a gentleman who happened to stroll out that way last Sunday. . . . The youngsters play base ball, and the men and women indulge in such as to do great violence to morality and decency."[23] Or,

there is a young man who resides on a hammock (or hummuck) of land on one of the sounds and there is a young woman of heretofore

20. Wilmington *Daily Journal*, November 5, 1871.
21. Wilmington Weekly *Journal*, July 23, 1883.
22. Wilmington *Daily Journal*, September 12, 1875.
23. Wilmington *Review*, May 31, 1881.

excellent character, who has been employed as a house servant . . . by a gentleman who resides on Wrightsville [Sound]. . . . The young man invited the young woman to come to the city with him and go to Coup's circus and she consented to do so. . . . She went with him in the boat and they were not seen again until the next morning when a fisherman . . . found the young man on the beach and assisted him in getting his boat afloat. As he did so he caught sight of a female figure in the bushes. . . . It is evident that they had passed the night together on the beach and had had a good breakfast there afterward.[24]

The year 1867, which had seen the *Dispatch* superseded by the *Star*, had also seen the creation of the Republican party of North Carolina and the establishment of a Republican paper, the *Post*, on the lower Cape Fear. One of the serious problems the North Carolina Republicans faced was the Conservative domination of the press. During Reconstruction, for example, there were seven Republican papers as opposed to twenty-six Conservative ones.[25] Yet this was despite the fact that the Republicans were able to win a number of elections and were credited with some 40 per cent of the votes throughout the rest of the nineteenth century.[26]

The entire seventeen-year history of the *Post* was a hectic one. Because the overwhelming majority of businessmen were Conservatives, the paper was never able to command much advertising; and, since those who had the means to pay the piper did not like the editorial tune, Republican editors found themselves almost constantly short of funds. Furthermore, since the Republicans had so few papers, their editors often tended to concentrate almost entirely on politics, trying to make up with partisan fervor all that they lacked in total volume of circulation. It is unlikely that the Republican papers attracted many readers who were not already intensely interested in politics and who did not share the editor's point of view. As a result, there was a noticeable tendency for circulation to sag in nonelection years.

24. *Ibid.*, October 31, 1881.

25. Joseph Grégoire de Roulhac Hamilton, *Reconstruction in North Carolina* (New York: Columbia University Press, 1914), p. 425, hereinafter cited as Hamilton, *Reconstruction.*

26. Helen Grey Edmonds, *The Negro and Fusionist Politics in North Carolina, 1895-1901* (Chapel Hill: The University of North Carolina Press, 1951), p. 24, hereinafter cited as Edmonds, *The Negro and Fusionist Politics.*

The period, 1867-72, was a particularly difficult one for the *Post*. At first the editors tried to publish daily. It appeared that Wilmington was the one place in North Carolina where there was a real basis for a Republican daily. After all, the city, which had a two-to-one Republican majority, was supporting two Conservative dailies. The effort failed probably because most Republicans there were poor and unlettered. The *Post* was pared down first to a triweekly, then finally to a weekly, though it was sometimes published more frequently during election campaigns.

Despite these economies, for the first three years, the Republican party had to subsidize the *Post* in order to publish a paper that would be competitive in price with the Conservative ones. This was done by means of an assessment levied on Republican officeholders.[27] But to make up the financial deficit by means of a party subsidy was to trade an old problem for a new one. By its dependence on party funds, the *Post* could not be a private concern, with a point of view that was the business of the editor, but rather it was more nearly the official voice of the party in the Cape Fear country, and its views were the business of every Republican. Thus the *Post* became caught in the internal factionalism of the Republican party, a recently formed, unstable coalition of antagonistic groups.

During the first five years that the *Post* was published, no prominent Republican served as editor. Furthermore there was a rapid turnover of editors, probably reflecting the shifting relationship between the various contending factions. In 1870, for example, a group of popular Negro neighborhood leaders temporarily gained the upper hand in the New Hanover County Republican Convention and roundly condemned the *Post*, demanding the removal of editor Charles I. Grady, whom they accused of being anti-Negro. They even refused to allow a copy of the official proceedings of the convention to be sent to the *Post*.[28] The fortunes of the paper took a turn for the better in 1872, however, when it passed under the control of an important Republican leader, William Parker Canaday.

27. Wilmington *Post*, July 23, 1883.
28. Wilmington *Daily Journal*, April 5, 1870.

"Who is W. P. Canady?" the *Journal* had inquired in 1869, misspelling his name. "We find him applying for one of the principal offices within the gift of the city . . . who this man is and what his record [is], we confess that we have some curiosity to know."[29] Certainly the name, "Canaday," did not bring to mind any great eighteenth-century rice dynasties. However, had the editors been more familiar with the Wilmington water front, with its odors of fish and tar, they might well have seen Canaday there, a twenty-five-year-old Confederate veteran busily weighing rosin.[30] His military record they could well approve: seventeen years old at the outbreak of war, he had volunteered as a private, but by Appomattox he had risen in rank to a first lieutenant. His political record, however, was not so favorable: Radicalized by war, he had joined the North Carolina Republican party the year it was founded.[31] He had been a popular figure among his comrades in "G" Company of the Tenth North Carolina.[32] He was also a popular figure in predominantly Negro Wilmington. The fact that as a political candidate he could win more votes than other Republicans running on the same ticket indicated that some men voted for him who were otherwise Conservatives or who did not vote at all.[33]

But, though Canaday was a man of many gifts, writing skill was not one of them. In fact, after examining some of his efforts in this direction, one might wonder how this "well-meaning but somewhat illiterate"[34] young man ever became the editor of a newspaper. The truth is, however, that the facility for constructing correct sentences was not the most important quality that one needed to be a successful editor in the late nineteenth-century South, particularly to be a successful Republican editor.

General Abbott, for example, had a beautiful writing style, but he had retracted and apologized for an article he had written for the *Post* rather than exchange gunfire with Major Joseph A.

29. *Ibid.*, January 17, 1869.
30. Ed[win] Brink *et al.* to William Woods Holden, November 23, 1868, William Woods Holden Papers, North Carolina Archives.
31. Wilmington *Post*, October 6, 1876.
32. Wilmington *Daily Journal*, January 23, 1869.
33. Wilmington *Star*, November 16, 1876.
34. Wilmington *Daily Journal*, January 23, 1869.

Engelhard, a Conservative who did not like his article.[35] *Post* editor, Charles I. Grady, had been able to quote Shakespeare, but the Negroes had reacted to his Negrophobia with a Grady-phobia that isolated him; and, when the editor was waylaid and beaten by one or more young Conservatives, no one lifted a finger to help him.[36] James C. Mann also had been assaulted for an article he had contributed to the *Post*.[37] Canaday did not always know the proper form of a verb to use, but he did know that, politically, he was on the side of the poor whites and the Negroes; and above all he was not gun-shy. He converted the *Post* into about the most badly written, the most scurrilous, the most scandalous, and the most consistently democratic paper that Wilmington had ever seen.

Newspaper readers on the lower Cape Fear, for example, were used to reading amusing little bits about the Saturday night scuffles of Negroes and other people enjoying little status, in such localities as Paddy's Hollow, Dry Pond, and Mount Misery. But the papers had a concept of editorial responsibility that would generally have restrained them from calling attention to trivial events that might reflect on some great family, or from suggesting that anything approaching a brawl might take place at such a high-toned establishment as the Purcell House, and involving members of the gentry.

Yet the *Post* could show such poor taste as to remark in a seemingly casual manner that "two young bloods got into a difficulty at the Purcell House on Saturday night last and quite a scuffle ensued, during which several friends of the respective parties showed a disposition to engage, but better counsels prevailed and the trouble soon came to an end."[38]

A newspaper editor was treading on dangerous ground when he reported such events. The editor of the *Herald* had been challenged to a duel because he had reported an illness and death in a way that a physician took to be a reflection on his professional

35. *Ibid.*, August 20, 1869.
36. *Ibid.*, August 13, 1869; Raleigh *Daily Standard*, January 20, 1870.
37. Joshua G. Wright to Julius Walker Wright, February 14, 1869, Murdock-Wright Papers.
38. Wilmington *Post*, October 12, 1883.

competence.[39] When General Abbott had been challenged, furthermore, following the publication in the *Post* of his article,
"Misrepresentation of Our Public Men . . ." he had discovered
that it is not always easy to decline a duel. He notified his challenger that "under no earthly consideration" would he fight a
duel. But this did not end the matter. Each time he appeared in
public thereafter, Engelhard confronted him trying to force him
into a fight.[40]

Canaday, however, made it plain that, as editor of the *Post*, he
was not running a "milk and cider concern." "We propose to call
the names of the men who try by their threats to intimidate the
editorial management of this paper, and if anyone feels that he
has cause for resentment it will not be hard for him to find the
man who is responsible."[41] However, the pugilists and lethal
weapons experts did not show the same readiness to apply censor-
ship as they had sometimes shown previously.

Nevertheless, during the twelve years that Canaday edited the
Post, at least one such effort was made. In 1876, he employed as
assistant editor Jesse J. Cassidey, a man who shared some of his
ideas on the operation of a newpaper. In one of his early articles,
Cassidey accused a Conservative congressman, Colonel Alfred
Moore Waddell, of having defaulted on a gambling debt. As a
member of the gentry, Waddell would have felt degraded to have
challenged to a duel a person having a more humble social origin
than his own. A Negro, or any other person unworthy of a
challenge, was supposed to be punished by means of a "caning."

Returning to Wilmington from Washington, the congressman
surprised Cassidey on the street, and caned or clubbed him
severely, while a group of Waddell's friends appeared "as if by
magic," from surrounding buildings to prevent anyone from coming to Cassidey's help.[42] Brought before a Conservative judge,
Waddell was fined ten dollars, which he promptly paid and returned to Washington. Cassidey, however, followed him to Washington, and there, singlehandedly, attacked him with a cane or

39. Wilmington *Herald*, June 29, 1865.
40. Wilmington Weekly *Journal*, August 20, 1869.
41. Wilmington *Post*, May 7, 1875.
42. *Ibid.*, May 5, 1876.

club, despite the fact that Waddell was at the time surrounded by a bodyguard of friends. In the fray that followed, Waddell and his friends administered some more rough treatment to Cassidey, including a broken nose; but the Democratic and Republican newspapers could not agree who came away with the honor and who with the humiliation.[43] Some of each may have gone both ways.

The *Post*, however, was not chastened by Cassidey's bruises. And, had Waddell and the other Conservative leaders wanted to do any further caning, they would scarcely have lacked provocation in the weeks and months that followed. When Waddell published a denial of the gambling debt charge, the *Post* published the name of a lawyer, who they said held three gambling debt acceptances which bore Waddell's signature and which were more than three years overdue. Cassidey added that he had previously called Waddell a "gambler, a drunkard and a defaulter. I now make the statement that he is a liar."[44]

To the editors who were inflaming the whites against the Negroes, and were thereby slowly breaking the back of the Republican party, the *Post* was capable of being equally vindictive, and personal. "And this buzzard . . . , is the fellow who wants to draw the 'color line.' We suggest to him to send to Charleston where he lived in 1866 and 1867, and bring to his home in Wadesboro those numerous mulatto childern of his that were begotten in adultery and born in bastardy. . . ."[45] On another occasion the *Post* published the name of the alleged Negro mistress of a Conservative editor who "preaches against civil rights in the daylight and *practices social* rights the balance of the time. . . ."[46]

Yet Canaday was never able to solve the most serious problem of his paper, the advertising boycott. It is ironical that a paper which at one time could claim the largest circulation of any in the state[47] would have difficulty soliciting advertising. "The *Post* don't [*sic*] ask anyone to advertise for charity," Canaday wrote,

43. *Ibid.*, May 5, 12, 19, June 2, 1876; Wilmington *Daily Journal*, May 17, 1876.
44. Wilmington *Post*, June 2, 9, 1876.
45. *Ibid.*, June 2, 1876.
46. *Ibid.*, July 23, 1875. (Emphasis in the original.)
47. *Ibid.*, July 9, 1875.

but the fact was he published "the only paper in the state that circulates in every county in North Carolina."[48]

But Canaday's difficulties in publishing the *Post* were overtaking him by degrees, as the strength of the Republican party slowly ebbed, and his old "Howe stop-cylinder" press gradually wore out. In 1884, he suspended operations, and his press brought ten dollars as junk.[49] The *Post* represented the closest approach the Republicans ever made to an effective, state-wide press.

The long-range reasons for the failure of Republican newspapers, and of the Republican party as well, were the magnitude of the goals which they set for themselves and the particular historical moment at which they attempted these objectives. They had tried to establish the principle of the equality of all men before the law. This notion had appealed strongly to those groups that had been deprived by the old society, those groups that felt an urgent need for change. But was it possible, in actuality, to make good the assertion of the political equality of all men in a society in which cultural inequalities were as marked as they were in the South?

At the end of the war there were many people in the North who, not content with the mere military conquest of the Confederacy, wanted to see the complete reintegration of the South into American society, and who did not believe that this could be done unless the educational gap that separated the former Confederacy from the rest of the country was greatly narrowed. As a result, beginning in 1865, there was a southward migration of hundreds of missionary-teachers, many of them men and women inflamed with an almost messianic zeal for mass education,[50] a movement that W. E. B. DuBois has characterized as the "Ninth Crusade."

48. *Ibid.*, December 11, 1881.

49. Wilmington *Star*, November 19, 1898.

50. Seventy-five of these were at one time engaged in Negro education in North Carolina, 22 from the American Missionary Association, also 22 from the New England Freedmen's Aid Society, 29 from the National Freedmen's Relief Association including two Negroes, and two persons who came to the state on their own initiative. Of these 75, all were women except 12. William T. Briggs, Annual Report of the Superintendent of Colored Schools in North Carolina, July, 1865, American Missionary Association Archives, Fisk University, hereinafter cited as Missionary Archives.

Coming in the wake of the conquering armies, settling in communities where but a few months before it had been a criminal offense to teach a Negro to read, these crusaders did not receive a uniformly friendly reception. Southern Conservatives were learning not to look on Yankees as one undifferentiated mass. Rather they were beginning to see that for some northerners the struggle had ended at Appomattox. These persons they sought out and courted. But there were others for whom the struggle still continued, having merely assumed political rather than military forms. Those who sought further changes in southern society, or Radicals, they regarded as their bitterest enemies.

On the Cape Fear, the teachers for the Freedmen's Bureau and the northern benevolent societies were generally suspected of Radicalism. They were the people who were stirring up the Negroes, putting ideas into their heads that would make it impossible for the Conservatives to piece together any of the broken fragments of a way of life that had endured in the region for seven generations. Occasionally there was violence: "Yesterday a colored girl was severely beaten for wanting to come to school," a representative of the American Missionary Association wrote from Wilmington in 1865.[51] More often there were only harsh words; and when it came to denouncing Radical agitators, no one was more bitter than the editor of the *Herald*, himself a New Yorker who had arrived with the Union navy.

Complaints reach us of the interference [,] by the enthusiastic school teacher who has come among us from the north [,] with the laboring portion of the community. We hear instances where this teacher enters the premises of employers and tampers with their servants to induce them to attend school to the neglect of their work. . . . If these servants are enticed away to schools for two or three or four or six hours in the day or evening they do not fulfill their contracts. It is their misfortune that they are poor and compelled to sell their time and therefore have none to bestow upon their educational pursuits. If we pay a nursemaid ten dollars per month for her time we are not disposed to allow her one-quarter or one-eighth of that time for educa-

51. Joseph G. Longley to George Whipple, May 31, 1865, Missionary Archives.

tional purposes. . . . The opulent can spare time in maturity for the further improvement of the mind; but the poor must work.[52]

But was it permissible for a zealous schoolmistress to "entice" children to attend her school? On one occasion a teacher walking along the street saw some Negro children playing. She stopped and asked them if they went to school. "They told her the people they worked for would not allow them to go to school, and while asking more questions about it, . . . a white man, attended by a boy, came along and roughly demanded 'Who are you?' " When she told him he "drove her away with terrible curses."[53]

How could a man attended by a servant, and hence from one of the affluent classes, with their cult of chivalry, their protective, almost worshipful attitude toward ladies, behave on this occasion so ungallantly toward a school mistress? Actually the women teachers from the Freedmen's Bureau and the benevolent organizations could expect little deferential treatment because of the ideas that Cape Fear males held toward women. If anything, the code of chivalry, like local notions of white superiority, was only part of a hostile wall of ideas and customs that confronted them in their work.

In the first place an upper-class male did not dissipate his gallantry upon women generally, but concentrated it mostly upon "ladies." A lady was a woman, not too far below his own social station, who observed a definite behavior pattern, defined by custom to form for her a fairly narrow prison. Like the Negro, she had a Place, albeit a more exalted one. Her Place was the parlor, perhaps also the kitchen and nursery, but better the parlor. If she wanted to do anything that had more far-reaching consequences than being "fair" and "virtuous," she stood in serious danger of overstepping the line that defined the limits of her

52. Wilmington *Herald*, February 23, 1866.

53. *Ibid.*, February 24, 1866. This reaction was by no means peculiar to the lower Cape Fear. By the end of 1865, the head of the Freedmen's Bureau believed that in the South a "majority of the white people to be utterly opposed to educating the negroes. . . . the teachers, though they may be the purest of Christian people, are nevertheless visited, . . . with undisguised marks of odium." U.S. War Dept., Bureau of Refugees, Freedmen and Abandoned Lands, *Report of the Commissioner*, 39th Cong., 1 sess., 1865, p. 33.

protected Place. If her behavior, in short, was unladylike, she could scarcely expect to be accorded the treatment of a Sir Walter Scott heroine.

Yet in the nineteenth century the upbringing of women was such that they were poorly equipped to engage in public, polemical exchanges with strange males. It would have been almost unthinkable for an educated woman to have returned in full-measure the volley of invectives and scurrility that she had received. Therefore women teachers sometimes found themselves in the unenviable position of being publicly humiliated without means or redress.

During the winter of 1866-67, however, between the smallpox epidemic and the cholera scare, an educator arrived in Wilmington who had spiritual resources that would prove more than ample for the many challenges that she would face. In her forties when she first came to the lower Cape Fear, Amy Morris Bradley was already no stranger to adversity. She had left her native New England in her youth to serve as a teacher in Central America where she sometimes had had to translate her own text books. Back in the United States at the outbreak of the war, she had volunteered as a nurse and served with the troops from Maine. Other crusaders on the Cape Fear would come and go, but Amy Bradley would still be standing her ground when she was eighty, she being one who feared God, but not many lesser beings.[54]

From the American Unitarian Association and the Soldiers' Memorial Society of Boston, she had a commisson to "do what good she could, not in interest of party or sect, but simply in love of God and man and in the spirit of Christ."[55] This was a broad commission. But she narrowed down her sights to one problem, that of education; and from this realistic, clearly defined objective she never relented. She avoided involvement in questions that were peripheral to this one. For example, she did not share the

54. Undated historical sketch of Tileston School, p. 5, Marcus Cicero Stephens Noble Papers, Southern Historical Collection, The University of North Carolina, hereinafter cited as "Tileston School," Noble Papers; Wilmington *Daily Journal,* April 22, 1873; Charlotte *Observer,* January 19, 1904.

55. Charles Lowe, "Miss Amy M. Bradley, and Her Schools in Wilmington," *Old and New,* I (June, 1870), 775-79, hereinafter cited as Lowe, "Bradley."

concern of southern whites that fearful consequences would follow if white and Negro illiterates learned to read in the same school, yet she never made an issue of this question. Her object was to teach people. She would teach the whites separately if they insisted.

It was probably from Silas Martin, or other members of Wilmington's ante-bellum New England community, that she acquired the use of a building for first school. The building was the empty shell of the "Union Free School," which Martin and others had founded in 1856 for the benefit of the underprivileged whites of the Dry Pond neighborhood. In 1863, however, as a result of war and the great yellow fever epidemic, the school had been abandoned.

On January 9, 1867, Amy Bradley reopened Union Free School with a student body consisting of three white children.[56] Nevertheless there were people who saw a sinister design in this move. A local paper warned its readers against this undertaking "by the societies of New England professing the doctrines of Free Loveism, Communism, Universalism, Unitarianism, and all the multiplicity of evil teachings that corrupt society and overthrow religion."[57]

This solemn warning notwithstanding, the children of the white poor were soon flocking to her school by the score for their share of the "evil teachings." By the end of the first year the enrollment had reached 140, the seating capacity of the building. But, even though prosperity was returning to the port, her efforts to promote free education were still more likely to inspire the local business community to make hostile pronouncements than to make generous contributions. Nevertheless her work attracted the attention of a wealthy Bostonian philanthropist, Mrs. Mary Tileston Hemenway, who donated enough money for the establishment of two more basic literacy or "grammar" schools, one more for whites and one for Negroes. In order to make more efficient use of these facilities she also opened an "industrial school"

56. "Tileston School," Noble Papers, p. 7.
57. Lowe, "Bradley," 775-76.

and a "Sunday school." In the meanwhile her sponsors, the New England societies, sent her some assistant teachers.[58]

Amy Bradley was concentrating largely upon the education of white children. A parallel campaign in Negro education was being carried out by the American Missionary Association, which as early as May, 1865, reported eleven schools and 1,575 pupils on the lower Cape Fear.[59] It was inevitable that she would be brought into working relations with other leaders of the mass education movement, both Negro and white. The editors of the *Star* were probably referring to her when they wrote that "we admire the consistency of the white Radical female who was seen riding the streets yesterday in company" of a Negro man. "May the Radical party long live to practice what it preaches."[60] But Amy Bradley, like some upturned slab of New England granite, was not likely to be toppled by such a gust of malice.

On the contrary, she was winning friends, and winning them right from the ranks of her former detractors. The overwhelming majority of the whites were Conservatives, yet from the beginning the children of the white poor had filled her schools to overflowing. The attitude of the Conservative leaders was now beginning to change. She in turn was anxious to make friends with them. For the 1870 graduation program of Hemenway Grammar School she invited as speakers two prominent Conservatives, one of whom was a former Confederate general, who, as a result of the misfortunes of history, had fallen in rank from the commander of a brigade to the commander of the Wilmington police force, a position he had held only to be again cast downward when the Republicans had taken over the administration of the city. They both accepted and spoke.[61] By 1873, even the *Journal* was willing to concede that the school mistress was "persevering and calm tempered, read in expedients [teaching methods] and utterly fearless."[62] "That woman could command an army," a visitor to Wil-

58. *Ibid.*, 776; Andrew J. Howell, *The Book of Wilmington* (n.p.: n.p., n.d.), pp. 155-56, hereinafter cited as Howell, *Wilmington.*
59. Joseph G. Longley, "Abstract Report: Colored Schools of the American Missionary Association, Wilmingon, N.C. [*sic*], May [*sic*], 1865," Missionary Archives.
60. Wilmington *Star*, May 14, 1868.
61. Wilmington *Daily Journal*, June 10, 1870.
62. *Ibid.*, April 22, 1873.

mington heard a local citizen remark as the two of them watched Amy Bradley going about her duties.[63]

Her position in the community was also influenced by the coming to power of the Republican on the lower Cape Fear. In 1870, the New Hanover County Board of Commissioners voted unanimously her appointment as County School Examiner. The *Journal's* world had been turned upside-down during the previous five years, a Negro even having served as mayor the past fall; but, at such an event, even the crusty voice of the ante-bellum Cape Fear could still express surprise: "This is the first instance within our recollection of a female having been appointed to a public office any where within the limits of New Hanover County. It is certainly, to us, a novel innovation [sic]."[64]

As County Examiner of Schools, she became acquainted with some of the broader problems of education. After Appomattox the South had become an educational wilderness. From the Potomac to the Rio Grande one saw abandoned schools and untutored children. Amid these scenes of ruin there was little to remind a person that ante-bellum North Carolina probably had had the best system of mass education in the South.[65] But, though the system was ruined, a tradition persisted of educating at least white children; and the Radical educators were making the most of it.[66] In the Constitution of 1868, they had devoted a complete article to the question of education, authorizing the legislature to levy taxes and appropriate other funds to support a system of free public schools for all children between the ages of six and twenty-one. County commissioners were subject to indictment if they failed to maintain at least one four-month school in each school district.[67] By the time the Conservatives captured control of the

63. "Tileston School," Noble Papers, p. 12.

64. Wilmington *Daily Journal*, June 7, 1870.

65. Edgar W. Knight, "The Influence of the Civil War on Education in North Carolina," *Proceedings and Addresses of the State Library and Historical Association of North Carolina*, 1917, compiled by R. D. W. Connor (Raleigh: Edwards and Broughton Printing Co., 1918), p. 54 and *passim*; R. D. W. Connor, "The Peabody Educational Fund," *The South Atlantic Quarterly*, IV (1905), 169-70.

66. See the remarks of a Radical Superintendent of Public Instruction, S. S. Ashley. North Carolina, *Report of the Superintendent of Public Instruction*, 1868, (n.p.: n.p., n.d.), p. 10, hereinafter cited as *Report on Schools*, 1868.

67. Constitution of North Carolina, 1868, IX, sections 2-4.

legislature, in 1870, the Superintendent of Public Instruction estimated that 25,000 white and 14,000 Negro children were attending public schools,[68] as opposed to an estimated "near" 150,000 children, all white, who had been attending in 1860.[69]

During Reconstruction and for several decades thereafter, the Conservatives or Democrats took a less friendly view of public school education than either the Whigs or the ante-bellum Democrats had taken a generation earlier. There were several reasons for this. For one thing there had always been strong opponents to public schools, though in ante-bellum days these had not been quite so concentrated in either of the major parties. The conditions prevailing during Reconstruction and after, furthermore were such as to discourage all but the most zealous friends of public schools.

The State Literary Fund, the main support of ante-bellum public schools, had been wiped out, a patriotic legislature having invested it in Confederate and other wartime securities that became worthless after Appomattox.[70] The economy of the state, moreover, did not fully recover until the beginning of the eighties. Also education had become a partisan issue. The Conservatives had come to associate the campaign for mass education with the Radical missionary-teachers, the Freedmen's Bureau, and the Republican party. To many, the campaign for public schools must have appeared as an effort to extract money from Conservative pockets, by means of a property tax that would be used to implant Radical notions in the heads of Negroes.

So, although in 1870 only about one-third as many children were attending school as were attending in 1860, the Conservatives took a series of measures that seriously hampered the recon-

68. North Carolina, *Annual Report Superintendent of Public Instruction*, 1870, ([Raleigh]: Jo. W. Holden [*sic*], State Printer and Binder, n.d.), p. 18.

69. North Carolina, *Report of the Superintendent of Common Schools. . . ,* 1860, ([Raleigh]: John Spelman, Printer to the State, n.d.), p. 4. A Republican Superintendent of Public Instruction in 1868 estimated that "not less than" 100,000 children attended ante-bellum public schools. *Report on Schools*, 1868, p. 3.

70. Jonathan Worth to E. P. Smith, June 13, 1860, Governor's Papers, Worth, North Carolina State Archives; Edgar Wallace Knight, *The Influence of Reconstruction on Education in the South* (New York: Teachers College, Columbia University, 1913), p. 16.

struction of the system of public schools. They greatly reduced the salary of the Commissioner of Education, also taking away from him allowances for clerical service and travel. They levied a school tax, but stipulated that the money collected was to be spent for schools only in the county in which the tax had been paid. The low tax rate, specified by law, placed the county commissioners of the poorer counties in a curious dilemma: A Republican Constitution directed them on pain of indictment to maintain a four-month school in each district. A Conservative legislature

	1870 (% illiterate, total pop.)		1900 (% illiterate, total pop.)		% total pop. that was Negro
Bladen	29.9%	12,831	20.8%	17,677	44.9%
Brunswick	35.6%	7,754	23.3%	12,657	38.4%
Columbus	10.1%	8,474	18.0%	21,274	29.5%
Duplin	41.3%	15,542	21.6%	22,405	35.4%
New Hanover	38.0%	27,978	18.0%	25,785	48.4%**
Pender	*	*	23.6%	13,381	48.9%
Robeson	40.5%	16,262	24.5%	40,371	40.8%
					9.7% "other non-white"
Sampson	43.0%	16,436	22.3%	26,380	30.6%

*Pender was created in 1875 out of New Hanover.
**New Hanover lost its Negro majority following the so-called "Race Riot" of Nov. 10, 1898. Compiled from the *Ninth Census*, 1870, *Statistics . . . Illiteracy*, Vol. I; and the *Twelfth Census*, 1900, Vol. II, *Population*, pt. II.

fixed a tax rate so low that they could not possibly carry out their constitutional duty.

In a legal sense this paradox was resolved by a Conservative State Supreme Court, when it ruled, in substance, that tax rates high enough to carry out the educational article of the Constitution were in conflict with another article in the same document, one fixing maximum tax rates, and were hence unconstitutional. The court also ruled unconstitutional any school tax, in addition to the small one passed by the state, that local townships or counties might institute on their own initiative.[71]

In one sense these efforts were highly successful: State-sup-

71. Lane *v.* Stanly, 65 N.C. 153 (1871).

ported schools remained scarce. But this proved more harmful to the white poor than to the Negroes. By means of such public schools as existed, by means of schools supported by churches and benevolent societies, Negroes were somehow learning to read. Their illiteracy rate in North Carolina fell from virtually 100 per cent in 1860 to 47.6 per cent in 1900. The illiteracy rate of whites, on the other hand, was at least as high in 1900 as it had been forty years before.[72]

"The democratic party is now like the attitude of the two men who went out to kill a beef," a certain "Mechanic" wrote to the Wilmington *Post*.

One of them was to hold it down while the other knocked it in the head; the latter being cross-eyed, when he drew the ax back to inflict the death blow, looked his friend full in the face, who asked "Do you intend to strike where you are looking?" "I do," was the reply. "Then I will turn loose" was the rejoinder. The democrats have used the poor white man to hold the negro down and now the axe is raised to inflict a mortal wound, but the cross-eyed democracy is looking the poor white men squarely in the face, and I for one say turn the negro loose before the blow has fallen.[73]

The Democratic position on education was an important reason why in the 1890's the poor white man did indeed, albeit briefly, "turn the negro loose," and the result was the Populist Revolt and Fusion movement.[74]

Because public schools were starved for funds, during the post-war nineteenth century, various types of private schools played an important role in education. So far as the Cape Fear country

72. The census reports would seem to indicate that "white illiteracy" stood at 19.5% in 1900, while the illiteracy of the "free population" had been only 10.3% in 1860. But other differences in methods of census taking rule out exact comparison of even these unlike categories: In 1860, an "illiterate" had to be twenty years old or more, while in 1900 he needed to be only ten. United States, Census Office, *Eighth Census of the United States: 1860. Statistics* (Washington: Government Printing Office, 1866), p. 347; ——, *Twelfth Census of the United States: 1900. Statistics*, 2 vols. (Washington: Government Printing Office, 1902), II, ciii.

73. Wilmington *Post*, August 3, 1875.

74. The momentary success of this movement did not mean that the white poor of eastern North Carolina had changed their opinion of the Negro. It did mean, however, that in their political behavior they were subordinating white supremacy to other issues. See Edmonds, *The Negro and Fusionist Politics*.

was concerned, these institutions were concentrated heavily in Wilmington; and, though many of them had limited resources, they were generally able to offer better education than the public schools. Nevertheless the private schools presented a wide variety of types.

There were the fashionable institutions that served a small group of families which could afford comparatively expensive tuition. These would include "Mrs. [Robert] Ransom's Female Seminary," with some eighty "scholars," directed by the wife of a former Confederate general; and the Cape Fear Academy, a military school, commanded by General Raleigh Edward Colston, C.S.A.[75] These relatively affluent schools had superior resources. Cape Fear Academy, for example, for the school year 1869-70 had three teachers for eighty-three cadets, while the Negro public schools in the same county at one time had six teachers for 634 children.[76] Unfortunately, however, the elite institutions did not give their pupils a forward-looking orientation. By means of Confederate flags, gray uniforms, and other symbols, they were almost perpetually re-enacting the tragic drama of the Lost Cause, keeping the eyes of their students focused backward toward the ante-bellum past.

The most interesting schools on the lower Cape Fear, however, were the private, free schools. If the fashionable academies were looking backward to an increasingly unrealistic image of the Old South, if the public schools were too hard-pressed to look anywhere, the private free schools, sponsored by northern benevolent societies and foundations, were squarely facing the problems of the present and were even charting a course for the future, toward high-quality mass education.

The largest potential source of northern aid was the George Peabody fund. But unfortunately few schools could qualify for a Peabody grant. In order to do so, an institution had to be able to raise funds locally that amounted to more than double the sum

75. Belle Thomas to George Gillett Thomas, January 19, 1868, Fuller-Thomas Papers, Department of Manuscripts, Duke University; Wilmington *Star,* September 16, 1868.

76. Wilmington *Daily Journal,* September 10, 1869; August 17, 1870; December 6, 1873.

the school received as Peabody aid. Furthermore, the school could not charge tuition, and had to operate ten months a year with a good attendance rate.[77] Thus Peabody money was well out of the reach of most educators in the Cape Fear country, though one Negro school in Wilmington was able to qualify.[78] More important, in the region were the schools conducted by Amy Bradley and supported primarily by Hemenway money.

The free, philanthropic schools did not actually educate a very large proportion of the children of the area, but they helped combat a large obstacle to mass education, a prejudice going far back into ante-bellum days that free education was pauper education. Institutions supported by Peabody and Hemenway funds were visible proof that free education can also be good education.

During her early years on the Cape Fear, Amy Bradley had concentrated upon basic literacy or grammar schools. But, in 1871, she obtained a thirty-thousand dollar donation from Mrs. Mary Tileston Hemenway for the construction of Tileston Normal School, which the philanthropist wished to have built in memory of her father.[79] By this time there were few people in the area not willing to concede the propriety of free grammar schools, established as a private charitable venture and therefore not making any demands upon the taxpayer. However, free "Normal" schools, where students from underprivileged homes might prepare for college and professional work, just as if they had been admitted into one of the academies, represented a bold new departure. Nevertheless, in the winter, 1871-72, an impressive building for such a venture was constructed, the cornerstone bearing the hopeful inscription, *Domus Haec Inimica Ignorantiae Et Superstitioni*, "this house is inimical to ignorance and superstition."[80]

Tileston was free, but associated with it was none of the squalor and brutality of pauper schools. Though corporal punish-

77. Edgar Wallace Knight, "The Peabody Fund and its Early Operation in North Carolina," *The South Atlantic Quarterly*, XIV (1915), 170.

78. *Proceedings of the Trustees of the Peabody Educational Fund* (Boston: Press of John Wilson and Son, 1875), I, 198; Howell, *Wilmington*, p. 164.

79. *Ibid.*, pp. 155-56; Ida Brooks Kellam *et al.*, *Wilmington: Historic Colonial City* (Wilmington: Stamp Defiance Chapter of the National Society Daughters of the American Revolution, 1954), p. 23, hereinafter cited as Kellam, *Wilmington*.

80. Wilmington *Daily Journal*, December 2, 1871.

ment was a standard of the day, in the matter of discipline, as in other respects, Amy Bradley charted her own c᷒ ᷑ᵣse, announcing that "moral suasion was her invariable . . . rule to govern children, and that if parents expected . . . her corps of assistants to use the rod they would be sadly mistaken."

Harsh discipline was hardly required at Tileston. The students were a select group. But, even though the school soon began to attract children from the well-to-do classes, Amy Bradley continued giving general preference to those from poor families.[81] During her first year of operation, the city administration granted a petition that she had presented, requesting free gas so that she could offer night classes to "a good number of scholars, of both sexes and almost all ages."[82]

By such methods she was able to expand the number of students that the building and staff could serve so that within ten years Tileston had an enrollment of more than five hundred,[83] dwarfing every other institution in the Cape Fear country. Nevertheless the *Post* reported that she was "forced, for want of room, to turn off hundreds every year. . . . It seems to us that there might be an addition put on . . . so she could provide for two or three hundred more."[84]

Yet there was a limit, not only to the number of students that one building operating night and day could accommodate, but also there was a limit to the generosity and resources of philanthropists. Tileston would not be able to enroll a large proportion of the children of the Cape Fear country. At most it could serve to prove a point. It could vindicate free schools and the sort of people who must attend free schools. There is reason to believe, in fact, that Amy Bradley compared Tileston to a lighthouse, pointing the way to a future in which all children would have equal opportunity to learn. She founded a student society, the "Lighthouse Club."[85] She founded a newspaper, *The Lighthouse*,

81. Wilmington *Review*, October 3, 1883.
82. Wilmington *Daily Journal*, March 6, 1873.
83. Wilmington *Review*, October 3, 1883.
84. Wilmington *Post*, October 5, 1883.
85. Wilmington *Daily Journal*, April 12, 1873.

published by Tileston students and teachers and publicizing the school's activities. Ten years later it was still being published.[86]

Many of Tileston's activities, furthermore, were worth noticing. It may have been due to its giant size, it may have been because the students shared some of the crusading zeal of their teachers; but Tileston could present school functions that would have been out of reach of the most expensive academies in the area: the publication of a newspaper, for example, or giving a benefit cantata for "sick, destitute and suffering poor in our midst."[87]

But academically it would also achieve some distinction in 1882 when a bright young graduate, William H. Chadbourn, was admitted to Massachusetts Institute of Technology. This was an event for the exclusive academies to consider: Coming from an affluent Republican lumber family, this youth well could have afforded to have attended a fashionable school. But he had gone to a crowded, free school, drawn largely from the underprivileged classes; and he had been admitted, "without conditions," to the finest engineering school in the nation.[88]

In 1871, at the groundbreaking ceremony that had launched the construction of Tileston, Amy Bradley was reported to have been ritualistically removing a few shovels of earth, when someone remarked, jokingly, that it looked as if she were digging a grave. "A grave," she had replied, "for burying much of the ignorance and vice that is growing up so freely in this town."[89] A grave to bury the ignorance and vice of Wilmington! What a vast chasm to dig with a shovel. But she was a person to undertake grandiose projects. And, while no one has quite succeeded in burying ignorance and vice in Wilmington or elsewhere, few would work at it with the persistence of Amy Bradley.

She was fortunate enough to live on into the twentieth century, long enough to see her thirty-year campaign for mass education take fire, as the Democratic party, somewhat chastened by its temporary loss of power in the 1890's, abandoned its unholy al-

86. *Ibid.*, January 9, 1872; Wilmington *Review*, February 2, 1882.
87. Wilmington *Star*, February 20, 1879.
88. Wilmington *Review*, June 7, 1882.
89. Wilmington *Daily Journal*, September 13, 1871.

liance with ignorance and began a vigorous campaign for free, tax-supported mass education. In her eighties at this time, it must have been a pleasure to her to have considered the relationship that her life had borne to the exciting events that were going on around her.

A minister, who had been in Wilmington in 1870, later tried to recall the impressions he had received from a visit to Amy Bradley's office: "I see a plainly dressed woman sitting in her bare room and talking to visitors, of whom I am one. There is a nervous energy in every word she says, and in every motion she makes. Hard work and anxiety of mind have left their marks upon her. But as the falling of the leaves in autumn only show better the fruit that has been ripening there; so the ripe results of a life-struggle, sacrifice, and victory, show themselves in the expression of this woman's worn face."[90] It is a credit to the people of the lower Cape Fear, and to the high regard with which they hold learning, that this saintly carpetbagger has come to occupy in their memory the honored place that she so positively earned.

During the postwar nineteenth century, Wilmington was important because of its newspapers and schools, but it was also important as the chief center in North Carolina for urban culture and amusement. In view of the fact that, during these years, the town had fewer than twenty thousand people, it seems surprising that it could symbolize city life to many persons. Perhaps the explanation is one of perspective. It is said, for example, that to a mouse a cat is the mightiest of beasts; certainly to rural and village North Carolina Wilmington was a mighty metropolis.

It was a place, during the fall and winter, where a back country merchant might buy stock for the coming year, where a Piedmont planter might find a buyer for his cotton, and where he might shop with a measure of choice. The coming of cool weather, furthermore, saw not only a quickening of economic life, but of high-toned social activity as well. This was the time of year that was still known as "the season" or "the pleasure season," though, since the war at least, it had probably been more business than pleasure that brought visitors to the city.

90. "Tileston School," Noble Papers, p. 11.

A planter or merchant reached Wilmington by one of the three railroads radiating from the city, or possibly by steamboat, and then engaged rooms at Purcell House or the Orton Hotel. The morning after his arrival he might learn with some pleasure that the local papers had taken notice of his presence, and had thus alerted his local friends and business associates of his arrival. He may well have been already familiar with these papers, perhaps having formed the habit of reading a Wilmington weekly or even a daily paper in his home community. He would doubtlessly scan the papers further to find out who else might be in the city, and what prospects there were for entertainment.

Ordinarily the papers showed a keen sensitivity for picking up any news item that might make Wilmington appear to be a place where an affluent planter or merchant might care to spend a few days. However, from an occasional lapse in this high sense of journalistic responsibility, the visitor might learn of the existence in the city, even the exact address, of "what is called a sailor boarding house, but which hardly deserves as respectable a name as that," where there were sometimes individuals "who, not satisfied with the orgies usually carried on under the shadow of night, were desecrating the Sabbath, and making the day hideous with their noise and tumult."[91] If his finer sensibilities were offended by this reminder of the seamy aspects of urban life, he could at least be assured that if such enterprises showed a tendency to wither before the scorching blast of journalistic disapproval, they could then be scarcely enjoying much prosperity.

For the more cultivated visitor there was the attraction of the Opera House, of which the people of the lower Cape Fear were justly proud. "In the whole Southern Country," the Journal bragged, only two opera houses surpassed it, the one at Mobile and the one at New Orleans.[92] A visitor could not only hear opera there, but could attend a variety of other programs as well. During a typical season one could look forward also to a concert, perhaps an operetta by Gilbert and Sullivan, an occasional lec-

91. Wilmington *Review*, August 4, 1881; Wilmington *Star*, September 2, 1879.
92. Wilmington *Daily Journal*, January 28, 1876.

ture, and a good play, usually by Shakespeare.[93] At the opposite end of the creative spectrum, a visitor could look forward to one of the almost artless, but tremendously popular, minstrel shows.[94]

But while burnt-cork buffoonery created the greatest sensation, apparently all productions were fairly well patronized by those who could afford them. It is interesting that in the nineteenth century the general public seemed eager to attend performances that, in an age of electronic entertainment, would enjoy the patronage of only a tiny clique.

When ever there is a performance at the Opera House, a gang of small boys white and colored gather around the entrance . . . and it is painful to witness their intense desire to get in. Having no money . . . these boys resort to all sort of dodges. . . . Some boys . . . resort to a desperate and dangerous method . . . . They go . . . upstairs over the police headquarters . . . climb out the window onto the cornill [cornice?], which is only seven or eight inches wide, and crawl fifty feet to the portico of the Opera House. They push up the window . . . and slide in. . . .[95]

And in order to see and hear what? Exotic costumes, strange music, far removed from the themes with which they were familiar, and sung in a language that was stranger still. But possibly herein lay the fascination. Perhaps for them the curtain rose not upon the "Barber of Seville," but upon a mysterious world of color and excitement that must have glowed somewhere beyond the horizon of each nineteenth-century provincial town.

In Wilmington one sometimes had an opportunity to hear distinguished lecturers, and, if fortunate, a chance to meet them socially as well. During William Cullen Bryant's visit, for example, Edward Kidder served as his host, taking the famous editor and poet to visit Tileston Normal School.[96] Although Oscar Wilde's lecture at the Opera House on "Decorative Art" attracted only "a fair" audience, the well-known young writer was nevertheless warmly welcomed by fashionable society: a house

93. *Ibid.*, March 27, 1868; Wilmington *Review*, December 7, 15, 1883, January 19, 1886.
94. Wilmington *Messenger*, January 13, 1891.
95. *Ibid.*, January 23, 1891.
96. Wilmington *Daily Journal*, April 8, 1873.

guest of Captain E. W. Manning at his place on the Sound, a dinner guest of Major C. M. Stedman, he took a trip to the beach and a swim in the ocean with a "party of young gentlemen."[97] When Carl Schurz lectured to "a good audience" on the "Problems of Education," it was the turn of the local German community to extend the usual hospitality to a celebrity.[98]

Some entertainment in Wilmington was more of a local nature. The Thalian Association, for example, probably the oldest amateur dramatics group in America, had been performing plays in the city since 1788.[99] There was also horse racing at Captain T. J. Southerland's track,[100] and the regattas that the Carolina Yacht Club had held since ante-bellum days.[101] "Lately we have enjoyed the sailing very much," wrote a gentleman who was scarcely enjoying his efforts to manage his plantation with free labor, "having strong easterly winds, the tide covering the marsh-grass, offering us delightful sport, shooting marsh-hens which hunting you know is enjoyed more than any other by sounders."[102] For high-toned social activities, there were the annual *"bal poudre"* and the masquerades that were held by societies flourishing such names as "L'Allegro Soiree Club," and "L'Arioso Pleasure Club."[103]

For persons with stronger intellectual interests, there was the Historical and Scientific Society of Wilmington. At its meetings one might hear a lecture on Colonial History delivered by George Davis, formerly Attorney General of the Confederacy; or one concerning the history of Fort Johnston, at the mouth of the Cape Fear, given by Edward Cantwell, a Republican judge and professor of law; or perhaps a lecture on the history of the University of North Carolina by Kemp Battle. On at least one occasion the society organized a party to excavate an Indian burial mound on

97. Wilmington *Review*, July 11, 1882.

98. *Ibid.*, January 21, 1885.

99. Kellam, *Wilmington*, p. 17; Wilmington *Daily Journal*, July 4, 1871.

100. Wilmington *Review*, October 25, 1887.

101. *Ibid.*, July 5, 1890; Kellam, Wilmington, p. 28.

102. Joshua G. Wright to Julius Walder Wright, September 23, 1869, Murdock-Wright Papers.

103. Wilmington *Daily Journal*, January 3, 1872, September 5, 1873; Wilmington *Messenger*, January 2, 1891.

Middle Sound, and the members puzzled over their finding that a prehistoric people in the area had buried their dead in standing or sitting posture.[104]

On one occasion the Historical and Scientific Society discussed problems of the economic development of the lower Cape Fear. They heard a report concerning the industries of the Bordeaux region of southwestern France, an area that shares a number of soil problems with the Piney Woods, but nevertheless one that has enjoyed a more satisfactory development of agriculture. They discussed local experiments that were being undertaken with planting vineyards, and the possibilities of establishing a grape and wine culture on the lower Cape Fear similar to that around Bordeaux.[105]

The concern that the society showed for the problems of agriculture is significant. Because, though the people of Wilmington might consider themselves urbane and cosmopolitan, in the final analysis they were a folk not far removed from the land; and the very tempo of their life was determined by the demands that the changing seasons made upon the cultivator of the soil. The "pleasure season," after all, was only a high-toned reflex of the harvest. Throughout the nineteenth century, the customs and ideas that one found on the Cape Fear bore the unmistakable earmarks of a people whose central concern was securing the bounty of the forest and fields.

Yet of all crops none was more intimately connected with the life of the region than the cultivation of rice. This had been clearly the case in ante-bellum days, when the industry had sustained the power and the culture of the gentry. But rice-growing, even in its Indian summer of the 1870's and 1880's, imparted a certain tone to the whole culture of the lower Cape Fear, and not simply to the gentry alone. Perhaps this can be best illustrated by the extent to which the requirements of the rice crop could become the preoccupation of the entire community, particularly at harvest time.

There is probably no more pleasant moment in the life of an

104. Wilmington *Star*, March 2, April 24, November 19, 1879, April 20, 1880.
105. *Ibid.*, April 27, 1881.

agricultural society than on the eve of the harvest, when a ripple of anticipation runs through the people. Who will not share a small measure of the bounty and leisure that lies just ahead? Even for the Negro the harvest held certain compensations for the mosquitoes and snakes that were in the flooded fields of July. For rice-growers, however, the autumn was not only a time of elation and anticipation, but also a time of still-lingering anxieties. Because the last great threat to the crop, the ricebird, arrived on the very eve of the harvest.

"My plantation record will show," a rice-grower wrote in 1886,

that for the past ten years, except when prevented by strong south or southwest winds, the rice birds have come punctually on the night of August 21st., apparently coming from seaward. All night their chirp can be heard, and millions of the birds make their appearance and settle in the rice fields. Curious to say, we have never seen this flight during the day time. From August 21st, to September 25th., every effort is made to save the crop. Men, boys, and women are posted with guns and ammunition every little ways, but all efforts are only partly successful.[106]

Yet this final defense of the crop was not regarded as an altogether unpleasant task, since ricebirds were counted a rare delicacy on the lower Cape Fear, and it was with a certain pleasure that one could learn that the "prevailing easterly winds have brought quantities of birds to the rice fields. In a few days they will be fat and luscious and you may expect to see them in the market."[107]

The arrival of the birds was even a festive occasion, as children turned out to the fields with bells, gourds, and other noisemakers to frighten the birds.[108] It was a time, also, that called for lowering a little the fences that men erect in order to estrange each other. It was a time when the fields were thrown open to hunters of all descriptions, Negroes, whites, men, or boys. And, Victorian etiquette notwithstanding, at such a time it was not unforgivable for members of the gentle sex to appear in the fields with firearms and make a little noise.

106. *Ibid.*, July 29, 1886.
107. Wilmington *Daily Journal*, August 28, 1875.
108. Lewis Cecil Gray, *History of Agriculture in the Southern United States to 1860* (2 vols.; Washington: Carnegie Institute of Washington, 1933), II, 729.

What if riotous parties of sportsmen of the most varied line-age and breeding should go rampaging through fields not their own startling clouds of birds? Or suppose bands of armed Negroes should appear wanting to earn some extra money by selling strings of fat ricebirds in the Wilmington market? They would be welcomed, perhaps given extra gunpowder, or lent a boat. There would be feasting in Wilmington. There would be more rice left for the planter. The birds were the enemy. People were friends. Autumn brought a curious convergence in human pur-poses.

"The rice fields are in all the glory of the rich, golden har-vest," the *Star* wrote, "and the booming guns are fired among the rice birds, which come in multitudes at this season. . . ."[109] The folk who lived along the lower Cape Fear were pitted against each other in many ways, alienated from one another by differ-ences of race, and by distinctions in human condition. But with the coming of the birds they stood as one people.

109. Wilmington *Star*, September 18, 1880.

IX ⤫ Summary and Conclusions

THE YEARS FOLLOWING THE CIVIL WAR SAW DRAMATIC CHANGES in the social institutions of the lower Cape Fear, important shifts in the economy and in the locus of political power. A number of the problems raised sharply at this time are still reverberating. The base line against which these changes must be measured is that provided by ante-bellum society, which had endured in the region for almost a century and a half.

While there is perhaps no static society, the prewar Cape Fear community was one that absorbed change slowly and with considerable difficulty. The story of the ante-bellum Cape Fear is largely a story of the forest industries, of rice, and of the families that were associated with these enterprises. The system of slavery had provided the large landholders with a highly successful means for producing these commodities by the simple techniques that had prevailed in the early eighteenth century. The assimilation by slave society of more recent productive methods, however, had been slow and painful.

Increasingly, the production of rice and naval stores lagged behind in the technical progress of the nineteenth century. The primitive character of these industries was reflected in the lives of the people who depended upon them. The people of the Piney Woods a hundred and fifty years after the area was first settled were still living in an essentially log-cabin culture, a way of life that was almost as changeless as the forest itself.

While the primary producers on the rice plantations, the slaves, lived under conditions at least as primitive as those in the

Piney Woods, and, although rice did not bring so much wealth into the region as did the forest industries, at the same time it exerted a stronger influence on the political power structure. Unlike naval stores and lumber, the rice economy produced a stable, hereditary, and cultivated gentry. The influence of the rice planter, however, went far beyond his plantation, and even beyond the Piney Woods. Indeed North Carolina counties such as Moore, Harnett, and Ashe, though located far from the ancient rice fields, nevertheless bear names that are an enduring testimony to the influence that the great rice dynasties once held.

For a century and a half the rice planter held sway over southern North Carolina and made his weight felt beyond. The old society did not fall, however, directly because of the obsolescence of its primary productive techniques. It is possible for an established industry to function with a measure of success even though its productive methods no longer reflect the best that science can offer. Economic developments, though of tremendous long-range importance, are rarely the immediate cause of an historical event. Before the Civil War, for example, it was possible for discerning men to foresee the ultimate submergence of southern sectional interests, if purely economic developments were allowed to proceed without corresponding changes in the political ground rules. A realization that the South was falling behind in the peaceful economic competition with the North prompted southern leaders to try their luck, first, in the somewhat less peaceful area of political conflict, and, finally, in a desperate contest of arms.

Thus it was not so much the prevalence of old-fashioned productive methods in the plantation area as it was an antagonism between an older and a newer view of the Constitution and the nation that helped precipitate a conflict fatal to the old society, as slavery became ever more conspicuously out of place in the nineteenth-century world and the planters demanded the ever stronger legal guarantees which they needed to maintain its stability. The lower Cape Fear was the strongest center that the secession extremists had in North Carolina, and the few Unionists in the area remained unorganized and intimidated.

The old way of life ended with the federal occupation, beginning in January and February, 1865. The six-month period from January 15 to June 20, 1865, in certain respects constitutes a distinct phase in the history of the lower Cape Fear. During these months presidential policy was committed inflexibly toward neither a Radical Reconstruction program, which sought a root-and-branch abolition of distinctly ante-bellum institutions and the establishment of American-style democracy from the ground up, nor toward a Conservative program, which sought some sort of compromise between the old society and democracy. As long as the President tried to steer a middle course between these two factions, Union field officers in the army of occupation enjoyed considerable latitude in shaping Reconstruction policy according to their own ideas.

The Military District of Wilmington, which embraced eight counties in southeastern North Carolina, was under the command of General Joseph Roswell Hawley, a veteran abolitionist, a Radical, and a native of North Carolina. Under Hawley's command, the pendulum of political change swept forward toward a Radical solution to the problem of Reconstruction. Radical military courts dispensed color-blind justice. Hawley seized large plantations and settled them with freedmen. Squatters were tolerated and even assisted by the military government. The Freedmen's Bureau was vigorously supported in its welfare and educational projects.

The spring of 1865 was a time when people suffered from famine and died from disease. But for the Negro it was also the springtime of freedom. Giant demonstrations marked the beginnings of a Negro political movement on the lower Cape Fear. A local Negro leadership began to emerge.

During the period from June 20, 1865, to July 26, 1868, the political pendulum in the Cape Fear country reversed its course, sweeping backwards toward a Conservative solution to the problem of Reconstruction. After some initial wavering, President Johnson became committed to a Conservative policy and began to assert strong executive leadership in this direciton. On June 20, 1865, he removed Hawley as commander of the eight-county

Military District of Wilmington, replacing him with General John Worthington Ames, a Conservative and a former member of Hawley's staff.

This period, characterized variously as "Conservative," or "Confederate," or "Presidential" Reconstruction, saw the restoration of the entire mechanism of political and military power to the ante-bellum ruling class on the lower Cape Fear. The municipal government of Wilmington was returned to the same individuals that had been in control before the withdrawal of Confederate troops. The ante-bellum county courts were revived, operating under a system of Black Codes, which assigned to the Negro the subordinate status of the prewar free Negro. To enforce this system, County Militia companies were formed. These appear to have been little more than the reincarnation of the ante-bellum County Patrols and the wartime Home Guards.

Plantations that had been seized by the Radical military government were now returned to their former owners. Squatters were violently evicted. Negroes were disarmed, their houses searched, and their possessions seized. The cowhide and the branding iron reappeared in the county courts, as the political pendulum swept backward toward 1860. But when the pendulum reached a point marked "January, 1865," the time of emancipation, it stopped abruptly. Slavery was one question that the war had settled.

The whole counteroffensive of the southern Conservatives existed only by the sufferance of President Johnson and his northern supporters, who were willing to uphold every type of southern property right except one, the right to possess human beings. At such times as it appeared that the southern Conservatives might be chipping away at such a basic result of the war as Abolition, as was the case in the Sampson County "orphan" raids of 1866, the supporters of the president closed ranks with the Radicals, and together they dramatically asserted the power of the federal government.

Presidential Reconstruction was thus characterized by a restoration of much of the political and military pattern of the old regime, but without the social and economic foundation that had given it a certain stability. Nowhere was this more obvious than on the lower Cape Fear. There, by ball and blade, the County Militia had been able to drive away the squatters. But growing rice required the use of a hoe and a spade, implements with which the gentry were less adept. The planters could restore some of the power relationships of a rice culture, but power relationships founded upon weeds instead of rice.

This effort to restore the old society, shorn of slavery, was not conducive to orderly government. It gave the South an opportunity to observe, not for the last time, how little tranquillity a society can enjoy if those in authority, lacking the full complement of repressive measures made possible by slavery, are nonetheless unwilling to extend to a large portion of their people the full complement of rights enjoyed by free men. The formidable military establishment that the Conservatives revived on the lower Cape Fear might well have been able to hold a large slave population in check, but it was less successful in dealing with Negroes who possessed at least mobility, and who had had a taste of freedom.

The city of Wilmington, for example, saw three major riots during Presidential Reconstruction. In August, 1865, Negro mobs forced the resignation of the municipal government, including the entire police force. Ironically, federal troops intervened to restore to power the same local administration that they had overthrown by the capture of the city six months before. There were other riots in February, 1866, and June, 1868, prompted in both instances by the efforts of mobs to set free city prisoners.

Despite the violence of Conservative repressive measures, Negroes continued to form organizations and to conduct demonstrations, a habit they had formed during the administration of General Hawley. In 1867, the Negroes joined forces with a handful of white Unionists to form the Republican party. They also enjoyed some success in hiding their weapons from the police who were periodically raiding their homes. This was not without significance early in 1868 when the Conservatives, doubtlessly noticing the loss of influence of their friends in Washington, began to rely increasingly on illegal rather than legal tactics with the formation of the Ku Klux Klan. The efforts of the Klan to influence the ratification election were unsuccessful and the Republicans carried all of the counties of the lower Cape Fear except Columbus. Presidential Reconstruction ended in the region on July 26, 1868, when Governor Holden, brandishing the threat of military force, brought about the capitulation of the local Conservative administrations.

The period from July 26, 1868, to August 4, 1870, the date when the Conservatives regained control of the legislature, was in certain respects the crest of Radical Reconstruction. Yet it is perhaps significant that during these years, unlike the period of Radical military Reconstruction in the first half of 1865, no assault was made on the concentration of economic power in the hands of a relatively few prominent families. By 1868, the idea of "forty acres and a mule" was virtually dead. Accommodating themselves to the economic status quo, the Republicans undertook to promote political equality in a society characterized by equality in almost nothing else.

Thus Reconstruction did not result in Negro domination, as one generation of southern historians thought, the Negro being too poor, too inexperienced politically, too culturally deprived to dominate, though his vote gave him some influence. Nor was southeastern North Carolina any longer dominated by the rice planter, his economic power having been broken, his political power compromised. If the Cape Fear country was dominated by anyone during these years it was by the men who were exploiting the wealth of the Piney Woods, by those who were speculating in timber and turpentine land, operating lumber mills and naval stores refineries, and controlling the railroads and export houses that shipped the forest products.

As was the case with rice, the forest industries used some primitive methods, probably reflecting the influence of slave labor. Yet there were some important differences between the two principal ante-bellum industries. The forest industries had never depended totally upon slave labor. Also a number of the families controlling these enterprises were newcomers to the region, including Scots and northerners. The latter, coming chiefly from

New England, had settled on the Cape Fear before as well as after the war.

The men engaged in the extraction, processing, and transportation of forestry products, furthermore, were able to make a much more satisfactory adjustment to free labor than were the rice planters. If one needed to curtail production because a particular area had been "cut over" or "boxed out," he no longer found himself with an enormous investment in slaves. The hands he laid off could eke out a meager existence in the Wilderness until they were again needed. On the other hand, if a rise in prices called for an expansion in production, a long-term investment in slaves no longer absorbed the bulk of his capital. The collapse of rice had filled the woods with Negroes. He could now expand more rapidly since investment in wages brought about a much steeper increase in production. Railroads, lumber, and turpentine were not languishing because of emancipation.

But whether it was because of their non-southern origins or because they were prospering in the employment of free labor, the men connected with the forest industries seemed to have had somewhat different views from those of the rice gentry. They could think in prose. They entertained few illusions that they were knights in shining armor. A number of them were Republicans, comprising most members of the "Ring" which dominated the party in the counties of the lower Cape Fear. But whether Republican or Conservative in their politics, they were generally progressive in their economic views, being responsible for most of the important technical innovations and new industries introduced into the area in the late nineteenth century.

Not all the members of the business community were as willing to accept change as those connected with the forest industries. Increasingly the Conservatives were drawing strength from the growth of a new type of landlord, the time merchant. Agriculture was reviving, slowly in rice, more rapidly in cotton on the fringes of the Cape Fear country. This did not mean that the antebellum-type planter was making a satisfactory recovery from war and emancipation.

The revival was being stimulated, rather, by merchant credit.

Though the time merchant operated a general store in some country town, his business did not consist mainly in retailing goods to the public. His store was primarily a credit institution that advanced supplies to flattened farmers and to his own tenants, the former often in the process of becoming the latter.

The time merchant owed his very existence to emancipation and the breakup of the plantation system. Indeed his domain, consisting of widely scattered tenant farms and the fragments of plantations, could scarcely have been operated with slave labor. At the same time his farming methods were sufficiently like those used in ante-bellum days as not to require the most skilled and strongly motivated labor. With the coming of the harvest, furthermore, the time when he had to reach a settlement with his debtors and tenants, he did not want to be negotiating with persons who were his equals before the law. A Conservative South, suspended somewhere between slavery and democracy, was tailor-made to suit the taste of the powerful and growing class of time merchants.

Granted the prevailing conditions of economic and cultural inequality, it was almost inescapable that with the collapse of the plantation system the businessman was going to dominate, regardless of which party he might choose to join and with or without universal manhood suffrage. It was of capital importance to the South, however, which party the business class chose. Even though in 1876 the Conservatives would adopt the name "Democratic party," their hostility to democracy was the principal difference they had with the Republicans. More was involved in this question than the equality of all men before the law and whether or not the businessmen were willing to accept the Negroes and plain whites as junior partners in the elective process, partners whose opinions were supposed to count. Involved also was the question of whether the South was to have a labor force modeled after the ante-bellum "free" Negro or one modeled after the white laborer of the North. A relatively free, skilled, and literate labor force would make it possible and even necessary for the South to undergo a rapid economic development, comparable to that that had been taking place in the North.

A spirited contest took place in the Cape Fear country between the two parties for the allegiance of the business class. The crucial phase of this encounter took place in 1868 and was centered in Wilmington. In apparent efforts to woo the business class the Republicans advanced conservative rather than popular candidates for the municipal administration in Wilmington and made special overtures to the Germans and the Jews. In seeming recognition of failure, the Republicans then replaced some of their conservative candidates with popular whites and with Negroes. The overwhelming majority of the businessmen had aligned themselves with the Conservatives.

In the years that followed the Conservatives were almost able to make good their claim of being the white man's party. In Duplin and Columbus counties, for example, with 65 to 70 per cent white majorities, they seem to have lost few white votes. New Hanover and Pender counties, on the other hand, with Negro majorities of about 55 per cent, generally returned Republican majorities of about two-thirds. Robeson, Bladen, and Brunswick, in each of which the whites had a slight majority, saw election contests between evenly matched parties. Sampson County, with a Negro population of about 30 per cent, usually returned a Republican vote of more than 40 per cent.

The Negro Conservative vote appears to have been a less significant factor than the white Republican vote. While there were always individual Negroes who were Conservatives, they did not play a conspicuous role in either Negro or Conservative circles. The "white man's party" did not make efforts to win Negro votes that were comparable to the efforts that the Republicans made to win white votes.

The Conservatives and Republicans conducted their organizations in vastly different ways. Conservative meetings were orderly affairs, characterized by little competition for control of the organization. The Conservatives could agree on candidates with little rancor, and it was only in rare instances that stories of their factional differences found their way into the newspapers.

The Republican party, on the other hand, was torn by bitter and open factionalism during its entire thirty-year life on the lower Cape Fear. There appears to have been no consistent difference in the political ideas of the feuding groups. The difficulty seems to have arisen from the fact that the party leaders could no longer do much for their supporters, and concentrated increasingly on trying to do something for themselves or for a few friends.

This problem was further complicated as a result of the dual control over the party by two distinct types of leaders: the wealthy patron, nearly always white, and the popular orator and debater, usually a Negro. Because of special discrimination of many employers against outspoken Republicans, popular orators had difficulty finding ordinary jobs. To make a living they became dependent upon various political jobs; and, to win these coveted positions, they had to compete with each other, not only for popular favor, but also for the favor of patrons. Thus each became the bitter rival of men having the same values and problems as himself.

Paradoxically, though the Republican party was torn by internal strife, it was nevertheless able to bring considerable peace and stability to those counties over which it obtained firm control. Of course, even at the height of their power, the Republicans were never able to deal successfully with the Ku Klux Klan in predominantly-white Sampson County. They were even less successful in dealing with the extremely complicated situation in Robeson County, in which the Klan and the Lowery Gang were engaging in acts of terror against each other, the latter enjoying broad popular support, especially among the Indians.

But the Pender-New Hanover area, with its Negro majority, was one of the most tranquil areas of the state after the Republicans assumed control. In Wilmington, especially, members of both parties enjoyed the freedom of being able to engage in lusty public debate, and of being able to organize noisy but nonviolent demonstrations, a degree of freedom, in fact, that has been all too rare in southern history. Even at the height of the Ku Klux Klan terror throughout Piedmont North Carolina, this freedom of assembly prevailed in the Wilmington area, and the courts continued to function in a normal manner.

The capture of the legislature by the Conservatives on August 4, 1870, initiated a long period during which the Republicans of the Cape Fear region were forced to give up one vantage point after another, a retreat interrupted by momentary successes, but one which finally ended in the destruction of the organization almost thirty years later. The new legislature began by gerrymandering the congressional district that embraced the Cape Fear country to include some strong Democratic Piedmont counties, thus making it extremely difficult for the Republicans to elect a candidate to Congress. Thereafter the nearest the party came to success was in 1878, when a lifelong Republican, Daniel Linsay Russell, by briefly bolting the party and running as a Greenback, was able to defeat his Democratic opponent.

Next the legislature created Pender County out of the northern end of New Hanover County in the belief that the Conservatives would be able to control the new county. The effort was largely unsuccessful as the Republicans continued to return majorities in both counties. The legislature had better luck gerrymandering the City of Wilmington and thereby turning over local control to a Democratic minority. Later they abolished local self-government in a series of predominantly Republican counties, including New Hanover and Pender. Thereafter the Board of Commissioners in each was appointed by a Conservative legislature. However, the Republicans continued winning legislative seats in New Hanover and usually Pender County until 1898, when Republican state leaders, acting upon an ultimatum in which some Democratic leaders threatened to resort to violence, agreed to allow the Democratic candidates for these seats to run unopposed, a concession that marked the end of the Republican party as a state-wide party in North Carolina.

In the eighteen seventies and eighties a high protective tariff along with slight improvements in techniques made possible a weak revival of rice-growing. At the end of the century, however, the rise of mechanized rice-production in Louisiana eclipsed the industry on the Cape Fear. The late nineteenth century also saw the virtual disappearance of naval stores, the other main antebellum industry in southeastern North Carolina. After more than a decade of prosperity following the war, production collapsed as a result of the "boxing out" of the Piney Woods. The conversion to free labor brought about more economical methods of exploitation, but it was in virgin forests of the Gulf states that the improved techniques flourished.

The virtual disappearance of the two major ante-bellum industries resulted in the stagnation, though by no means the total collapse, of the Cape Fear economy. Fortunately there were also economic developments that sustained the economy. The completion of the Wilmington, Charlotte, and Rutherfordton Railroad and the improvement of the port facilities of the Cape Fear estuary converted Wilmington into an important cotton market. The lumber industry took on a renewed significance with the establishment of the creosote process in the area. The economy of the region also received strength from the increasing importance of truck farming and from the establishment of a fertilizer industry in the area. The development of textile manufacturing, however, was comparatively slight. This may have been due to the lack of water power and to the lack of a dense and stable population. Throughout the latter half of the nineteenth century Wilmington continued to be the largest city in the state and, for a large area, an important center for trade, urban entertainment, and culture.

This study does not sustain the belief of certain historians of the Dunning school that Reconstruction was characterized by Negro domination. The Cape Fear region was dominated for a time by a group of men who could be regarded as carpetbaggers, though some had lived in the area since the eighteen twenties. A number of these men co-operated with native-born Conservatives in a campaign to bribe the legislature to make large appropriations to the Wilmington, Charlotte, and Rutherfordton Railroad. This impropriety evoked little criticism from either their friends or their enemies in the Cape Fear country, the region as a whole having apparently benefited from the results. The carpetbaggers and others who repudiated the ante-bellum traditions were generally a stimulating influence in the area, there being a close correlation between political and economic innovation.

The history of the Cape Fear country during Reconstruction also suggests that, in a society characterized by serious cultural and economic inequalities, the establishment of democratic political institutions, such as universal manhood suffrage, does not necessarily diffuse political power, and may substitute one form of minority control for another, as those men having economic power may also have the means to dominate the elective processes as well. This study may also indicate that, during times when the constitutional basis for government is being debated, when there is no general agreement as to ground rules for resolving political differences, orderly government then depends upon two conditions: a measure of popular support and a politically reliable mechanism of force.

Appendix A

Agricultural Descriptions of the
Lower Cape Fear Counties, 1880

BLADEN

Population: 16,158.—White, 7,598; colored, 8,560.

Area: 1,026 square miles.—Woodland, 297,237 acres.

Tilled lands: 37,990 acres.—Area planted in cotton, 1,618 acres; in corn, 21,556 acres; in wheat, 109 acres; in oats, 362 acres.

Cotton production: 683 bales; average cotton product per acre, 0.42 bale, 603 pounds seed-cotton, or 201 pounds cotton lint.

Bladen county lies south of Cumberland, and, like it, on both sides of the Cape Fear river. It has narrow zones of pine barrens running parallel to the river courses nearly the whole length of the county, and it also abounds in cypress swamps and alluvial "bottoms" along its streams. There are also large bodies of level piny woods. Marl is found in the bluffs of the river. On many of the streams are extensive bodies of gum and cypress swamps. This county has a very limited agriculture, the chief crop being corn; and very little cotton is produced, turpentine and lumber being still among the chief interests. Of the county area, only 5.79 per cent is tilled land of which 4.26 per cent is cultivated in cotton.

Abstract of the Report of D. A. Lamont, of Brinkland

The upland soils vary greatly in appearance and quality, and may be found in spots and patches of from 1 to 300 acres. Cotton in the lowlands will not mature, and is subject to be killed by frost; therefore the uplands are always preferred.

Three kinds of soils may be distinguished:

(1) The *gray gravelly* soil, with clay subsoil, forming about one-third of the land in this region. Its natural timber is cypress, oak, poplar, ash, hickory, gum, pine, and walnut. The crops are corn, cotton, and small grain, but the soil is best adapted to cotton, corn, and oats. The cotton crop occupies about one-fourth of the lands, and is most productive when 3 feet high. It is inclined to run to weed in the richest land and in wet seasons, and efforts are made to restrain this tendency by topping and by using less heating manures. The product from fresh land ranges from 1,200 to 1,500 pounds of seed-cotton per acre, 1,425 pounds making a 475-pound bale, which rates in the market as good middling. After three years cultivation the land yields from 800 to 1,000 pounds per acre, from 1,425 to 1,540 pounds being required to make a bale, which rates as low middling. Ragweed and hog-weed are most troublesome. About one-third of the land once cultivated now lies turned out, but when it is again taken in it is found to be much improved. The valleys are considerably improved by the washings of the uplands.

(2) *Chocolate-colored* soil, rich by deposits, occupies one-sixth of the lands in a belt one-half a mile wide by from 12 to 15 miles long. The average thickness is 2 feet before changing into that of the subsoil, which is heavier and sticky. This soil is best adapted to corn, wheat, and oats. Cotton runs to weed under all circumstances.

(3) *Black soil*, mixed with coarse and fine sand, occupies one-half as much surface, and is about 10 miles long by 2 miles wide. This soil is timbered with pine, bay, black gum, and gallberry. The subsoil contains pipe-clay, and is adapted to corn, potatoes, and cotton; but one-fifteenth of this soil is planted in the latter crop. Fresh land produces from 600 to 1,000 pounds of seed-cotton per acre, which rates in the market as middling.

Cotton shipments are made by steamboat to Wilmington. Rates of freight, per bale, 50 cents.

BRUNSWICK

Population: 9,389.—White, 5,227; colored, 4,052.

Area: 814 square miles.—Woodland, 304,722 acres.

Tilled lands: 18,006 acres.—Area planted in cotton, 385 acres; in corn, 4,915 acres; in wheat, 8 acres; in oats, 240 acres.

Cotton production: 244 bales; average cotton product per acre, 0.63 bale, 903 pounds seed-cotton, or 301 pounds cotton lint.

Brunswick county lies on the west side of the Cape Fear river, and touches the Atlantic on the south. Its central and western portion is occupied by the great pocoson known as Green swamp, which, with its many projections, covers nearly half of the territory of the county. This swamp is bordered by wide tracts of canebrakes, and contains extensive areas of gum, cypress, and juniper swamps, which have been for half a century the center of a large lumber trade. The various streams which flow from this swamp to all points of the compass are bordered by oak flats, tracts of semi-swamp, and often by canebrakes, and in the body of it are numerous hummocks or flat ridges having a silty soil and a growth of short-leaf pine and small oaks. Between the arms of the swamp, on the narrow divides, and particularly in the southern portion of the county, near the sea-shore, are patches of long-leaf pine lands with sandy soils, and elsewhere of level piny woods, valuable for lumber and naval stores. Along the Cape Fear are large bodies of alluvial lands of unsurpassed fertility, which are among the best rice soils in this country. Waccamaw lake occupies the highest part of Green swamp, and covers an area of about 40 square miles. Naval stores and lumber are, of course, the principal interest, agriculture being of subordinate importance, and limited mainly to the cultivation of rice, of which its product is more than double that of any other county in the state. Of the county area, 3.46 per cent is tilled land, of which 2.14 per cent is cultivated in cotton.

Abstract of the Report of W. G. Curtis, of Smithville.

The chief soil cultivated in cotton is a *fine sandy loam*, and the most of the land in this region is of this description, extending fifty miles in each direction. Its natural timber is pine, intermixed with black-jack and other varieties of oak. The soil is gray to the depth of

6 inches, but the subsoil is heavier, being a clay intermixed with sand. The chief crops are corn, sweet potatoes, cotton, and rice, and the soil is about equally adapted to all, except that sweet potatoes will grow in poorer land than the others. The height usually attained by cotton is from 2½ to 3 feet, and it is most productive at that height. When planted on very rich lowlands, or on soils having a sandy subsoil, the cotton-plant is inclined to run to weed. Fresh land produces 900 pounds of seed-cotton per acre, 1,425 pounds making a 475-pound bale, which, when clean, rates as low middling and middling. After years of cultivation it rapidly depreciates, unless kept up by manuring, and 1,660 pounds are then needed for a 475-pound bale. The staple is much shorter than that from fresh land. Crab- and cane-grass are troublesome. Very little of such land originally cultivated now lies "turned out." It does very well after resting a year or two, but it is subject to gullying, and the damage is serious. The valleys are benefited by the washings of the uplands.

Shipments are made by rail and river, in December and January, to Wilmington; rate of freight per bale, 40 cents.

COLUMBUS

Population: 14,439.—White, 8,926; colored, 5,513.
Area: 895 square miles.—Woodland, 357,014 acres.
Tilled lands: 38,293 acres.—Area planted in cotton, 2,113 acres; in corn, 15,723 acres; in wheat, 38 acres; in oats, 267 acres.
Cotton production: 930 bales; average cotton product per acre, 0.44 bale, 627 pounds seed-cotton, or 209 pounds cotton lint.

Columbus county lies farther inland and contains a larger proportion of upland piny woods soil than Brunswick. It is penetrated through all its parts by narrow belts of gum and cypress swamp and considerable tracts of oak and pine flats. The average soil of its upland piny woods is of moderate fertility, well adapted to the growth of cotton, but the richer swamp and gray-loam lands are devoted principally to corn. Brown marsh and White marsh are two large bodies of swamp in the eastern side of the county, and Gum swamp and others of less extent are found in the south and west. The production of cotton, potatoes, and rice divides with lumber and naval stores the interest of its people. Marl is found in several parts of the county. Of the county area 6.69 per cent is tilled land, of which 5.52 per cent is cultivated in cotton.

Abstract of the Report of D. S. Cowan, of Robeson.

The oak and hickory ridges have a light loam soil and a clay subsoil. The pine lands are stiff and heavy, and have a clay subsoil, generally underlaid with hard-pan. Marl underlies this whole region. Cotton in the lowlands runs to weed, and does not fruit well. The kinds of soils cultivated in cotton are: first, the oak and hickory ridges; second, the lowlands of Livingston creek above overflow; third, the cypress swamps, reclaimed. The *oak and hickory* is the chief soil, the proportion of this kind of land being about 40 per cent. Its natural timber is pine, oak, hickory, dogwood, maple, holly, walnut, and chincapin. The soil is a light clay loam, prairie-like, the color being brown or orange red, which does not bake or become sticky, and the average thickness 9 inches. The subsoil is heavier, the color being generally a light red, sometimes gray, and sometimes underlaid with hard-pan, which is quite impervious, and contains a limy substance, underlaid by clay at from 1 foot to 3 feet. The chief crops are corn, potatoes, cotton, pease, oats, rye, and vegetables of every description, the soil suiting them all remarkably well. The proportion of cotton planted is one-tenth, which is most productive at 3½ feet, but in very wet weather it is apt to run to weed. Fresh land produces 800 pounds of seed-cotton per acre, 1,400 pounds making a 475-pound bale, which, when clean, rates as good middling. After four years cultivation the yield is 500 pounds per acre, and then 1,425 pounds are needed to make a bale, but it does not compare favorably with that from fresh land. Cocklebur and hog-weed are most troublesome. About 5 per cent of such land originally cultivated lies turned out, and when again taken in, if marled, it does well. It is subject to gullying on the slopes, but the damage is not serious.

The soil of the *level pine lands* (pine flats) is heavy, black, and smooth, with no sand in it, and forms about 20 per cent of the lands. The average thickness of the soil is 2 inches. The subsoil is a sticky, fine clay, sometimes pure white, resembling kaolin, with hard-pan underneath, and impervious; it is difficult to till in wet and in dry seasons, and is too flat to drain cheaply. Native grasses for pasturing are apparently best adapted to this soil.

Cotton shipments are made in December by rail to Wilmington; freight, $1 per bale.

DUPLIN

Population: 18,773.—White, 10,587; colored, 8,186.
Area: 832 square miles.—Woodland, 228,505 acres.

Tilled Lands: 69,314 acres.—Area planted in cotton, 9,654 acres; in corn, 36,813 acres; in wheat, 1,031 acres; in rye, 422 acres; in oats, 433 acres.

Cotton production: 4,499 bales; average cotton product per acre, 0.47 bale, 663 pounds seed-cotton, or 221 pounds cotton lint.

Duplin county lies southward of the two preceding counties, and partakes of their general topographical and agricultural features. It is drained by the Northeast Cape Fear river, which flows southward through its middle section, and both this and the numerous tributaries are bordered by belts of alluvial and often swampylands. Near its northern and eastern borders are two small pocosons, and within its southern section lies one-half of the great Angola Bay pocoson, an almost impenetrable jungle of the average character of pocoson lands, with fringes of rich swamp lands on the streams that issue from it. This pocoson is flanked on the westward toward the Northeast Cape Fear river by a fringe of fertile white-oak flats and semi-swamp lands. Between the tributaries of the river, on the divides, are several tracts of sandy pine hills, which are very unproductive. The cotton lands, which are of limited extent, are the level piny woods of the usual description; but corn is a more valuable crop, and the product of potatoes and rice are of considerable importance. The county has still valuable resources in timber and turpentine lands. Marl (blue and white) is abundant, though but little used. Of the county area, 13.02 per cent is tilled land, of which 13.93 per cent is cotton.

Abstract of the Report of J. A. Bryan, of Kenansville.

(J. B. Oliver, of Mount Olive, also furnished a report.)

The uplands of the county, comprising all kinds of soils, after being fertilized, are planted in cotton to a small extent. These uplands are all sandy, but vary in color and quality. Drought in May retards the cotton growth and renders it too late to make a full crop, and excessive rains, with cold weather during the month of May and early in June, affect the plant. Excessive drought in July and August induces rust sometimes where the soil is not manured heavily, but otherwise the cotton-plant will thrive under as unfavorable weather as corn or the other crops usually raised in this county.

The soil principally cultivated in cotton is the *stiff upland or loamy soil.* About one-third of the land in this region is of this kind, and it occurs in all parts of the county in areas of from 5 to 1,000 acres each. Its timber growth is long- and short-leaf pine, black and sweet gums, oak, hickory, and black-jack. The soil is a fine sandy loam, which varies in color from a gray to buff, yellow, brown, black, and chocolate. The average thickness of the surface soil is from 10 to 12 inches, with a subsoil that is heavier and is of a yellow or red clay, that bakes hard when exposed to the sun. These clays have from 50 to 75 per cent of sand in their composition. The soil is easy to till. Corn, pease, sweet potatoes, wheat, and cotton are the chief crops of the region, but the soil is best adapted to corn, cotton, and sweet potatoes. The most productive height of the cotton-plant is 4 feet, but it runs to weed on alluvial or creek bottoms where there is an excess of moisture and organic matter. Fresh lands produce 300 pounds of seed-cotton per acre, and 1,545 pounds will make a bale of lint. After four years cultivation the product falls off, but the staple rates about the same. Crab-grass is the most troublesome weed. Very little land once cultivated now lies turned out.

The naturally drained land, or *sandy upland*, occupies one-third of this region, and extends 20 miles through the central portion of the county, not entirely uninterrupted, and is timbered with pine, black-jack, red oak, chincapin, hickory, and sourwood. The average thickness of the surface soil is 6 inches before its color changes into that of the subsoil, which varies from a red to yellow clay, while in places a brown sand intervenes between the soil and clay. It is easy to till, and is early, warm, and well-drained. The proportion of cotton planted is about one-twentieth of the area under cultivation. Fresh land produces about 200 pounds of seed-cotton per acre, 1,545 pounds of which make a bale of lint, rating as middling when clean.

Gallberry lands occupy one-thirtieth part of the county, but are located mostly in the southeastern part, and are timbered with pine, gum, maple, etc.

Cotton shipments are made by rail to Wilmington at $1.25 per bale of 450 pounds.

Mr. J. B. Oliver, of Mount Olive, divides the soils into *fine sandy uplands*, with red oak, short-leaf pine, hickory, and dogwood, amounting to one-eighth of the land, and having a soil 6 inches deep, one-fourth of its surface being planted in cotton; and *pine uplands*, with a long-leaf pine growth, making one-fourth of the lands in the section, one-fourth of which is in cotton. Another kind of land—*second pocoson*—timbered with water oak, white oak, overcup oak, rosemary pine (P. *taeda*) , and sweet and blue gum, has a clay-loam soil 4 feet deep and a subsoil of whitish, sticky clay. Very little of this soil is planted in cotton, as it is better for corn. The troublesome weeds are hog-weed, yellow-top, and crab-grass. The seasons are short between late and early killing frosts, April 20 and October 20.

NEW HANOVER

Population: 21,376.—White, 8,159; colored, 13,217.

Area: 182 square miles.—Woodland, 39,603 acres.

Tilled lands: 7,396 acres.—Area planted in cotton, 142 acres; in corn 2,008 acres; in oats, 86 acres.

Cotton production: 66 bales; average cotton product per acre, 0.46 bale, 663 pounds seed-cotton, or 221 pounds cotton lint.

New Hanover is one of the smallest counties in the state, and consists of a narrow triangular wedge between the Cape Fear river on the west and the Atlantic coast on the east, with its narrow fringe of sounds, marshes, and dunes. The margins of the streams and sounds are bordered in many places by narrow strips of oak and pine flats with a gray silty soil. The central portion of the county, a swell as the dunes along the shore, are sandy and unproductive; but there are tracts of alluvial and swamp-land river bottoms along the Cape Fear which produce large crops of rice. The county contains the largest city in the state, Wilmington (population nearly 20,000). It is also the most important seaport, and has a large foreign as well as inland trade in lumber, naval stores, and cotton, both by means of its railway and navigable rivers. Of the county area, 6.35 per cent is tilled land, of which 1.92 per cent is cultivated in cotton.

Abstract of the Report of A. R. Black, of Wilmington.

Cypress swamps are not, but sand flats (pocosons) are, very extensive in this county. Very good alluvial lands are to be found on both branches of the Cape Fear river, and sandy loams abound near these rivers and along the coast. The kinds of soils cultivated in cotton are pine, oak, and hickory flats, with clay subsoils which are inclined to be stiff. The proportion of the lands in the region of this kind is very small, not exceeding 3 per cent. The cotton lands are generally found near the streams and interspersed along the coast, and are timbered principally with long-leaf pine, with some short-leaf pine, hickory, dogwood, red oak, chincapin, and sweet gum. The average thickness of the soil is from 4 to 6 inches, with a subsoil of clay, mixed more or less with sand, under cotton lands. The chief crops are peanuts, corn, rice, sweet and Irish potatoes, and garden truck, but the soil is best adapted to peanuts and rice. The proportion of cotton planted is not one acre in one hundred. The height usually attained by the cotton-plant is 3 feet, and it is most productive at that height. It inclines to run to weed when planted in swamp lands, but guano or manure favors bolling. Fresh land produces from 500 to 1,000 pounds of seed-cotton per acre, about 1,540 pounds making a 475-pound bale, the staple rating as middling when clean. After several years cultivation the product ranges from 400 to 800 pounds per acre, the staple rating the same as that from fresh land. Crab-grass is the most troublesome. About 5 per cent of land once cultivated now lies turned out.

Cotton is generally hauled to Wilmington during November by river and rail.

PENDER

Population: 12,468.—White, 5,509; colored, 6,959.

Area: 889 square miles.—Woodland, 287,700 acres.

Tilled lands: 38,156 acres.—Area planted in cotton, 1,463 acres; in corn, 16,550 acres; in wheat, 7 acres; in oats, 183.

Cotton production: 835 bales; average cotton product per acre, 0.57 bale, 813 pounds seed-cotton, or 271 pounds cotton lint.

Pender county, like the preceding, is bounded in part on the south by the Atlantic ocean, with its fringe of sounds, marshes, and dunes, and is drained southward by the waters of the Northeast Cape Fear river. Holly Shelter pocoson occupies a large part of the southeastern section, and from it flow numerous creeks into the above-mentioned river, while others flow directly into the Atlantic. The central portion and larger part of this great pocoson, which contains about 100 square miles, is quite barren, but around its margin, especially toward the river, are considerable tracts of white-oak flats, canebrake, and swamp lands, with their characteristic growths and soils. In the northeastern section lies the half of another similar pocoson nearly as large, called Angola bay, and in the center of the western half of the county is a third but much smaller swamp of the same general character. The western side of the county for the breadth of from 6 to 8 miles belongs to the region of upland piny woods, the principal growth being long-leaf pines, with an under-growth of oaks, hickory, dogwood, etc., and a sandy soil; but some of it approaches the character of the regular "sandhills," with pine and oak flats here and there. Along the streams are generally alluvial belts or swamps and oak flats, which are the corn lands of the county. A savanna of several square miles is found in the upper end of the county, which merges northward into a barren pocoson of still greater extent. Marl abounds in all parts of the county, and Eocene limestone is found along the principal river above named. These add greatly to its agricultural advantages.

The cotton product is inconsiderable; the remaining products are corn, rice, potatoes, lumber, and naval stores.

Of the county area, 6.71 per cent is tilled land, of which 3.83 per cent is cultivated in cotton.

Cotton and other products are shipped to Wilmington and Norfolk by rail, or to the former by the two Cape Fear rivers, which form the boundaries east and west.

ROBESON

Population: 23,880.—White, 11,942; colored, 11,938.

Area: 1,039 square miles.—Woodland, 383,093 acres.

Tilled lands: 103,055 acres.—Area planted in cotton, 21,607 acres; in corn, 49,961 acres; in wheat, 875 acres; in rye, 1,548; in oats, 2,814 acres.

Cotton production: 8,846 bales; average cotton product per acre, 0.41 bale, 582 pounds seed-cotton, or 194 pounds cotton lint.

The soils of Robeson county are mainly those of the ordinary level piny woods, but there are belts of gum and cypress swamp along nearly all of its water-courses, those on the two main streams being quite large. The county is drained by the upper waters of Lumber river, which enters the Atlantic through the state of South Carolina at Georgetown. On the higher divides between the streams the soil is sometimes quite sandy, in some places reaching the character of pine barrens. The lands are chiefly devoted to the culture of cotton and corn, but the value of the potato and rice crops is quite considerable. Turpentine and lumber are also large interests. Marl is found abundantly in the lower half of the county. Of the county area, 15.50 per cent is tilled land, of which 20.96 per cent is cultivated in cotton. Shipments are made by rail to Wilmington.

SAMPSON

Population: 22,894.—White, 13,347; colored, 9,547.

Area: 964 square miles.—Woodland, 374,576 acres.

Tilled lands: 116,892 acres.—Area planted in cotton, 15,346 acres; in tobacco, 28 acres; in corn, 53,951 acres; in wheat, 1,249 acres; in rye, 409 acres; in oats, 654 acres.

Cotton production: 6,291 bales; average cotton product per acre, 0.41 bale, 585 pounds seed-cotton, or 195 pounds ᴄotton lint.

Sampson county lies in the middle of the long-leaf pine belt, and much the larger part of its territory represents the average character of the soils and forests of that belt. It is drained by South river, one of the principal tributaries of the Cape Fear, whose streams divide its territory into north- and south-lying belts or zones—flattish swells, the higher portions of which are characterized by sandy soils and forests predominantly of long-leaf pine. In places near the southern and western margins, and again near the northern end, there are tracts which are quite sandy and approach the character of pine barrens. There are also extensive pine flats, especially on the waters of Six Runs, with here and there considerable bodies of pine and oak flats.

The corn crop of the county is much more important than that of cotton, reaching nearly 500,000 bushels, and the crops of potatoes and rice are both unusually large. There are also large bodies of virgin pine timber, still valuable both for turpentine and for lumber. Marl is abundant, and is used with the best results in some sections, chiefly the northern. Of the county area, 18.95 per cent is tilled land, of which 13.13 per cent is cultivated in cotton.

Abstract of the Report of A. A. M'Kay, of Clinton.

Cotton depends very much upon a warm spring, so that it can start up sufficiently to get out of the way of the grass. Since commercial fertilizers have come into use, the cotton has been so pushed that the frost in the fall scarcely ever catches it, or at least few green bolls are affected. The kinds of soils cultivated in cotton are generally a soil that is stiff, caused by the clay being near the surface, and the rich and sandy loams.

The chief soil is a *clayey and sandy loam,* which occupies about two-thirds of the lands in this region, and is timbered principally with long-leaf pine; many oak ridges have a growth of maple, popular, black and sweet gum, elm, hickory, cypress, juniper, ash, beech, holly, dogwood, and cedar. The chief crops are cotton, corn, pease, sweet potatoes, wheat, rye, oats, tobacco, etc., but the soil is best adapted to corn and cotton, and about one-fourth of every farm is planted in cotton. The plant usually attains a height of from $3\frac{1}{2}$ to 4 feet, and is most productive at that height. It does not incline to run to weed, except on alluvial lands or lands very highly manured; topping favors bolling.

Fresh land produces about 750 pounds of seed-cotton per acre, about 1,425 pounds making a 475-pound bale of lint, which, when clean, rates in the market as low middling. After ten years cultivation the yield per acre is 300 pounds. Cocklebur is the most troublesome weed. About two-fifths of land once cultivated now lies turned out, and when again taken in produces better than if cultivated every year. The valleys are improved by the washings of the slopes. Efforts have been made to check the damage done to the slopes, by plowing in curved lines and by hillside ditching, with profit to the lands and to the crops.

Cotton shipments are made in November by rail to Wilmington. The rates of freight are 50 cents per bale to Wilmington and $2.50 to New York. Most of the cotton in the county is sold to merchants in Clinton, the county-seat.

United States, Census Office, *Tenth Census of the United States: 1880*, in 15 volumes. *Cotton Production in the Eastern Gulf, Atlantic, and Pacific States* (Washington: Government Printing Office, 1884), VI, 37-49.

Appendix B

AGRICULTURAL PRODUCTION, 1870

Counties of the Cape Fear Region	Acres of Land			Cash Value in 1870				Orchard Products	Produce of market gardens	Forest Products	Value of Home Manuf's	Value of Animals Slaught'd or sold for Slaughter
	Improved	Unimproved		Farms	Farm implements & Machinery	Wages P'd in yr, includ'g board	Est'd Value of all farm Products, Improvements & Additions to Stock					
		Woodland	Other Unimproved									
	Number in Thousands						Dollars in Thousands					
Bladen	28	268	15	222	21	39	371	—	—	118	5	75
Brunswick	21	260	2	376	24	40	291	—	3	63	7	32
Columbus	26	24	243	161	21	47	691	—	—	110	54	66
Duplin	84	311	12	650	34	87	810	1	1	44	7	181
New Hanover	46	274	30	651	37	179	634	—	12	114	8	103
Pender	Created in 1875 out of New Hanover.											
Robeson	78	314	51	552	48	124	809	9	—	102	29	126
Sampson	84	323	14	513	53	101	914	4	—	128	30	202

United States, Census Office, *Ninth Census of the United States: 1870. Wealth and Industry* (Washington: Government Printing Office, 1872), III, 214-21.

Appendix C

AGRICULTURAL PRODUCTION, 1870

	Tobacco	Cotton	Wool	Peas & Beans	Irish Potatoes	Sweet Potatoes	Wine	Butter	Cheese	Milk Sold	Hay	Clover	Sorghum	Beeswax	Honey
	lbs.	bales	lbs.	bu.	bu.	bu.	gals.	lbs.	lbs.	gals.	ton	bu.	gals.	lbs.	lbs.
Bladen	789	146	6,151	6,700	882	68,123	2,342	2,814	25	—	59	10	42	2,795	27,381
Brunswick	528	119	3,775	6,482	1,890	129,168	446	9,815	—	42	—	—	—	974	11,035
Columbus	2,430	119	7,993	4,149	1,791	79,307	12,910	4,719	115	40	3	—	73	2,124	24,006
Duplin	275	1,785	9,522	12,304	4,319	135,581	2,451	4,687	150	—	972	—	368	2,222	38,309
New Hanover	—	70	11,629	88,892	11,192	94,713	4,622	7,480	—	3,065	261	—	—	3,014	29,950
Robeson	653	2,109	14,081	21,261	5,495	84,784	1,358	21,934	200	—	—	—	10	2,303	25,199
Sampson	7,523	1,231	11,437	21,950	1,662	141,373	73	35,554	—	—	2	615	—	1,624	22,664

United States, Census Office, Ninth Census of the United States: 1870. *Wealth and Industry* (Washington: Government Printing Office, 1872), III, 214-21.

AGRICULTURAL PRODUCTION, 1870

Counties of the Cape Fear Region	Livestock								Wheat		Grain Crops					Rice
	All Livestock	Horses	Mules & Asses	Milch Cows	Working Oxen	Other Cattle	Sheep	Swine	Spring	Winter	Rye	Indian Corn	Oats	Barley	Buckwheat	
	Dollars	Numbers							Bushels		Bushels					Pounds
BLADEN Area 1,013* Pop. 13,000	191,000	478	360	2380	621	4079	4398	11,526	26	57	846	86,986	3214	—	—	38,187
BRUNSWICK Area 812 Pop. 8,000	161,000	372	168	2777	892	3403	3555	10,485	—	12	65	56,211	10	—	—	748,418
COLUMBUS Area 685 Pop. 8,000	121,500	368	219	1960	854	2696	5383	12,759	79	18	1013	65,972	209	—	—	216,964
DUPLIN Area 830 Pop. 16,000	302,500	1176	466	3100	994	4626	5698	20,767	1974	402	2607	291,633	1470	10	—	155,599
NEW HANOVER Area 1,082 Pop. 28,000	230,500	633	410	2456	605	4083	3736	14,712	—	—	20	133,176	540	—	—	398,925
ROBESON Area 1,043 Pop. 16,000	314,500	1152	741	2915	928	5511	8396	18,751	1304	968	5838	138,545	9603	8	—	69,486
SAMPSON Area 921 Pop. 16,000	394,000	1441	605	3378	1149	5267	6732	22,524	1617	1022	2369	281,381	8775	96	—	19,837

*Areas in square miles
United States, Census Office, Ninth Census of the United States: 1870. Wealth and Industry (Washington: Government Printing Office, 1872), III, 215, 219.

Appendix E

NORTH CAROLINA FORESTS

The forests of North Carolina were once hardly surpassed in variety and importance by those of any other part of the United States. The coast region was occupied by the coniferous forests of the southern Maritime Pine Belt; the middle districts of the state by a forest of oaks and other hard-wood trees, through which the old-field pine is now rapidly spreading over worn-out and abandoned farming lands. The high ridges and deep valleys of the Appalachian system which culminate in the western part of the state are still everywhere covered with dense forest of the most valuable hard-wood trees mingled with northern pines and hemlocks. The inaccessibility of this mountain region has protected these valuable forests up to the present time, and few inroads have yet been made into their stores of oak, cherry, yellow poplar, and walnut. The hard-wood forests of the middle districts, however, have been largely removed or culled of their finest timber, although the area of woodland in this part of the state is now increasing. These new forests, usually composed of inferior pine, are of little economic value, except as a source of abundant fuel and as a means of restoring fertility to the soil, preparing it to produce again more valuable crops. A larger proportion of the pine forest of the coast has been destroyed in North Carolina than in the other southern states. This part of the state has long been the seat of important lumbering operations, while the manufacture of naval stores, once almost exclusively confined to North Carolina, and always an important industry here, has seriously injured these forests. The original forests have been practically removed from the northeastern part of the state, the great region watered by the numerous streams flowing into Albemarle and Pamlico sounds; and although some lumber, largely second-growth pine trees of poor quality, is produced here, the importance of these forests is not great. The merchantable pine, too, has been removed from the banks of the Cape Fear and other rivers flowing through the southern part of the state, and although these streams still yield annually a large number of logs, they are only produced at a constantly increasing distance from their banks and with a consequent increasing cost for transport.

Forest fires inflict serious damage upon the pine forests of the south. During the census year 546,102 acres of woodland were reported destroyed by forest fires, with a loss of $357,980. The largest number of these fires were traced to the carelessness of farmers in clearing land, to locomotives, hunters, and to malice.

Manufacturers of cooperage and wheel stock, industries which once flourished in the eastern and central portions of the state, already suffer from the exhaustion and deterioration of material. Such industries, however, are increasing in the extreme western counties, and promise to attain there an important development.

The following estimate, by counties, of the merchantable pine standing May 31, 1880, south of the Neuse river, the only part of the state where it is of commercial importance, was prepared by Mr. Edward Kidder, of Wilmington. It is based upon actual surveys and the reports of a large number of timberland experts familiar with the different counties still occupied by the forests of long-leaved pine:

LONG-LEAVED PINE (Pinus palustris)

Counties	*Feet, board measure*
Bladen	288,000,000
Brunswick	141,000,000
Chatham	448,000,000
Columbus	288,000,000
Cumberland	806,000,000
Duplin	21,000,000
Harnett	486,000,000
Johnston	563,000,000
Moore	504,000,000
New Hanover	96,000,000
Onslow	34,000,000
Robeson	864,000,000
Sampson	602,000,000
Wake	48,000,000
Wayne	40,000,000
Total	5,229,000,000
Cut for the census year ending May 31, 1880, exclusive of 50,190,000 feet cut in the counties adja-	108,411,000

cent to Albemarle and Pamlico sounds and along the
Pamlico and Neuse rivers,
which is largely loblolly
pine (Pinus Taeda).

NAVAL STORES

Small quantities of crude turpentine were produced upon the coast
of North Carolina, between the Pamlico and Cape Fear rivers, soon
after the earliest settlement of the country. It was sent to Great
Britain or converted into spirits of turpentine and rosin for home
consumption. The demand for ships' stores had greatly increased the
North Carolina production as early as 1818, although the field of
operations was not extended south of the Cape Fear river, nor more
than 100 miles from the coast, until 1836. The large demand for
spirits of turpentine created during that year induced manufacturers
to test the yield of trees on the west side of the Cape Fear river, up
to that time considered unproductive. The result was satisfactory,
although overproduction and low prices deferred until 1840 the development of this region. Since 1840 this industry has been gradually
carried southward. Naval stores were produced in South Carolina in
1840, and in Georgia two years later. Turpentine orchards were
established in Florida and Alabama in 1855, and more recently in
Mississippi and eastern Louisiana.

The naval stores manufactured in the United States are principally produced from the resinous exudations of the long-leaved pine
(*pinus palustris*), and in small quantities from the loblolly pine
(*Pinus Taeda*), and the slash pine (*Pinus Cubensis*) of the Florida
coast. The trees selected for "boxing" are usually from 12 to 18
inches in diameter, although trees with trunks only 8 inches through
are now sometimes worked. A deep cut or "box" is made in the trunk
of the tree, by a cut slanting downward, some 7 inches in depth, and
generally 12 inches above the ground, and met by a second cut started
10 inches above the first and running down from the bark to meet it.
In this manner a segment is removed from the trunk and a triangular
trough formed 4 inches deep and 4 inches wide at the top.

Two such boxes, or upon a large trunk sometimes four, are made
on each tree. A "crop," the unit of production among large operators,
consists of 10,000 such boxes. The boxes are cut early in November
with a narrow-bladed ax specially manufactured for the purpose, and

the trees are worked on an average during thirty-two weeks. As soon as the upper surface of the box ceases to exude freely, it is "hacked" over and a fresh surface exposed, the dried resin adhering to the cut having been first carefully removed with a sharp, narrow, steel scraper. The boxes, especially after the first season, are often hacked as often as once a week, and are thus gradually extended upward until upon trees which have been worked during a number of seasons the upper surface of the box is often 10 to 12 feet above the ground. For these long boxes the scraper is attached to a wooden handle, generally loaded with iron at the lower end to facilitate the operation of drawing down the resin. Once in four weeks, or often less frequently, the resin caught in the bottom of the box is removed into a bucket with a small, sharp, oval steel spade attached to a short wooden handle. The product of these "dippings," as this operation is called, is placed in barrels and transported to the distillery. The first season a turpentine orchard is worked boxes are usually dipped eight times, yielding an average of 300 barrels of turpentine to the crop. The second year the number of dippings is reduced to five, the product falling off to 150 barrels, while for the third season 100 barrels are considered a fair yield from three dippings. To this must be added the yield of the "scrapes," which for the first year is estimated, for one crop, at from 60 to 70 barrels of 280 pounds each, and for succeeding years at 100 barrels.

Trees can be profitably worked in North Carolina by experienced operators during four of five years, or, upon a small scale, in connection with farming operations and by actual residents, several years longer; farther south the trees seem to possess less recuperative power, and in South Carolina four years is given as the outside limit during which an orchard can be profitably worked, while in Georgia, Florida, and Alabama they are often abandoned as distillers, coopers, and laborers can work ten crops. The average wages of such a force is $1 a day per man, so that the cost of labor necessary to work a crop during the season of thirty-two weeks is $480.

The following grades of turpentine are recognized in the trade: "Virgin dip," or "Soft white gum turpentine"—the product the first year the trees are worked; "Yellow dip"—the product of the second and succeeding years, and becoming darker colored and less liquid every year; "Scrape" or "Hard turpentine,"—the product of the scrapings of the boxes.

Rosin is graded as follows: "W"—Window-glass; "N"—Extra pale;

"M"—Pale; "K"—Low pale; "I"—Good No. 1; "H"—No. 1; "G"—Low No. 1; "F"—Good No. 2; "E"—No. 2; "D"—Good strain; "C"—Strain; "B"—Common strain; "A"—Black.

Window-glass is the lightest grade, and is only produced from the first dippings of "virgin" trees—that is, trees worked for the first time. The resinous exudation becomes darker colored and less volatile every year, as the box grows older, and the rosin produced is darker and less valuable. Trees worked during several years produce a very dark brown or black rosin. Spirits of turpentine made from virgin trees is light colored, light, in weight, and free from any taste; the resinous matter yielded in succeeding years gains more and more body, and the additional heat required in distilling it throws off some resin combined with the spirits, producing in it a strong, biting taste and greater weight.

Tar, produced by burning the dead wood and most resinous parts of the long-leaved pine in covered kilns, is graded as follows: "Rope yellow," or Ropemakers' tar—the highest grade, produced with a minimum of heat from the most resinous parts of the wood; "Roany," or "Ship smearing"—the next running of the kiln; "Black" or "Thin"—the lowest grade, made from inferior wood, or the last running of the kiln, and therefore produced with the maximum of heat.

The following statistics of the production of naval stores during the census year were prepared by Mr. A. H. Van Bokkelen, of Wilmington, North Carolina, to whom I am indebted for such information in regard to the methods used in carrying on this industry:

States	Turpentine Gallons	Rosin Barrels
Alabama	2,005,000	158,482
Florida	1,036,350	68,281
Georgia	3,151,500	277,500
Louisiana	250,000	20,000
Mississippi	250,000	20,000
North Carolina	6,279,200	663,967
South Carolina	4,593,200	333,940
	17,565,250	1,542,170

Eighty thousand barrels of tar were manufactured during the census year in North Carolina, and 10,000 barrels in the other southern states.

The total value of this crop of naval stores at centers of distribution, and of course including freight from the forest and different brokerage charges, was not far from $8,000,000. The net profits of the industry, even in the case of virgin trees, is very small, and at present prices is believed to be unprofitable except to the most skillful operators. The low price of southern timber-lands and the facility with which rights to operate tracts of forest for turpentine have been lately obtainable in several states have unnaturally stimulated production. The result of this has been that manufacturers, unable to make a profit except from virgin trees, abandon their orchards after one or two years working and seek new fields of operation; the ratio of virgin forest to the total area worked over in the production of naval stores is therefore constantly increasing. It is estimated by Mr. Van Bokkelen that during the years between 1870 and 1880 an average of one-third of the total annual product of the country was obtained from virgin trees, and that in 1880 one-fourth of the crop was thus produced, necessitating the boxing in that year of the best trees upon 600,000 acres of forest. The production of naval stores is carried on in a wasteful, extravagant manner, and the net profits derived from the business are entirely out of proportion to the damage which it inflicts upon the forests of the country; the injury is enormous. Lumber made from trees previously worked for turpentine is of inferior quality, although it is probably less injured than has been generally supposed. Comparatively few trees, however, once boxed are manufactured into lumber. It is estimated that 20 per cent of them weakened by the deep gashes inflicted upon their trunks, sooner or later are blown down and ruined; fires, too, every year destroy vast areas of the turpentine orchards, in spite of the care taken by operators to prevent their spread. It is customary in the winter, in order to prevent the fires which annually run through the forests of the Southern Pine Belt from spreading to the boxes, to "racket" the trees; that is, to remove all combustible material for a distance of 3 feet around the base of each boxed tree. Fire, carefully watched, has then been set to the dry grass between the trees, in order to prevent the spread of accidental conflagrations, and to give the box-choppers a firmer foothold than would be offered by the dry and slippery pine leaves. In spite of these precautions, however, turpentine orchards, especially when abandoned, are often destroyed by fire. The surface of the box, thickly covered with a most inflammable material, is easily ignited, and a fire once started in this way may rage over the thousands of acres before its fury can be checked.

The manufacture of naval stores, then, decreases the value of the boxed tree for lumber, reduces the ability of the tree to withstand the force of gales, and enormously increases the danger to the forest of total destruction by fire.

Wilmington, the most important distributing point for this industry in the United States, handles 80 per cent of all the naval stores manufactured in North Carolina. Previous to 1870 Swansboro, Washington, and New Berne were also large shipping points.

United States, Census Office, *Tenth Census of the United States: 1880*, in 15 volumes. *Forests* (Washington, 1884), IX, 515-18.

Appendix F

MANUFACTURES, 1870

Counties & Industries	Establishments	Hands Employed	Capital	Wages	Materials	Products
Bladen						
Cooperage	3	7	$3,100	$500	$12,400	$13,707
Lumber, sawed	2	55	105,000	13,000	12,600	29,280
Tar & turpentine	21	112	41,200	18,250	164,718	268,117
Brunswick						
Cars, freight	1	18	10,000	6,000	1,900	27,000
Tar & turpentine	5	15	23,700	4,715	82,576	111,595
Columbus						
Lumber, sawed	3	27	10,500	2,600	4,400	10,000
Duplin						
Flouring-mill products	5	10	4,200	900	23,000	26,900
Lumber, sawed	2	16	3,500	2,525	775	11,000
Tar & turpentine	7	17	5,300	3,325	93,869	130,596
New Hanover						
Bread & other bakery products	5	15	4,600	4,405	20,190	30,250
Brick	1	11	1,000	800	2,000	10,800
Carriages & wagons	3	14	2,100	4,121	3,918	10,320
Cars freight & passenger	2	100	27,000	54,000	19,500	73,500
Clothing, men's	3	28	6,000	9,170	6,955	20,000
Coffins	2	6	2,200	1,400	967	10,800
Cooperage	5	27	5,600	7,676	8,999	19,592
Fertilizers	1	54	250,000	8,700	100,000	120,000
Flouring-mill products	3	25	67,000	11,806	463,630	507,940
Gas	1	10	100,000	8,000	4,000	35,150
Iron, castings	2	8	15,000	5,400	11,960	17,360
Lumber, planed	5	46	45,000	22,970	69,500	96,500
Lumber, sawed	7	150	138,000	71,082	293,483	425,250
Machinery (not specified)	1	33	30,000	23,430	25,000	60,000
_____, railroad repairing	2	37	50,000	25,600	28,300	53,900
Printing & publishing	3	49	20,500	33,000	9,050	47,810
Shipbuilding & repairing	1	17	15,000	10,000	700	15,000
Tar and turpentine	8	69	110,000	28,510	311,376	388,291
Tin, Copper & sheet-iron ware	2	15	15,500	7,200	7,950	16,150
Upholstery	4	19	7,500	3,575	6,935	13,303
Pender (no data)						
Robeson						
Lumber, sawed	1	10	7,000	2,500	5,100	14,000
Tar & turpentine	15	141	$33,900	$23,530	$110,550	$198,443
Sampson (no data)						

United States, Census Office, *Ninth Census of the United States: 1870. Wealth and Industry* Washington: Government Printing Office, 1872), III, 709-10.

Appendix G

MANUFACTURES, 1880

Counties & Industries	Number of Establishments	Capital	Average No. Employed	Total Wages, Per Year	Value of Materials	Value of Products
Bladen						
Lumber, sawed	4	$36,700	48	$10,925	$35,325	$61,290
Tar & turpentine	15	25,800	49	8,385	42,135	86,300
Brunswick (no data)						
Columbus						
Lumber, sawed	3	12,500	45	9,000	34,800	56,000
Tar and turpentine	21	26,265	147	18,300	63,017	158,745
Duplin						
Flour- and grist-mill products	27	28,900	34	3,978	55,488	62,068
Tar & turpentine	13	31,250	46	5,290	33,500	69,250
New Hanover						
Cotton goods	1	60,000	107	18,900	34,507	81,388
Fertilizers	1	350,000	125	40,000	150,000	300,000
Flour- and grist-mill products	4	125,000	37	13,229	219,292	253,652
Foundry and machine-shop products	1	65,000	50	25,000	40,000	70,000
Lumber, sawed	5	193,000	181	64,989	235,980	385,300
Tar & turpentine	8	99,000	123	32,279	265,916	416,641
Printing & publishing	5	19,000	31	13,156	12,828	35,427
Tobacco Manufactures	1	25,000	78	15,000	47,000	72,600
Pender (no data)						
Robeson						
Flour- and grist-mill products	33	44,645	43	3,192	63,571	72,900
Lumber, sawed	18	45,000	86	13,169	56,379	91,590
Tar & turpentine	36	65,000	646	57,692	131,480	305,397
Sampson						
Flour- and grist-mill products	16	29,800	25	1,625	49,772	57,760
Tar & turpentine	17	31,550	58	10,853	112,170	149,245

United States, Census Office, *Tenth Census of the United States: 1880*, in 15 Volumes.   *Manufactures* (Washington: Government Printing Office, 1884), III, 317-19.

Appendix H

ANTE-BELLUM VOTES FOR PRESIDENTS

	1836		1840		1844		1848		1852		1856		1860		
	Hugh White	Van Buren	Wm. Harrison	Van Buren	Clay	Polk	Zach. Taylor	Cass	W. Scott	Pierce	Buchanan	Fillmore	Breckinridge	Bell	Douglas
Bladen	—	69	346	414	280	486	280	341	371	582	—	—	601	463	3
Brunswick	123	88	350	230	351	283	319	237	51	—	364	384	—	60	—
Columbus	—	110	204	315	135	363	169	274	175	—	530	207	413	—	—
Duplin	197	662	253	807	223	936	318	939	187	930	1,173	117	1,380	149	3
New Hanover	150	738	293	1,042	383	1,123	464	1,255	383	1,400	1,472	577	1,617	644	5
Pender	—	—	—	—	—	—	—	—	—	—	—	—	—	—	—
Robeson	293	472	579	506	558	580	633	545	—	62	673	566	720	646	135
Sampson	297	559	553	741	533	860	612	741	603	867	927	359	977	529	6

J. Bryan Grimes et al. (ed.), *North Carolina Manual, 1913* (Raleigh: Edwards and Broughton, 1913), pp. 983-86.

Appendix I

VOTES CAST FOR PRESIDENT, 1868-1900

Counties	1868		1872		1876		1880		1884		1888		1892			1896		1900	
	Seymour	Grant	Greely	Grant	Tilden	Hayes	Hancock	Garfield	Cleveland	Blaine	Cleveland	Harrison	Cleveland	Weaver	Harrison	McKinley	Bryan	Bryan	McKinley
Bladen	1,079	1,372	758	1,409	1,397	1,390	1,278	1,537	1,410	1,532	1,820	1,375	1,228	321	1,205	1,865	1,256	1,102	1,112
Brunswick	698	878	490	857	1,002	1,044	746	889	928	936	1,023	965	755	685	446	1,279	878	525	643
Columbus	951	512	730	777	1,431	770	1,597	922	1,867	948	1,078	893	1,532	635	813	1,908	1,161	1,623	1,207
Duplin	1,580	1,025	1,211	1,039	2,195	1,253	2,015	1,228	2,247	1,181	2,209	1,135	—	—	—	2,409	1,147	1,879	1,081
Pender	—	—	—	—	1,172	1,252	1,007	1,234	1,207	1,246	725	758	872	137	960	1,276	1,164	1,137	593
New Hanover	2,344	3,915	1,870	3,443	1,634	2,994	1,438	2,200	1,745	2,894	1,670	2,856	2,408	38	1,500	2,100	3,183	2,247	60
Robeson	1,337	1,318	1,051	1,503	2,117	1,739	2,235	1,960	2,508	2,278	2,879	1,970	2,312	842	1,117	3,457	2,429	3,280	1,174
Sampson	1,447	1,026	889	1,470	2,100	1,667	2,122	1,626	2,551	1,591	2,390	1,608	1,299	1,619	1,235	2,789	1,271	1,257	2,002

J. Bryan Grimes et al. (ed.), *North Carolina Manual, 1913* (Raleigh: Edwards and Broughton, 1913), pp. 987-90.

VOTES CAST FOR GOVERNOR, 1884-1900

Counties	1884		1888			1892			1896			1900	
	Scales	York	Fowle	Dockery	Wm. Walker	Carr (Dem)	Furches (Rep)	Exum (Pop)	Russell	Watson	Guthrie (Pop)	Aycock	Adams (Rep)
Bladen	1,426	1,511	1,541	1,365	—	1,292	904	546	1,263	1,361	288	1,589	1,375
Brunswick	921	926	1,010	965	4	767	140	745	890	820	410	915	948
Columbus	1,867	923	2,072	910	1	1,618	755	648	1,014	1,420	731	2,178	1,201
Duplin	2,239	1,174	2,205	1,154	6	1,502	970	817	1,145	1,551	868	2,125	1,297
New Hanover	1,751	2,878	1,880	2,856	4	2,447	1,326	187	3,145	2,218	75	2,963	3
Pender	1,215	1,240	721	757	—	901	957	132	1,159	1,089	186	1,260	276
Robeson	2,361	1,992	2,823	1,899	44	2,270	1,121	1,129	2,282	2,176	1,294	4,100	557
Sampson	2,525	1,536	2,370	1,616	12	1,370	1,266	1,585	1,258	1,270	1,561	1,356	1,954

J. Bryan Grimes et al. (ed.), *North Carolina Manual, 1913* (Raleigh: Edwards and Broughton, 1913), I, pp. 987-90.

Appendix J

VOTES CAST FOR GOVERNOR, 1860-1880

Counties	1860		1862		1864		1865		1866		1868		1872		1876		1880	
	Ellis	Jno. Pool (Whig)	Vance	Johnston (Dem)	Vance	Holden	Worth	Holden	Worth	Dockery	Holden	Ashe	Caldwell	Merrimon	Vance	Settle	Jarvis	K. P. Buxton
Bladen	660	553	332	344	724	77	416	90	427	—	1263	957	1448	1208	1395	1390	1278	1530
Brunswick	410	420	316	204	592	19	—	—	335	—	783	781	708	711	1006	1041	902	896
Columbus	718	430	297	496	463	116	208	285	259	—	434	823	639	1024	1438	767	1577	922
Duplin	1358	197	100	961	985	65	462	161	433	4	961	1488	1032	1750	2194	1244	1963	1214
New Hanover	1549	713	287	1237	1641	53	764	114	498	2	3568	2231	3614	2261	1622	2988	1359	2349
Pender	—	—	—	—	—	—	—	—	—	—	—	—	—	—	1166	1252	998	1246
Robeson	844	681	931	320	1108	131	620	243	309	69	1615	1252	1583	1631	2096	1757	2253	1934
Sampson	1042	590	463	704	873	172	449	208	465	38	1018	1168	1434	1697	2071	1669	2108	1638

J. Bryan Grimes et al. (ed.), *North Carolina Manual, 1913* (Raleigh: Edwards and Broughton, 1913), pp. 987-90.

Appendix K

POPULATION INCREASE, IN THE CAPE FEAR REGION, 1790-1910
(in thousands)

	1790	1800	1810	1820	1830	1840	1850	1860	1870	1880	1890	1900	1910	Areas (in sq. miles)
Bladen	5	7	5	7	8	8	10	12	13	16	17	18	18	1,013
Brunswick	3	4	5	5	7	5	7	8	8	9	10	12	14	812
Columbus	—	—	3	4	4	4	6	9	8	14	17	21	28	685
Duplin	6	7	8	10	11	11	14	16	16	19	19	22	25	830
New Hanover	7	7	11	11	11	13	18	22	28	21	24	26	32	199
Pender	—	—	—	—	—	—	—	—	—	12	13	13	15	883
Robeson	5	7	8	8	9	10	13	15	16	23	31	40	51	1,043
Sampson	6	7	7	9	12	12	14	17	16	23	25	26	30	921

R. D. W. Connor (ed.), *Manual of North Carolina* (Raleigh: Edwards and Broughton, 1915), pp. 224-27.

Appendix L

CHURCHES IN THE CAPE FEAR REGION, 1870

Counties	All Denominations				Baptist		Christian		Episcopal		Friends		Lutheran		Methodist		Presbyterian		Reformed	
	Organizations	Edifices	Seating Capacity	Property	Organizations	Seating Capacity	Organizations	Seating Capacity	Organizations	Seating Capacity	Organizations	Seating Capacity	Organizations	Seating Capacity	Organizations	Seating Capacity	Organizations	Seating Capacity	Organizations	Seating Capacity
Bladen	28	28	5,300	25,500	14	2,500	—	—	—	—	—	—	—	—	9	1,700	5	1,100	—	—
Brunswick	22	20	5,125	5,300	11	2,500	—	—	1	125	—	—	—	—	10	2,500	—	—	—	—
Columbus	37	30	5,800	9,600	26	4,000	—	—	—	—	—	—	—	—	10	1,300	1	500	—	—
Duplin	31	31	5,650	14,360	14	3,550	—	—	—	—	—	—	1	300	14	1,200	3	900	—	—
New Hanover	27	27	10,875	399,100	6	2,350	—	—	3	1,700	—	—	—	—	10	4,225	5	1,500	—	—
Robeson	39	37	19,600	33,800	14	5,000	—	—	—	—	—	—	—	—	15	6,600	10	8,000	—	—
Sampson	42	41	11,700	27,450	24	6,800	3	600	1	300	—	—	—	—	10	3,000	3	500	—	—

United States, Census Office, *Ninth Census of the United States: 1870*, in 3 volumes, *Population* (Washington: Government Printing Office, 1872), I, 549-50.

Appendix M

CHURCHES IN THE CAPE FEAR REGION, 1890

Counties	Organizations	Church Edifices	Approx. Seating Capacity	Hall, etc.	Seating Capacity	Value of Church Property	Communicants or Members
Bladen	100	100	37,900	—	—	$68,099	11,410
Brunswick	74	68	18,990	2	300	41,000	5,714
Columbus	108	107	36,430	2	—	75,535	12,107
Duplin	94	88	29,550	7	675	85,640	11,680
New Hanover	57	59	22,740	3	650	405,675	12,424
Pender	73	70	21,125	3	160	55,890	8,750
Robeson	144	140	49,855	—	—	136,792	17,024
Sampson	121	114	37,340	4	200	97,175	14,762

United States, Census Office, *Eleventh Census of the United States: 1890. Churches* (Washington: Government Printing Office, 1894), IX, 74-75.

✑ Bibliography

I. Primary Sources

A. MANUSCRIPTS

American Missionary Association Archives, Fisk University.

Catherine (McGeachy) Buie Papers. Department of Manuscripts, Duke University.

De Rosset Papers (Group II). Southern Historical Collection, The University of North Carolina.

Fuller-Thomas Papers. Department of Manuscripts, Duke University.

Governor's Papers. North Carolina State Department of Archives.
    Benjamin Smith, 1811.
    William Woods Holden (Provisional Term), 1865.
    Jonathan Worth, 1865-68.
    William Woods Holden (Elected Term), 1868-70.
    Tod R. Caldwell, 1871-74.
    Curtis H. Brogden, 1874-76.

Joseph Roswell Hawley Papers. Manuscripts Division, Library of Congress.

William Woods Holden Papers. Department of Manuscripts, Duke University.

Andrew Johnson Papers. Manuscripts Division, Library of Congress.

Hugh MacRae Papers. Department of Manuscripts, Duke University.

Murdock-Wright Papers. Southern Historical Collection, The University of North Carolina.

[Marcus Cicero Stephen Noble?]. "Tileston Normal School," undated, unsigned, 36-page historical sketch in typescript, contained in the M.E.S. Noble Papers. Southern Historical Collection, The University of North Carolina.

Henry Nutt Scrapbook. Contains reports of navigation committees, newspaper clippings, and letters, all related to the problems of the Cape Fear Harbor. Southern Historical Collection, The University of North Carolina.

————. [Report to General Joseph G. Totten, Chief Army Engineer], March 30, 1853. Report signed by Henry Nutt is contained within the Nutt Scrapbook but paginated separately. Southern Historical Collection, The University of North Carolina.

Matt Whitaker Ransom Papers. Southern Historical Collection, The University of North Carolina.

Daniel Lindsay Russell Papers. Southern Historical Collection, The University of North Carolina.

David Schenck Diary. Southern Historical Collection, The University of North Carolina.

Thomas Settle Papers. Southern Historical Collection, The University of North Carolina.

John Swinton Papers. Southern Historical Collection, The University of North Carolina.

B. PUBLIC DOCUMENTS

Confederate States of America. *Statutes at Large.*
North Carolina.
  Cases
    Lane *v.* Stanly, 65 N.C. 153 (1871).
    Van Bokkelen *v.* Canaday, 73 N.C. 198 (1875).
  Law
    Ordinances of the Convention, 1865-66.
    Public Laws, 1865.
    Public Laws, 1866.
    Constitution of North Carolina, 1868.
    Laws, 1868. Special sess.

Private Laws, 1874-75.

Ordinances, Passed by the N.C. [sic] Constitutional Convention of 1875.

Laws and Resolutions, 1876-77.

Reports

Railroad Investigations

Report of the Railroad Investigation Commission [Bragg Report]. Raleigh: James H. Moore, 1871.

Report of the Commission to Investigate Fraud and Corruption Under Act of Assembly Session 1871-1872 [Shipp Report]. Raleigh: James H. Moore, 1872.

Schools

Report of the Superintendent of Common Schools, 1860. [Raleigh]: John Spelman, n.d.

Report of the Superintendent of Public Instruction, 1868. n.p.: n.p., n.d.

Annual Report Superintendent of Public Instruction, 1870. [Raleigh]: Jo. W. Holden [sic], n.d.

Senate

Trial of William W. Holden, Governor of North Carolina . . . , 3 vols. Raleigh: "Sentinel Printing Office," 1871.

United States

Bureau of the Census. *A Statistical Abstract Supplement: Historical Statistics of the United States, Colonial Times to 1957.* Washington: Government Printing Office, 1960.

Bureau of Refugees. Freedmen and Abandoned Lands Published Reports.

Report of the Commissioner, 1865.

Report of the Commissioner, 1866.

Report of the Commissioner, 1868.

Bureau of Statistics (Treasury Department). *Annual report . . . in regard to imported merchandise . . . ,* 1875, 1880, 1885, 1890, 1895, 1900, 1905, 1910.

Census Office. *Eighth Census of the United States: 1860. Statistics.* Washington: Government Printing Office, 1866.

———. *Ninth Census of the United States: 1870. Population,* I. Washington: Government Printing Office, 1872.

———. *Ninth Census of the United States: Wealth and Industry,* III. Washington, 1872.

——. *Tenth Census of the United States: 1880. Manufactures*, II. Washington: Government Printing Office, 1884.

——. *Tenth Census of the United States: 1880. Cotton Production in the Eastern Gulf, Atlantic and Pacific States . . .* , V. Washington: Government Printing Office, 1884.

——. *Tenth Census of the United States: 1880. Forests.* Washington: Government Printing Office, 1884.

——. *Twelfth Census of the United States: 1900. Population,* II. Washington: Government Printing Office, 1901.

Congress, Joint Committee on Printing. *Biographical Directory of the American Congress, 1774-1949.* Washington: Government Printing Office, 1950.

——. Joint Committee on Reconstruction, *Report of the Joint Committee: Part II, Virginia, North Carolina, South Carolina,* Reports of the Committees, Vol. II, 39th Cong., 1st Sess., 1866.

Department of Agriculture. *The Naval Stores Industry: Bulletin No. 229, July 28, 1915.* Washington: Government Printing Office, 1915.

——. *Soils: The Yearbook of Agriculture, 1957.* Washington: Government Printing Office, [1957].

Navy Department. *Official Records of the Union and Confederate Navies in the War of the Rebellion,* Ser. I, Vol. III. Washington: Government Printing Office, 1896.

War Department. *The War of the Rebellion: A Compilation of the Official Records of the Union and Confederate Armies,* Ser. I, Vols. XI, XLVII (Parts I, II, and III). Washington: Government Printing Office, 1895.

Unpublished Records

"North Carolina, CXLVII: Lumberton Sub-District, Letters Sent." National Archives (R.G. 105 N.C. 147).

——. General Orders . . . Monthly and Annual Reports . . . , [Annual Report, Superintendent Southern District North Carolina, 1866] by Allen Rutherford, Wilmington, October 29, 1866. National Archives (R.G. 105 N.C. Box 423).

C. OTHER DOCUMENTS

Aptheker, Herbert (ed.). *A Documentary History of the Negro People in the United States.* New York: The Citadel Press, 1951.

Brown, Frank C. (ed.). *North Carolina Folklore, II*. Durham: Duke University Press, 1952.

Proceedings of the Trustees of the Peabody Educational Fund, I. Boston: Press of John Wilson and Son, 1875.

D. NEWSPAPERS

Charlotte *Observer*, 1904.

New York *Herald*, 1865.

Philadelphia *Inquirer*, 1865. A correspondent for this paper visited the lower Cape Fear in the summer of 1865 and wrote a detailed account of the conditions prevailing there.

Raleigh *Sentinel*, 1868.

Raleigh *Standard*, 1868.

Wilmington *Dispatch*, 1865-66.

Wilmington *Herald*, 1865-66. This also appears as *Herald of the Union* and *Daily Herald*.

Wilmington *Journal*, 1864-98. This paper presents some special problems in citation. The *Journal* and the *Daily Journal* often appear on the same day, but contain different material. Also after the financial failure of the owners in 1876, the *Journal* continues to appear, but as the weekly edition of the Wilmington *Review*. Furthermore the editors were sometimes careless about getting the proper date on an issue. Occasionally several successive issues appear under a single date, or more than one date appears over the various pages of a single issue.

Wilmington *Messenger*, 1890-91.

Wilmington *North Carolinian*, 1864-65.

Wilmington *Post*, 1867-84. Also appears as the *Daily Post* and the *Tri-Weekly Post*.

Wilmington *Review*, 1876-98.

Wilmington *Star*, 1867-99. Originally appeared in 1867 as *The Evening Star*, but changed within a few months to *The Morning Star*.

E. ARTICLES

Burkhead, Reverend L. S. "History of the Difficulties of the Pastorate of the Front Street Methodist Church, Wilmington, N.C., For the Year 1865," *Historical Papers of Trinity College*,

Ser. VIII. Durham: Trinity College Historical Society, 1909, pp. 33-118.

Lowe, Charles. "Miss. Amy M. Bradley, and Her Schools in Wilmington," *Old and New*, I (June, 1870), 775-79.

F. CONTEMPORARY REFERENCE WORKS

Haddock, T. M. *Haddock's Wilmington, N.C., Directory and General Advertiser Containing a General and Business Directory of the City, Historical Sketch, State, County, City Government, etc., etc. [sic]* Wilmington: P. Heinsberger, 1871.

Reilly, J. S. (ed.). *Wilmington, Past, Present, & [sic] Future.* n.p.: n.p. [c. 1884].

Shotwell, R. [andolph] A. [bbott] and Atkinson, Nat. *Legislative Record Giving Passed [,] Session Ending March [,] 1877: Together with Sketches of the Lives and Public Acts of the Members of the Houses.* Raleigh: Edwards and Broughton, 1877.

Smaw, Frank D. *Wilmington Directory Including a General and City Business Directory for 1865-66.* Wilmington: P. Heinsberger, 1865.

Sprunt, James. *Information and Statistics Respecting Wilmington, North Carolina, Being a Report by the President of the Produce Exchange Presented to its Members, April, 1883.* Wilmington: Jackson and Bell, Water-Power Presses, 1883.

G. BOOKS

Andrews, Sidney. *The South Since the War and Shown by Fourteen Weeks of Travel and Observation in Georgia and the Carolinas.* Boston: Ticknor and Fields, 1866.

Avirett, James Battle, *The Old Plantation: How We Lived in Great House and Cabin Before the War.* New York: F. Tennyson Neely Co., 1901.

Brickell, John. *The Natural History of North Carolina.* Dublin, Ireland: James Carson, 1737.

Curtis, Walter Gilman. *Reminiscences*, 1848-1900. Southport, N.C.: Herald Job Office, n.d.

Howell, Andrew J. *The Book of Wilmington.* n.p.: n.p., n.d.

James, Joshua T. *Historical and Commercial Sketch of Wilmington.* [Wilmington?]: n.p., [1867].

Michaux, Francois Andre. *North American Sylva*, II. Paris: C. d'Hautel, 1819.

Moore, Frank. *The Civil War in Song and Story*. Chicago: P. F. Collier, 1889.

Olmsted, Frederick Law. *A Journey in the Seaboard Slave States in the Years 1853-1854 With Remarks on Their Economy*, II. New York: G. P. Putnam's Sons, 1904.

Sprunt, James. *Tales of the Cape Fear Blockade*. Ed. Cornelius M. D. Thomas. Winnabow, N.C.: Charles Towne Preservation Trust, 1960.

Waddell, A. [lfred] M. [oore]. *The Last Year of the War in North Carolina*. . . . Richmond: William Ellis Jones, 1888.

———. *Some Memories of My Life*. Raleigh: Edwards and Broughton, 1908.

II. Secondary Sources

A. ARTICLES

Alexander, Thomas B. "Persistent Whiggery in the Confederate South, 1860-1877," *The Journal of Southern History*, XXVII (August, 1961) , 305-29.

Connor, Robert Diggs Wimberly. "The Peabody Educational Fund," *The South Atlantic Quarterly*, IV (1905) , 169-81.

Dailey, Douglas C. "The Election of 1872 in North Carolina," *The North Carolina Historical Review*, XL (1963), 338-60.

Gabriel, Ralph H. "Joseph Roswell Hawley," *Dictionary of American Biography*, (New York: Charles Scribner's Sons, 1932), IV, 421-22.

Gamble, Thomas (ed.). "Charleston's Story as a Naval Stores Emporium," in *Naval Stores: History, Production, Distribution and Consumption*. Savannah: Review Publishing and Printing Co., 1921.

———. "Pages from Wilmington's Story as America's First Great Naval Stores Port," in *Naval Stores: History, Production, Distribution and Consumption*. Savannah: Review Publishing and Printing Co., 1921.

———. "The Production of Naval Stores in the United States: How the Industry Has Moved from the Carolinas to Texas," in *Naval Stores: History, Production, Distribution and Consumption*. Savannah: Review Publishing and Printing Co., 1921.

Knight, Edgar Wallace. "The Influence of the Civil War on Education in North Carolina," *Proceedings and Addresses of the*

State Literary and Historical Association of North Carolina,
1917, compiled by Robert Diggs Connor (Raleigh: Edwards
and Broughton Printing Co., 1918), XVIII, 52-60.

———. "The Peabody Fund and its Early Operation in North
Carolina," *The South Atlantic Quarterly,* XIV (1915), 168-80.

Moore, Louis Toomer. "Colonial Plantations of the Lower Cape
Fear." Contained in Ida Brooks Kellam *et al., Wilmington:*
Historic Colonial City (Wilmington: Stamp Defiance Chapter
of the National Society Daughters of the American Revolution,
1954), pp. 46-53.

Olsen, Otto H. "The Ku Klux Klan: A Study in Reconstruction
Politics and Propaganda," *The North Carolina Historical Re-*
view, XXXIX (August, 1962), 340-62.

Ostrom, Carl E. and John W. Squires. "Naval Stores: The
Forest," United States Department of Agriculture, *Trees: The*
Yearbook of Agriculture, 1949. Washington: Government
Printing Office [1949], pp. 291-98.

Price, Charles L. "The Railroad Schemes of George W. Swepson,"
East Carolina College Publications in History: Essays in Ameri-
can History, ed. Hubert A. Coleman *et al.* (Greenville, N.C.:
Department of History, East Carolina College, 1964), I, pp. 32-
50.

Ruark, Bryant Whitlock. "Some Phases of Reconstruction in Wilmington and the County of New Hanover," *Historical Papers*
of Trinity College, Ser. IX (Durham: Trinity College Historical Society, 1915), pp. 79-112.

Russ, William A., Jr. "Radical Disfranchisement in North Carolina, 1867-1868," *The North Carolina Historical Review,* XI
(1934), 271-83.

Stoess, A. D. and Robert L. Brown. "Stabilizing Sand Dunes,"
United States, Department of Agriculture, *Soil: The Yearbook*
of Agriculture, 1957. Washington: Government Printing Office,
[1957], pp. 321-26.

Truax, Thomas R. "Preservative Treatment of Wood," United
States, Department of Agriculture, *Trees: The Yearbook of*
Agriculture, 1949. Washington: Government Printing Office,
[1949], pp. 623-25.

Ward, Jay. "Naval Stores: The Industry," United States, Department of Agriculture, *Trees: The Yearbook of Agriculture, 1949.*
Washington: Government Printing Office, [1949], pp. 286-91.

B. BIOGRAPHY

Bailey, Joseph Cannon. *Seaman A. Knapp: Schoolmaster of American Agriculture*. New York: Columbia University Press, 1945.

Daniels, Jonathan. *Prince of Carpetbaggers*. Philadelphia: Lippincott, [1958].

Seitz, Don Carlos. *Braxton Bragg: General of the Confederacy*. Columbia, S.C.: The State Co., 1924.

Soley, James Russell. *Admiral [David Nixon] Porter*. New York: D. Appleton & Co., 1903.

Tucker, Glenn. *Zeb Vance: Champion of Personal Freedom*. Indianapolis: The Bobbs-Merrill Co., 1965.

C. GENERAL WORKS AND SPECIALIZED MONOGRAPHS

Barrett, John G. *The Civil War in North Carolina*. Chapel Hill: The University of North Carolina Press, 1963.

Bloodworth, Mattie. *History of Pender County, North Carolina*. Richmond: the Dietz Printing Co., 1947.

Carse, Robert. *Blockade: The Civil War at Sea*. New York: Rinehart & Co., 1958.

Cochran, Hamilton. *Blockade Runners of the Confederacy*. New York: The Bobbs-Merrill Co., 1958.

Coleman, Charles H. *The Election of 1868*. New York: Columbia University Press, 1933.

Edmonds, Helen Grey. *The Negro and Fusion Politics in North Carolina, 1895-1901*. Chapel Hill: The University of North Carolina Press, 1951.

Gray, Lewis Cecil. *History of Agriculture in the Southern United States to 1860*, 2 vols. Washington: Carnegie Institute of Washington, 1933.

Hamilton, Joseph Gregoire de Roulhac. *Reconstruction in North Carolina*. New York: Columbia University Press, 1914.

Horn, Stanley Fitzgerald. *This Fascinating Lumber Business*. Indianapolis: Bobbs-Merrill Co., 1951.

Knight, Edgar Wallace. *The Influence of Reconstruction on Education in the South*. New York: Teachers' College, Columbia University, 1913.

Lefler, Hugh Talmage and Albert Ray Newsome. *North Carolina:*

The History of a Southern State. Chapel Hill: The University of North Carolina Press, 1963.

Moore, Louis Toomer. *Stories New and Old of the Cape Fear Region*. Wilmington: Published by the author, 1956.

Singletary, Otis A. *The Negro Militia and Reconstruction*. Austin: The University of Texas Press, 1957.

Sitterson, Joseph Carlyle. *The Secession Movement in North Carolina*. Chapel Hill: The University of North Carolina Press, 1939.

Sprunt, James. *Chronicles of the Cape Fear River*. Raleigh: Edwards and Broughton Printing Co., 1914.

Woodward, Comer Vann. *Reunion and Reaction: The Compromise of 1877 and Reconstruction*. Rev. ed. with a new introduction and concluding chapter. Garden City, N.Y.: Doubleday, 1956.

D. PAMPHLETS

De Rosset, William Lord. *Pictorial and Historical New Hanover County and Wilmington, North Carolina, 1723-1938*. Wilmington: Published by the author, 1938.

Kellam, Ida Brooks *et al. Wilmington Historical Colonial City*. Wilmington: Stamp Defiance Chapter of the National Society Daughters of the American Revolution, 1954. Contains a valuable essay by Louis Toomer Moore giving historical sketches of some fifty plantations of the lower Cape Fear and a map locating them.

[North Carolina State Archives]. *Colonel William Lamb Day: Souvenir Booklet*. Wilmington: Carolina Printing Co., 1962.

Schorger, A. W. and H. S. Betts. *The Naval Stores Industry: United States Department of Agriculture Bulletin No. 229, July 28, 1915*. Washington: Government Printing Office, 1915.

E. REFERENCE WORKS

North Carolina Historical Commission. *North Carolina Manual, 1913*, prepared by J. Bryan Grimes, R. D. W. Connor *et al*. Raleigh: [Edwards and Broughton], 1913.

Woodward, Comer Vann. *Origins of the New South*. Vol. IX. eds. Wendell Holmes Stephenson and Ellis Merton Coulter. *A History of the South*. Baton Rouge: Louisiana State University Press, 1951.

F. UNPUBLISHED WORKS

Beeker, Henry Judson. "Wilmington During the Civil War." Unpublished master's thesis, Duke University, 1941.

Brewer, James H. "An Apocalypse on Slavery: The Story of the Negro Slave in the Lower Cape Fear Region of North Carolina." Unpublished doctoral dissertation, University of Pittsburgh, 1949.

Kirkland, John Robert. "Federal Troops in North Carolina During Reconstruction." Unpublished master's thesis, The University of North Carolina, 1964.

Nowaczyk, Elaine Joan. "The North Carolina Negro in Politics, 1865-1871." Unpublished doctoral dissertation, The University of North Carolina, 1959.

Perry, Percival. "The Naval Stores Industry in the Ante-Bellum South." Unpublished doctoral dissertation, Duke University, 1947.

Price, Charles Lewis. "Railroads and Reconstruction in North Carolina, 1865-1871." Unpublished doctoral dissertation, The University of North Carolina, 1959.

Randall, Peter Duncan. "Geographic Factors in the Growth and Economy of Wilmington, North Carolina." Unpublished doctoral dissertation, The University of North Carolina, 1965.

Raper, Horace Wilson. "The Political Career of William Woods Holden with Special Reference to His Provisional Governorship." Unpublished master's thesis, The University of North Carolina, 1947.

Williams, S. P. "The Problem of Redistricting in North Carolina." Unpublished master's thesis, Duke University, 1935.

ᏋᎦ *Index*